ARE YOU ★★★ TOUGH ENOUGH?

ARE YOU
★★★ TOUGH
ENOUGH?

ANNE BURFORD
WITH JOHN GREENYA

McGRAW-HILL BOOK COMPANY

New York   St. Louis   San Francisco   Hamburg   Mexico   Toronto

1 2 3 4 5 6 7 8 9 D O C D O C 8 7 6 5

ISBN 0-07-008940-X

LIBRARY OF CONGRESS CATALOGING-IN-PUBLICATION DATA

Burford, Anne M. (Anne McGill), 1942–
   Are you tough enough?

   1. United States.   Environmental Protection Agency.
2. Environmental policy—United States.   3. United
States—Politics and government—1981–
I. Greenya, John.   II. Title.
HC110.E5B883   1986   353.0082'321   85–18062
ISBN 0–07–008940–X

Book Design by Patrice Fodero

To my husband and my children

—A.B.

For Suzanne and the boys

—J.G.

ACKNOWLEDGMENTS

I want to thank my husband, Robert Burford, for being there when I needed him—always.

I want to thank my children, Neil, Stephanie, and J.J., for just being, but also for believing in their mother.

I want to thank, in alphabetical order: Cristy Bach, Kathleen Bennett, Stanley Brand, John D. Dingell, Eric Eidsness, William Hedeman, John Horton, Morgan Kinghorn, Elliott J. Levitas, Mary Ellen Lynch, Lee Modesitt, Patricia Payne, Frieda Poundstone, Ralph Ross, Jim Sanderson, John Skinner, Lester Sutton, John Todhunter, James Watt, and Gerry Yamada.

John Daniel, whose keen intellect and unflappable Southern manner clearly make him the best "fire fighter" in town, was a resource without which this book would not have been "lived," much less written.

As for John Greenya, he is a marvelous craftsman who, notwithstanding his liberal Democratic background, has become a treasured friend.

CONTENTS

RONALD REAGAN
PRESIDENT OF THE UNITED STATES

to all who see these presents, Greeting:

Know ye that reposing special trust and confidence in the integrity and ability of ANNE MCGILL GORSUCH of Colorado, I have nominated, and by and with the advice and consent of the Senate, do appoint her Administrator of the Environmental Protection Agency and do authorize and empower her to execute and fulfill the duties of that office according to law . . . during the pleasure of the President of the United States for the time being.

by the President: Ronald Reagan

done at the City of Washington, the Seventh day of May in the year of our Lord One Thousand Nineteen Hundred and Eighty-one.

THE WHITE HOUSE

March 9, 1983

It is with regret that I have accepted the resignation of Anne McGill Burford as Administrator of the Environmental Protection Agency.

I am grateful to Anne for her fine work during the past two years and for the courage and dedication that she has continually displayed.

At the same time I am greatly disappointed that some persons have unjustly attacked her and have made unfair judgments based upon allegation and innuendo alone. The unfortunate actions have so interfered with her sound management of the Agency that Anne has unselfishly concluded that she should step down to best serve the interests of the Agency and the country.

I am proud of her and glad that she has agreed to continue to serve this Administration in a position which will soon be announced.

Ronald Reagan

Politics in Washington is omnipresent. It is a one-industry town. Everyone that comes there has interests in government and everyone has one thing on their mind: Politics.

Robert Burford,
quoted in the *Rocky Mountain News*,
May 24, 1981

Anne's biggest weakness was her loyalty to the President. And in that loyalty she believed the members of the President's team would be loyal to her and to other team members. Contrary to the advice that I gave her, she took actions that were very unfair to herself, and thus indirectly unfair to the President. She did what she was told to do by the President's team members. And I would say, "Anne, you are being misled by the Department of Justice; you're being misled by the President's Counsel; they do not have the President's best interests at heart. They are using you for their legal purposes—not the President's program."

James Watt,
February, 1985

First of all, large amounts of people actively associated with the environmental movement had come into EPA during the Carter Administration, and because of their political appointments and the fact that they did not share the views of the Reagan Administration, their departure was almost sudden after the election. Secondly, I think a large number of the staff within the Agency associated with those people began to forecast nothing but doom. Thirdly, when Anne arrived, she was preceded by a barrage of press accounts of her performance in Colorado, dubbing her "the Wicked Witch of the West." She certainly did not gain the positive entrée of the news media that every other Administrator of the Agency that I had seen had gotten when she came, so before she had an opportunity to present herself and her direction, she had been pre-judged by a large number of people. Fourthly, she was in the process at that time of preparing the President's budget for the following fiscal year, and that did call for significant cuts. In addition, people who worked for her *did* eliminate or significantly reduce the number of offices.

I felt that all of the people who had been selected had come on board, they had filled the key political positions, but there was a lack of cohesiveness unlike anything I had ever seen in government, and, essentially, a trial period in which each individual was attempting to establish their own notoriety and their own recognition within the agency, perhaps at the expense of their peers. One of Anne's problems was that she was was not able entirely to select her own people. Some of them, whom she did select, such as Kathleen Bennett and Eric Eidsness, were very eager to get about the business of protecting the environment and carrying out the programs in a way that was not disruptive. Others, I think, had no business ever even being considered for government service and were a disgrace to the federal government, clearly were operating off their own personal agenda rather than any Administrator's or Administration's agenda but what they perceived as the Administration's agenda, had relatively little ethics or integrity, and are a disgrace to any group that they become associated with.

> William Hedeman, EPA
> Director of Superfund,
> February, 1985

Part I

WELCOME TO WASHINGTON

1

WILL YOU HOLD
FOR THE PRESIDENT?

When the President called I was standing in my kitchen in my blue jeans making lunch.

"This is the White House. Will you hold for the President?"

What a question. "Yes, of course."

"Hello, Anne. This is the President. I'm calling to ask you to be the Administrator of the Environmental Protection Agency. Will you accept?"

"Mr. President, I'd be honored."

He went on to mention that he would also be naming Dr. John Hernandez, a college professor from New Mexico, as my Deputy Administrator. I told him I understood that, and agreed. He welcomed me aboard, and said he was looking forward to having me on his team. I thanked him, and we hung up.

I immediately forgot all about lunch. I yelled to my friend Mary Wiggington, who was in another room, "That was the President! I've got the job! I'm the head of EPA! Let's pack the bags!"

In addition to my excitement at being asked to be part of the administration of a man I admired more than anyone else in American political life, a man I had admired deeply for years, I was also relieved that the waiting was over. It had all taken so long. There had been so many false starts, so many steps and levels in the interview process, that I had come to the point where

I'd told myself the whole dream would not be true until Ronald Reagan himself actually called and asked me to be the Administrator of the Environmental Protection Agency.

And now it had happened. He had called, and the dream was coming true. I smiled at Mary, who was already pulling my luggage out of the closet.

Two and a half years later, give or take a few weeks, it was all over.

What began with such great expectations turned into, if not a nightmare, then certainly a very bad dream. I became the increasingly lonely buffer between an angry Congress, an entrenched and secretive senior White House staff, and the Department of Justice. A few paces behind them were a small but effective cadre of environmental extremists and a hostile, confrontational press.

At least nominally, the issue in question was the doctrine of executive privilege, a doctrine that I as a lawyer and a conservative Republican felt was being mistakenly asserted. The real issue, however, was one of trust. Was my team at EPA out to rape and pillage the environment, as the most extreme of our critics assumed, simply because we had been put in office by Ronald Reagan? Or were we applying such respectable conservative principles of government as efficiency and sound management to the job of protecting the environment? Unfortunately, the debate never got down to the fundamental issues involved. With very few exceptions, whenever our critics saw smoke, they *believed* fire.

All this high drama was being played out on the front pages and on the morning and evening news, to the increasingly great disruption of my life and the lives of my family and staff. It ended, in March, 1983, with my resignation.

Later in 1983, I was on an airplane, and the man seated next to me kept glancing at me. Finally he said, "You look so familiar. Shouldn't I know you?" (At least he didn't say, as a woman once did, "Didn't you use to be somebody?") I tried to deflect his curiosity, but when he persisted, I said simply, "I'm Anne Burford. I used to be the head of EPA, but it didn't work out."

In some ways it really was that simple. In others it was incredibly complex, fraught with backstage maneuvering that would have done Machiavelli proud, as people in positions of public trust pursued private agendas with barely concealed glee. Promises were not just broken, they were halved and then quartered. And all of it was done in the name of Ronald Reagan, though seldom, I am sure, with his complete understanding.

Now that time has passed, friends ask me if I would do things differently—if I would even take the job, if history were somehow to offer me another chance. To the surprise of most of them, I answer that while I would make a few alterations in our game plan, I certainly *would* take the job again.

I left the Environmental Protection Agency a better and more efficient place than it was when I found it, and I'm more than willing to let history be the judge of that. Within the context of my political philosophy (which is basically the same as that of Ronald Reagan) and given the economic realities of the day, I believe EPA was doing just what it should have been doing, and, certainly by midterm, doing it damn well.

As for my opinion of all the President's men, and the very few women in high places, that's a different story.

Am I saying I didn't make any mistakes? Of course not. But the mistakes that I or we made had little or nothing to do with the headline charges of which we all stood accused at the time of my resignation, and which the public most likely believes today. Within my team, it was never a question of whether or not we would have clean air and water, but *how* we would have them.

My twenty-two months as head of EPA were quite a trip, and quite a costly educational experience. My story should also be seen as a cautionary tale, one to be read with care not just by women and conservatives, but also by men and liberals, by anyone who is concerned with the nature of our political leadership and the fair and proper functioning of our system of government.

As for me, I'm very much a survivor. I'm alive and well, even if I still work in Washington. On the first business day of 1985, I opened an office on Thomas Jefferson Street, Northwest, about twelve blocks from the White House. To the *west*. On the same day I got my first client—a politically conservative legal foundation. As they say, the more things change, the more they stay the same.

My Washington odyssey began with another phone call. In the

fall of 1980, shortly after the election, I heard from Frieda Poundstone, a dynamic and very politically active fellow Colorado conservative. I was somewhat surprised that Frieda was inviting me
to go to Washington, D.C. with her and several others from the
state to work on the transition team that would pave the way for
the Reagan administration; there were other conservatives (and
other women) who knew her better than I did. But I was clearly
flattered.

I think I got the call because I was considered a "comer."
Although I had only recently announced my intention not to run
for reelection, I had been an active and highly visible member of
the Colorado House of Representatives for two terms (four years).
Of those predominantly Democratic districts in the state that had
elected Republicans, my East Denver district was probably the
most Democratic, by about a factor of *ten*. And I had been reelected in 1978 by a margin of 4 percent. Registration in my district
was about 49 percent Democratic, 18 percent Republican, and the
rest Independents. What's more, when I was first elected, I had
replaced a fairly powerful two-term incumbent.

I had decided not to seek reelection for a number of reasons.
Those of us young conservatives who had entered the legislature
at about the same time had accomplished our mutual goals. And
we had a wonderful time doing it. Another reason is that while I
had continually received a great deal of publicity, at one point
having been on the front pages of the Denver papers for weeks
at a time, I had never felt comfortable with all that publicity. I
didn't like it for myself, and I definitely didn't like it for my
children.

Finally, it had become apparent that my husband, who was
also a Denver lawyer (he was with a private firm; I worked for
the legal department of Mountain Bell, the telephone company,
during the more than six months when the legislature was not in
session), and I were going to get a divorce. I didn't need to be
going through *that* while trying to get reelected in a tough district.

It was a time to regroup personally and professionally. In
addition to beginning the steps leading to the divorce, I felt it was
time to go back to being a lawyer for Mountain Bell, which I had
been doing since 1975.

After all that political involvement, though, I couldn't just walk
away from active, elective politics, especially not at just the moment

when Ronald Reagan and what he so ably and effectively stood for were about to be given a vote of confidence by the American electorate. So I had agreed to be an active campaigner in a number of races on the state level, and I had also signed up to be a surrogate speaker for Reagan.

Frieda Poundstone's call struck a very receptive nerve. Not only was it a compliment to be asked, it offered me a chance to do something worthwhile *and* have some fun, an activity in which I have never been a reluctant participant. So I said yes, and began to make the kind of arrangements that are necessary when an about-to-be-divorced mother of three children under the age of thirteen is going to be out of town for several weeks.

Our assignment from transition leadership (Meese, Baker, et al) was to examine the entire range of independent government panels and commissions from the standpoint of budget, personnel, and policy, and then to recommend necessary changes. All the excitement of the Reagan victory was still very much in the air, and I viewed the trip as a chance to begin to put the Reagan philosophy of regulatory reform, New Federalism and reduced government size and expense into practice.

I welcomed the chance to go to Washington. I had visited the capital before, but had never spent any length of time there, nor, for that matter, in any of the big Eastern cities. To me Washington was a cosmopolitan center, and I looked forward to an exciting time.

My friend Katy Lewis, the press person for Republicans in the Colorado House, and I flew out a day after Frieda. She had made reservations for us at a downtown motel best left unnamed. In Washington, as I was about to learn, there's downtown and there's *downtown*, and while this place, which had been converted from a seedy apartment house into a seedy hotel/motel, was near 14th Street, Northwest, it was definitely not at the attractive end. The good part of 14th Street intersects Pennsylvania Avenue just two blocks from the White House. The motel was one of those places you have to buzz to get into, and the glass seemed to be about four inches thick. When we got to the room, we discovered the shower didn't work. If you wanted to rinse your hair, you had to use an old pan from the kitchenette.

Although it was 10:00 P.M. in Washington, Katy and I were still on Denver time two hours behind, so we did a quick about-face and headed for the ground-floor bar, which turned out to be a windowless smoke-filled room. Almost all its space was taken up by a boisterous group of labor union organizers—the kind of guys who go around with clubs!—and the 14th Street hookers who had latched on to them.

Katy and I just wanted to have a drink by ourselves, but the union boys wouldn't leave us alone. Even the fact that all I could talk about was the greatness of Ronald Reagan and his election didn't deter them. Finally we gave up and went back to the room, but at 2:00 A.M. they were pounding on our door, inviting us to join them in their rooms for a drink!

The next morning we called down for room service, only to find out that there wasn't any. I had to put on my raincoat over my nightgown and go downstairs to get our coffee. We called Frieda and pleaded with her to find us someplace else, fast.

She contacted someone at transition headquarters, who found us the River Inn, a very nice place in the Foggy Bottom area of Northwest Washington, near the Kennedy Center and Rock Creek Park, but still close enough to the main downtown business section, the major tourist attractions, and the best restaurants. We rented a number of apartments there for our whole group. The River Inn became a home away from home. In Washington, I was learning, the difference of a few blocks can represent different worlds.

While our work was interesting, it was hardly exhausting, and we were able to go out to dinner and parties at night and generally to enjoy life in Washington. But as the days passed we (especially Frieda) began to notice that while the conservatives were still in the trenches drinking bubbly and celebrating Ronald Reagan's victory, a whole slew of nonconservative Republicans—holdovers or returnees from the Ford and even Nixon administrations—were quietly moving in and taking the powerful positions.

I had thought that transition would be transition—you would come in and be assigned a specific task; you would do it; and then you would make your recommendations to the President. But it wasn't that at all. Transition was the biggest cattle market I had ever seen.

In some ways serving on the transition team was an additional campaign contribution—we paid for our own transportation, rooms, and meals, and in exchange we received one dollar. I had figured it was all for a good conservative cause. Instead it was becoming apparent that all the conservatives were being shunted off into a corner, really isolated. Finally, Frieda said, "Whoa. We'll continue to do the substantive work, but I'm also going to get busy politicking, because if we don't do something fast, we won't have any conservatives in this administration."

Fortunately, Frieda was very good at both the substantive work and the politicking. She was instrumental in getting a number of fellow conservative Coloradoans appointed, among them James Watt as Secretary of the Interior, and Robert Burford, a Grand Junction rancher and former Speaker of the Colorado House, who had been one of my close colleagues in public office and would become my husband two years later. Frieda was also the person who got me interested in serving in the Reagan administration.

Frieda's initial thought was that with my background I should naturally be interested in a position with the Justice Department. But I wasn't. If all I wanted was to go on being a lawyer, then I might as well stay with the job and the client I had, Mountain Bell. The small change that one could effect in a legal job at the Department of Justice wouldn't be worth it to my family. If one wanted to make a difference as a member of a new conservative Republican administration, it didn't seem to me that being a lawyer at the Justice Department would give me, or anyone else, much of an opportunity to do so. I surprised Frieda by telling her, "What I'd really like is to be the Deputy Administrator of the Environmental Protection Agency."

In answer to her "Why?" I said, "A. Even though I've had a lot of publicity in the last four years, I've never liked it; in fact, I've hated it. It would be the Administrator, not the Deputy, who'd get the publicity. B. I could really run that agency, which traditionally has been run by the Deputy, not the Administrator, and it desperately needs to be run. C. I could really make a difference. And D, everything the President has talked about doing—regulatory reform, the New Federalism, getting better results with fewer dollars—is possible at EPA."

And there was one more reason: my dealings with EPA as a state legislator had taught me that the head of EPA has more unfettered power than anybody else in town. I don't care if you're the Secretary of *Defense*. The Administrator of EPA has more discretionary power (all of which, incidentally, had come from

Congress), which means someone could get in there and really do a job.

Frieda didn't say much, but I had the feeling she filed the information away mentally.

Transition ended, and I went home to Denver. If I had needed any reminder that I was a mother, homemaker, and soon-to-be-single parent, as well as an attorney and an active conservative Republican, I got it that Christmas when all three of my children came down with chickenpox. Welcome home, Mom.

I'm not exaggerating when I say I dislike publicity. The history of my relationship with the press is rather unusual. In 1976, when I was first elected as a Colorado legislator, I was the *darling* of the press. As far as they were concerned I could do no wrong.

A wise friend warned me not to expect it to continue. U.S. Congressman Ken Kramer, my old desk mate in the Colorado House, said, "Watch out, Anne. The press may be all over you now, doing these female-mother-of-three-exciting-new-legislator puff pieces, but when they find out how conservative you are, they'll turn on you like hounds!" And he was absolutely right.

In my first year as a legislator I rewrote and carried through to passage a piece of legislation that essentially rewrote the entire sentencing scheme for the state of Colorado. That got me a great deal of attention from the press, but I should have realized right there that I was going to have trouble with the press eventually, because they never really got that story straight. They didn't even get the facts right, let alone explain the impact. It was a very controversial bill, and the governor vetoed it, but the leadership of the House and Senate called a special session of the legislature to reconsider it, and then it passed. In fact, in the House there was only one vote against it.

We felt the indeterminate sentencing system used in Colorado should be changed. In theory it was considered the more humane method because it allows the judge to take individual differences into consideration. In actuality, however, and as I had learned when I'd gotten interested in the question as an assistant D.A., it was neither humane nor fair. What would happen is that the judge would sentence someone to, say, five to forty years for committing a felony, but that person would serve on the average only about eighteen months.

The villain was the parole board. This group of faceless, name-less, nonelected people were the ones who decided how long a person actually spent in jail for his or her crime. We did a study of Colorado's five classes of felonies, and learned that the average time served, as opposed to the formal sentence, was about eighteen months. Our bill would base the sentences on reality. It wasn't an attempt to make people spend more time in jail; I told my col-leagues they could do that in the next session if we had the money to build new prisons. The idea was to bring the sentences in line with terms actually being served, along with some judicial leeway, say, six months, in order to make things fairer for everyone con-cerned.

One of the problems was that the public was being misserved because they thought felons were actually doing the "heavy time" they heard about from the media; judges were misserved because their intentions were being thwarted by the parole board; and even the prisoners themselves were misserved because they never knew for sure when they would get out.

I had come to the view that the presumption behind indeter-minate sentencing—that a group of people can figure out when someone has been rehabilitated—was an enormously subjective one, which also happened to be wrong. I had come to believe that prisons do not rehabilitate, but merely punish, and, as a result, that punishment was being meted out most unfairly. Blacks and chicanos regularly served much longer sentences than whites. So we produced a giant revamping of the system, with a bill that I carried in my freshman year in the legislature.

The whole issue was controversial. And it was not very well understood, in part because the press reported it so poorly, giving people the impression that it was somehow a conservative bill. If they'd done their homework they would have known that Senator Ted Kennedy had been unsuccessfully introducing a similar bill on the federal level for years (a version passed in 1984).

Nonetheless, at the end of my first year in office I was pleas-antly surprised at being voted—in a poll in which both the press and the members of the House cast ballots—the Outstanding Freshman Legislator. There was even a certain humor to the way it came about. The awards were given out during an informal House session, and early in the presentation, during which all sorts of different awards were given, the presenter announced that I had been voted "Best-dressed Legislator." I thought, good grief, just think of going down in history as the best-dressed Colorado legislator of 1976. I was really disappointed. I thought that having successfully introduced and carried twenty-six bills—an unheard-of number—would have qualified me for something more substantive. And I knew that they almost never gave anyone more than one award. But then near the end of the ceremony, they announced my award as Outstanding Freshman Legislator. I was very proud.

The fact that the press started to do a job on me simply because I was a conservative disappointed me. Perhaps it indicates my naïveté, but in some ways that's the attitude that got me involved in politics in the first place. And I have never regretted that involvement.

Some years ago, my former husband was asked if he would be interested in running for office in Colorado, and he said no. While I understood all his reasons, his decision always kind of bothered me. It seemed to me that you had a certain obligation, especially if life had worked out well for you, to give something back, to reinvest in the community that had invested in you. And I was always active in the Republican party, but as a worker for a given candidate, never as a candidate myself.

Then in 1975 an interesting thing happened. Bill Brock, now Secretary of Labor, but then Chairman of the Republican National Committee, had the firm belief that you built a political party from the courthouse up, not from the White House down, and he sent people all around the country to preach that gospel. They spent a good deal of money on computer profiles of the Democratic incumbents around various states, and they did profiles of the ideal candidates to oppose them. When they had their information they went out and recruited candidates to run against those incumbents. And by so doing they got a lot of people involved in elective politics who probably would not been involved otherwise, including myself.

By 1976 those efforts in Colorado had produced a number of new members of the House, people who in years past would not have run for the General Assembly because they didn't have "political ambitions" in the traditional sense. A lot of good businesspeople, good teachers. I certainly would not have run if they hadn't come to me and said they thought I could do so and win.

I had considered myself simply a good Republican, not a potential candidate. In fact, my parents, especially my father, didn't exactly look at politics as a noble profession. In his view, while politics may not have been as declassé as being a go-go dancer (which I once wanted to be until he made his viewpoint known), it was one of those certain things one just doesn't do. Working for the government was another one of his no-nos.

My East Denver district was represented by a rather strong incumbent, who had been in office for two terms and was on the Joint Budget Committee, a very powerful committee because Colorado is one of the few states in which the legislature actually designs the budget. And, as I mentioned, the numbers were horrible for a Republican challenger, what with 19% Republicans, over 40% Democrats, and the rest independent. The incumbent had the added advantage of being Jewish in a heavily Jewish district. But he also had a problem that year.

He was a lawyer who had not yet passed the bar. In fact, he had failed the bar examination twice. He then made the mistake of taking it for the third time—if you flunked three times you had to get special permission from the State Supreme Court to try again. And just before the election he got the news that he had failed the bar exam this time too.

One of the liberal local papers, in a real eat-your-own move, ran a most unflattering photograph of the incumbent along with his exam results. The Jewish community happens to be proud of and impressed with high academic credentials, and the incumbent was embarrassing them on this score. In contrast, I looked terrific. With my academic honors *and* a Fulbright Scholarship, I look golden on paper. So all of this was thrown in the hopper and helped to contribute to a most unusual—and in some ways downright funny—election.

Unbeknownst to me there was some Republican infighting going on, and the district captain had become miffed with another Republican challenger, so he tapped me as his new candidate, without telling me that he had really written off any chance of my beating the incumbent. He just wanted to oppose the other Republican. Well, once I learned that, and realized he was not going to help me much even if I survived the primary, I got mad and decided to do it all myself, or at least with a team of my own choosing.

Some members of my husband's family turned out to be very good campaigners. His family name was well known in the area, as was my maiden name, and with my five sisters and one brother— and my father being a well-known and well-liked surgeon—I wasn't exactly helpless when it came to support troops.

Shortly before the primary, I learned that my "swell" district captain was not going to come across with any money. So I had to go out and raise all my own funds. This did me a lot of good in the long run; that way I didn't owe him.

We did the classic door-to-door campaign, and we did it well. One of my problems was the response I got when I pushed door-bells of homes of Jewish voters, and a little old Jewish woman would say, "Well, Mrs. Gorsuch, of course we will vote for you. You're one of us." At first I came clean every time, and I even gave my little speech—to them and to the so-called feminists who said they would vote for me just because I was a woman—about how you should vote for the best-qualified candidate. But after a while (and especially after the campaign manager and treasurer I'd been promised by the district captain never showed up) I must admit I was so pleased to hear anybody say he or she was going to vote for me that I skipped the speech.

My sister-in-law Diane was a big help. She had called and asked what she could do to help, and I suggested fund raising. When she said she didn't know how, I told her how. And together we planned a fund-raising cocktail party that people are *still* talking about in Denver. Traditionally, fund-raisers had been kind of casual, wine-and-cheese or beer-and-pretzel affairs. No way, I said, and we planned just the opposite, a real *soirée*.

Diane called all her Junior League buddies, and asked each one to bring trays of their fanciest hors d'oeuvres. Then we borrowed the home of a friend whose backyard is on the edge of a beautiful park, and rented a tent, and told everyone to dress up. We threw the fanciest cocktail party of the summer, and collected fifty dollars a head!

As a fundraiser, it couldn't be beat. We easily brought in enough to finance the entire campaign without having to go to the district captain, who still didn't think I had a chance to win. It was a great time.

I was different and I was "news" when I entered politics. But as Ken Kramer had predicted, when the liberal press (if that isn't a redundancy) found out how fundamentally conservative I am, it turned on me. In all, the honeymoon lasted about six months.

Something not unlike what happened to me also happened to Vice-President George Bush, who is in reality more conservative than the press had been painting him during the first Reagan-Bush term in office. When he began to sound much more conservative, toward the end of the reelection campaign in 1984, the press treatment began to change, and the stories became much harsher.

One political rule I established at the very beginning was always to take the high road. Some of my supporters were overjoyed at that most unflattering picture of the incumbent that accompanied the story of his having flunked the bar exam, and they wanted to reproduce it and distribute it as a leaflet, especially in Jewish neighborhoods. When I got wind of that, I said absolutely not. In fact, I called my opponent and told him that we weren't going to do anything with that horrible picture. And my people didn't, though some of them were certainly frustrated.

Then I learned another lesson about politics. The opponent to whom I had just been so fair turned around and played a dirty trick on me. He got the Colorado Attorney General, who was a Democrat, to write a letter (on official state stationery, which made it look as if it were an official opinion of the State Attorney General) stating that I had a conflict-of-interest problem because I was a corporate attorney for Mountain Bell. It was just off the wall, and had no merit.

I was furious. And, again, my district captain was no help at all. So I sat down and wrote one of the best letters I have ever written. It not only explained perfectly that there was no conflict, but it also exposed my opponent's attempt to call me unethical for the shabby trick it was.

It should be remembered that this was 1976, the year Jimmy Carter nosed out Gerald Ford for the presidency. There were no Ronald Reagan coattails to ride in on. We were clearly four years ahead of the mood in the country that would produce the Reagan victory in 1980. And we went right to work, that term and especially the next, to carry out a conservative agenda. In that first term we passed the criminal sentencing restructure. In the second, we made Colorado political history by replacing an incumbent Republican speaker with a conservative Republican. By then we really had the place hopping. We repealed five different taxes, and were the first state in the country to index income tax. We also passed regulatory reform measures, and limited the growth of state government. Because we were passing measures that represented a conservative revolution, the liberal press tagged us with the term "House Crazies," which they meant to be pejorative. They didn't like us because we were conservative, and they didn't like us because we were effective. And we were very effective indeed.

I was the legal brains of the outfit. Steve Durham, who later worked for me at EPA as Region Eight Administrator, and who has an amazing ability to speak forcefully and eloquently on any issue, was the spokesperson. Robert Burford was the Boss. He made Durham chairman of the Business Affairs Committee, and me the head of State Affairs, which were two of the three most important committees in the House, the other one being the Judiciary Committee. In a smart conciliatory move he gave Judiciary to the former Speaker, the man he had defeated.

State Affairs was quite a plum. Traditionally it had been the Speaker's own committee, so anything that was problematic, from either a legal or a political point of view, went to State Affairs. But I told Burford that I wouldn't take it if he was going to call the shots; he would have to have enough confidence in my judgment to know I would run it right. And he did.

What's more, he gave me the best possible group of people as my committee members. We absolutely stuck together. There wasn't anything that came out of there that I didn't want to come out of there. It just ran like a clock, which of course was a source of great frustration to the Democrats because they knew that if a bill came to my committee it was going to come out looking the way I wanted it to look—or it wasn't going to come out at all.

I was playing a very controversial role. And I—and all of us—got a lot of bad press.

One of my problems with the press was that I have always been somewhat hard to pigeonhole, and the press loves to pigeonhole people, in large part because then it doesn't have to do as much thinking or as much work. This difficulty of categorization was especially clear when I opposed a Republican severance tax bill, and later introduced the auto emission inspection and maintenance bill, voted to abolish the sales tax on food, and sponsored a bill that removed what amounted to an unfair tax on people who had cooperated with the government and then lost their homes by adverse condemnation procedures, a tax not paid by people who *hadn't* cooperated. The last one so confused the press that one paper ran a story based on the speculation that there had to be some "special interest" behind the bill, otherwise why were the infamous House Crazies in favor of it? They were in favor of it because I had studied the matter and pointed out to them the basic unfairness of the situation.

We did "Reaganism" in the Colorado legislature before Reagan did it. But no one in the press ever wrote about that. Frankly, I think they all just missed it. While the press and the activists were screaming, we were going about our business, streamlining the state government and in the process bringing Colorado into the twentieth century. That, in brief, was the conservative background that brought me, somewhat tardily, to the attention of the new team in Washington.

2

WHY SETTLE FOR NUMBER TWO?

When Frieda Poundstone saw that conservatives weren't getting enough of the jobs, results started showing in January, 1981. I got a call from Washington asking me to come out and talk to the Secretary of Energy, a wonderful South Carolina gentleman by the name of James Edwards. He offered me the job of Assistant Secretary for Environment and Emergency Preparedness in the Department of Energy. He was such a charming and impressive man that I almost took the job just to work for him. But, I thought, why disrupt my whole family for a position that won't really allow me to make a difference. As far as I was concerned, the job at Energy should probably have been abolished; and, indeed, since then it has been deemphasized as part of a reorganization.

So I said, "No, thanks." But before I left Washington I called the office of Sen. William Armstrong, Colorado's Republican Senator (Democrat Gary Hart is the other Senator). I reminded his office that I had applied for the job of Deputy Administrator at EPA. His office said they had no idea where that application stood in terms of its "viability," but they promised to call the man in charge of personnel at the White House and find out.

Like most hopefuls, I'd followed the time-honored procedure of papering the town with my résumé, and I tried to make sure it came from as many different influential directions as possible.

I'd applied through the Republican National Committee (RNC), which had a special search group for women; through Senator Armstrong; through trade associations; and I had done it directly myself. My résumé must have wended its way to the White House personnel office from at least ten different directions. Conspicuous by their absence on my list of sponsors, however, were womens' groups or hard-core conservative groups or individuals.

Theoretically, RNC had the duty of looking for strong conservative Republican women, with the very able Sally Buikema in charge of that program. And another very able woman, Wendy Borcherdt, from California, was in the White House personnel office, specifically as a conservative female to try to recruit others like herself. So there *were* conservatives in places of some power; the question was the extent to which they would be allowed to exercise that power.

Bob Potts, Senator Armstrong's Administrative Assistant, called the White House personnel office and got an appointment for me with Alexander Armendaris, a Hispanic businessman who had taken leave to work on the transition. One of his tasks was to interview plausible candidates for the top posts in agencies and departments immediately below the Cabinet, such as NASA and EPA.

When I got over there I was startled to find that even though I had been aiming copies of my résumé at the White House from a dozen different directions, Mr. Armendaris did not have a single one. The White House had lost *all* the résumés of women! I don't think there was a deep, dark plot involved. I suspect what happened is that all the résumés of women seeking jobs with the new administration were put in a box over at the headquarters of the transition team, and were then shipped to the personnel office in the Old Executive Office Building (OEOB) next door to the White House. And somewhere en route, or somewhere in the cavernous bowels of the OEOB, they got lost. Even if the loss was accidental, it was hardly a good omen.

I ended up having to jump into a cab and go back to Senator Armstrong's office to get a copy of my own résumé, and then cab it back to 16th and Pennsylvania Avenue, pronto. Not an auspicious beginning.

The interview went very well. Mr. Armendaris and I hit it off beautifully. Unlike a number of the people under consideration for the job—all of them men—I'd had extensive legislative dealings with EPA, and was very familiar with its impact "in the field," as applied in the states, where the agency's policies are actually implemented. I later learned that a number of the candidates were scientists or consultants whose connections to either industry or academia were too strong and too recent.

Mr. Armendaris told me candidly that although I was applying for the post of Deputy Administrator, he felt that I was qualified to be the Administrator. That took me back a bit, but it also intrigued me. He explained that the job called for someone who could articulate the agency's positions to Congress, and it would be a big plus to have someone in the job who had a legislative background. He had carefully interviewed all the candidates to see if they had a "private agenda," as opposed to their being willing to carry out the goals of the President. He was convinced I would be "a good soldier," and he told me he particularly liked what I said about believing that EPA could be getting "more for its buck" in protecting the environment.

He was concerned that I had come to his attention rather late in the interviewing process, but said he would rush my name over to the personnel people at the White House. He asked if I could remain in Washington for a few more days. On the strength of his positive—and flattering—reaction, I decided to do so. As things turned out, it was a good idea. But what I had envisioned as the scenario of my hoped-for entry into the administration of Ronald Reagan seemed to be changing daily.

Within days I got a call from James Watt, a fellow Coloradoan and the new Secretary of the Interior. At the time he called, Jim had been confirmed by the Senate and had held the post for some time. Jim's natural combativeness and outspoken views had kept him in the news almost daily. He called to say he'd been asked by the President to help screen candidates for the top slots at the Environmental Protection Agency. He said he knew I was interested in the Deputy position, and wanted to interview me.

I had known Jim Watt for some years—and I liked him, although we were not close personal friends. I looked forward to the interview. One of the last times we'd done business together he'd filed suit against EPA over the mandatory auto emissions testing requirements, and I was his opponent by virtue of being the prime sponsor of the bill that would require such testing.

Under the federal government's Clean Air Act, states that did not pass laws requiring emission and maintenance testing for autos would lose their federal transportation funds. Watt, the head of the Mountain States Legal Foundation, a conservative organization actively backed by Joseph Coors (who was also a supporter of mine) felt that this requirement was unconstitutional because it amounted to blackmail.

As a lawyer I believed that the law probably *was* unconstitutional, but as a resident of and representative from Denver I knew just how bad our air pollution was, and I knew that auto emissions were contributing to the problem. So I introduced a bill that required auto emission inspection in Denver and the surrounding counties. My bill passed, and Watt lost his lawsuit on a technicality. Jim and I remained on friendly terms. After all, we were both conservatives and both staunch Reagan supporters.

The interview with Watt began on a friendly basis. It was almost a carbon copy of my interview with Alex Armendaris; Jim seemed to become increasingly impressed with my background and experience, a lot of which he'd known nothing about because of our somewhat limited professional contact back home. Finally, he said much the same thing that Armandaris had said—that I was actually more qualified than the people they'd been considering for the Administrator's job.

Then he said something he shouldn't have. Jim Watt has, as most Americans now know thanks to the power of television and the other media, a characteristic grin that can easily be mistaken for a smirk. And at that moment it seemed to me he was smirking as he said, in all seriousness, "Anne, you are undoubtedly the most qualified candidate, on all counts, for the *top* job, but I am not going to recommend you," and then he paused, "because you are not tough enough."

I happen to be slow to anger. Though I may show annoyance quickly, it usually takes something major to make me angry instantly. That remark, however, did it. *Not tough enough?* Who did this guy think he was? And who did he think he was talking to? I blew my stack.

"You, Jim Watt," I raged at him, "who has never even practiced law or been elected to public office and had this cushy little job with a legal foundation, while I've been elected twice from the most Democratic district in the state of Colorado by a factor of about ten, and at the head of every conservative cause in the legislature for the last four years, and on the front pages almost every day for the last four years—you have the nerve to tell me that I'm not tough enough? That's the most chauvinistic remark I've ever heard!"

His jaw didn't quite drop, but the smirk vanished. And then, as I stared at him, it occurred to me that if he and Alex Armendaris were right that I was the best qualified candidate for the job of EPA Administrator, then, damn it, that's the job I ought to have.

"I'm not leaving this office," I told a startled Jim Watt, "until I have two things. One, your personal apology. And, two, your promise that you will recommend to the President that I should be the Administrator of the Environmental Protection Agency."

To Jim Watt's credit, I got both.

In early January an article in the *Rocky Mountain News* by reporters Daniel Taylor and Al Gordon turned out to be more than a little prophetic. It read, in part:

GORSUCH, EPA CRITIC, SEEKS AGENCY POST

Two-term state Rep. Anne Gorsuch, a Republican who didn't seek re-election to the Legislature this year, is seeking appointment as deputy director of the U.S. Environmental Protection Agency—an agency she has frequently criticized.

She could wind up as its director.

Gorsuch, 38, confirmed Tuesday that she is seeking the post and was interviewed for it while in Washington working on President-elect Ronald Reagan's transition team.

During her tenure in the Legislature, Gorsuch, a Mountain Bell attorney, was a vehement foe of the agency, frequently criticizing EPA officials for promulgating environmental regulations that, she contended, made no sense.

Gorsuch said Tuesday that she thinks the agency should continue to exist, but its direction should be changed.

"I do believe we need an Evironmental Protection Agency," she said. "And I think EPA's role should be performed by the federal government instead of the states because of the technical nature of the agency's work. But, in many cases, the agency has developed regulations without any consideration of the cost to the public."

While Gorsuch has applied for the Agency's number two post, Washington sources say she may be under consideration as its director. A transition committee source in Washington said the decision is down to "a couple of dozen" people to head the EPA, but would neither confirm nor deny that Gorsuch was among those.

Gorsuch frequently has been mentioned as a possibility to head the EPA's regional office in Denver, and as a possibility to be the next U.S. Attorney in Denver. But she said she would rather work in Washington, where the top policy decisions are made.

"I'm really not looking for the director's job," she said. "I think I would have more of a chance to affect policy in the deputy director's job. That's really the workhorse position."

She said it was time someone brought "some common sense to the EPA."

In the decade of EPA's existence, the Administrator had always been the one who spoke for the agency on the Hill and around the country in speeches and appearances, whereas someone else actually ran the agency. It was my intention if I got the job to reverse that arrangement. I wanted the chance to make the EPA an efficient and effective agency.

Once James Watt made his recommendation to the President, the process began to move, but the movement was neither swift nor sure. And there was a stumbling block in the person of someone back home who'd always been a friend and a supporter.

The White House personnel system is a pyramid through which one moves, level by level, until reaching the top. The "top" was Pendelton "Penn" James. When it became apparent that my candidacy for Administrator was real, Penn James was not exactly enthusiastic about considering me. There were two reasons. One reason was Joe Coors, the Colorado brewer and Ronald Reagan confidant who was an early and influential member of Reagan's kitchen cabinet.

Joe Coors is an awfully nice gentleman, a friend from way back, and I really like him. But he is from a generation that is unused to and therefore uncomfortable with women in top management positions. And so when my name got all the way up to the kitchen cabinet, even though we were both from Colorado and knew and respected and liked one another, he was a reluctant supporter. Penn James, I am afraid, shared that reluctance. It was at this point that Wendy Borcherdt went to bat for me. She took me on as a cause, and forced Penn James to act favorably on my recommendation.

Reason number two was somewhat more pragmatic. Once we began to talk seriously about me as Administrator, it was always with the understanding that I would accept Dr. John Hernandez, professor and environmental consultant from New Mexico, as Deputy Administrator.

John Hernandez had been the choice of New Mexico Senator Pete Domenici, a fine man with an enviable record of placing his people in top spots around Washington, for Director of EPA. The idea of Hernandez as my deputy bothered a number of influential conservatives, because John was not one of us politically or philosophically. So it was by no means clear—and certainly not to me—that I had anything resembling the inside track for the job.

That the conservatives were initially happy with me and displeased with Dr. Hernandez now strikes me as an irony, since from the beginning to the bitter end I received almost no help from any of the high-profile conservatives.

By February 1981 I felt as if I were supporting United Air Lines. I made at least a half a dozen trips to Washington to talk to people or to be interviewed officially by various members of the White House personnel hierarchy. And I paid for every one of those trips, plus expenses, myself. I didn't know if I was getting any closer to the job, but at least I was learning my way around the city.

As the interviews progressed, they fell into a predictable and rather odd pattern: Each one began with a recitation of my background and accomplishments, whereupon the interviewer was duly—and I felt sincerely—impressed. There followed a brief period of small talk near the end, and then each man (all of my interviewers were men) ended the interview with the same question: "But are you tough enough?"

In view of the pervasiveness of that attitude, which may or may not have been a true concern, in time I actually became grateful to Jim Watt for causing me to blow up at him. Having lost my temper with him, I was able to contain it when all the interviewers asked the same question.

My last interviewer was Edwin Meese III, then the President's counsel and now Attorney General. A disciple of Ronald Reagan for decades, Californian Ed Meese was my last hurdle. I had been able to keep my cool when the other men in the interviewing chain asked the tough-enough question. But when Meese ended the interview with that very same query, I decided to give him the same double-barreled answer I gave Jim Watt.

"No," I snapped. "I graduated from law school at the age of twenty, passed the bar at twenty-one, served in two D.A.'s offices, was elected twice from a heavily Democratic district, and was at the head of every conservative cause for the last four years—I've obviously been a marshmallow."

Ed Meese did not laugh, but I could tell he liked my answer. A few days later I learned that he had recommended me.

Then everything seemed to stop. President Reagan had been in office for more than a month, then six weeks, then seven, and I had yet to receive a yes or no. I became quite discouraged, and at one point, when Wendy Borcherdt called from Washington and said, "Get back out here," I told her I was tired of going back and forth. "Are you guys serious or not?" I asked.

"*I* am," was Wendy's reply.

Still, I was getting just plain disgusted. "Look," I said, "I've been out there at least a half a dozen times. Frankly, right about now I don't care *whom* you appoint, but you sure as hell better get somebody in there in a hurry. Just from a private citizen's point of view, I can tell you that you're two months too late right now. EPA is too damn important an agency to be without a head for so long."

I don't know exactly what caused the lengthy delay in appointing me to be the head of Ronald Reagan's EPA. But I find it very hard to resist the impression that David Stockman had a lot to do with it.

One of the most brilliant young men I have ever met, David

Stockman is also one of the most driven and calculating. And when he gets fixed on an idea, he does not easily let it go. It is a matter of record that he hates the legislation that established the Environmental Protection Agency. In facts, he hates EPA. Period.

David has the soul of a conservative—at least I think he does. From his days in Congress, both as an aide to John Anderson and as a member himself, he has frequently opposed pro-EPA legislation. Philosophically, I can understand his position. And I think he was right. Many of the areas are so technical that Congress left a great deal of rule-making authority, which should really be legislative authority, to the discretion of the Administrator. And that, from a conservative point of view, is making government highly unresponsive.

To this day he remains very strongly opposed to the legislation that EPA is charged with implementing. And though that may be correct from a conservative point of view, that won't make the agency go away.

It has always been my feeling that Stockman was instrumental in delaying the decision on my appointment—and perhaps that of others, too. I believe this because in the leadership vacuum that resulted, he did an awful lot of the running of the agency. He proposed the first budget, and he drafted legislation that changed the water laws with regard to grants for sewage treatment plants. He had all that done by the time I got to town. I agree that these very dramatic changes were necessary, and it was David Stockman who got them through, not me. I think he would have been perfectly happy to continue running the agency—through the budget— forever.

As evidence of my thesis that Stockman was perfectly happy with the vacuum of power and that he continued to exercise an unwholesome degree of power over EPA, I offer a letter he wrote to his House colleagues at the time the Superfund legislation was pending. I did not learn of the letter's existence until we did the research for this book. I wish I had seen it before taking office.

DAVID A. STOCKMAN
4th District, Michigan

Congress of the United States
House of Representatives
Washington, D.C. 20515

September 15, 1980

RE: SUPERFUND OR EPA POWER GRAB?

Dear Colleague:

When you vote on H.R. 7020—the chemical superfund proposal—please set-aside the "agit-prop" issued by EPA's mis-education division, and recall the following basics:

Abandoned Sites Only

H.R. 7020 has nothing to do with current and future waste production or midnight dumping and other improper disposal of hazardous waste. Every pound of the estimated annual 34.4 million metric tons of hazardous industrial waste will soon be tightly regulated under a cradle-to-grave control system established by the Resource Recovery and Conservation Act. Penalties for violation are severe. That's why the stock market value of high technology disposal companies like Waste Management, Inc. and SCA has skyrocketed and midnight dumpers are on the run.

Superfund is concerned only with *abandoned* and *inactive* sites—with the unfinished business left by inadequate disposal standards and practices in the past.

The Documented Problem is Limited

Thus far, only 400-800 abandoned dump-sites that may pose threats to public health or safety have been reliably identified. The 30,000 to 50,000 estimate tossed out by the EPA is rank speculation. It was based on a contractor's tally of hurried, unstandardized, arm-chair guesses made by EPA regional offices, some of which even included ordinary municipal landfills containing rusting refrigerators and rotting garbarge. The study was termed "little better than a guesstimate" by The Eckhardt subcommittee.

Tailor Made for the States

This particular pollution problem is tailor made for state rather than Federal action. Unlike air, water and current hazardous waste pollution, abandoned dump sites *don't travel across state lines*. In fact, EPA estimates that 41 states will assume responsibility for [clean-up].

Given these conditions, I am proposing something quite novel in the environmental field: let the states investigate, inventory and clean-up their own abandoned dumps! The Federal role would be limited to providing no strings financial aid ($500 million over five years) and technical assistance.

LET'S GET OFF THE SUPER BUREAUCRACY KICK

Prior to 1970, this solution would have appeared quite sensible. But for ten years we've been in an environmental time-warp. EPA and its minions in the press and the professional environmental lobbies have assumed an absolute monopoly right to flood the American economy with regulations, litigation and compliance costs that are out of proportion to any environmental problem—real and imagined—that has reached the Congressional calendar.

Its time to get off this super bureaucracy kick—unless you really believe that the present drastic deterioration of our economy, productivity, international competitiveness, and living standards will soon miraculously fade away.

It won't happen so long as we keep writing blank checks that authorize hot-shot junior lawyers and zealots ensconced in the EPA to bleed American industry of scarce funds needed for investment, modernization and job-creation. Like every other major environmental enabling act of the past decade, H.R. 7020 has absolutely no definitions of the waste sites being regulated, no cost-benefit limitation on the monitoring and clean-up expenditures being incurred, and ample authorization for punitive litigation, taxes, and penalties against every "deep pocket" business it can haul into court. The only saving note is that after Chrysler,

Ford, U.S. Steel, Firestone, White Motors, etc., there aren't many deep pockets left to prosecute.

In subsequent letters I intend to itemize the horrors for small business, local governments, non-chemical business firms and the national economy and job creation which lie buried in this bill. But for now let me just remind you of two things the committee report and proponents have not bothered to mention.

1.   *This bill was written at 2:00 A.M. in the morning in a smoke filled room by a handful* of lobbyists, subcommittee members and staff. The full Commerce Committee membership did not even have a print until 10:00 A.M. the next morning—at which point it was gaveled through under a gag rule by the end of the day. As such, it consists of a series of sloppy compromises grafted onto an EPA proposed empire expansion—Superfund—for which absolutely no solid case has been made.

2.   *Not a pittance of evidence for a dominant Federal role.* As written, every decision to define, identify, monitor, clean-up abandoned sites or sue for cost recovery will be made by EPA bureaucrats pursuant to five different rule making exercises required by the bill. Yet this pre-emptive extension of Federal power was not based on even a shred of evidence that state environmental officials are so morally benighted or technically inept that they could not handle the abandoned site problem on their own, given modest financial help.

The discussion of "inadequate state and local responses" in the Commerce Committee report on page 19 is an insult and a joke. It cites three instances, one of which occurred in 1958 and another of which could not occur under the new RCRA regulations.

Rather than unleash another multi-thousand bureaucratic army, new taxes on business, new powers to litigate and punish, and a new multibillion drain on our faltering national economy, I would urge that you consider a policy more in conformity with the economic exigencies of the present hour. Let's help the states protect their own citizens and water supplies from threats posed by a modest number of abandoned industrial dump sites. My substitute is designed to do just that in a simple and effective manner.

With all best wishes, I am

Yours very truly,

DAVE STOCKMAN
Member of Congress

DS/ms

No matter who was behind the delay in the nomination, it finally ended on February 20, 1981, when Ronald Reagan caught me in my kitchen and asked me to be the EPA Administrator.

3

ADVISE AND CONSENT

Early in 1985 I had lunch with a lawyer friend now working for a legal foundation who'd been with me at EPA from the beginning, and after a while the conversation turned to the topic of Fred Fielding. Mr. Fielding, Watergate buffs may recall, was a lawyer in the Nixon White House. In fact, Fielding had worked for John Dean, the President's counsel, and had been the one who called Dean in California to inform him of the break-in at the Democratic headquarters. He was a real survivor.

My lunch companion said, "I've often thought the reason Fred Fielding is still with the administration and all of us are gone is that he was the first one we all talked to, the one who interrogated everybody to see what skeletons they had in their closets. Hell, he probably knows so much dirt about people that the White House wouldn't *dare* get rid of him!"

I laughed, but I knew what he meant. Although hardly a Reaganite, Fred Fielding had materialized on the White House steps immediately after the election, proclaiming himself to be Mr. Ethics, and offering to do the kind of hard questioning that is supposed to turn up those details of one's past which could embarrass the administration. Fielding was probably the prime example of the Nixon-Ford Republicans who had surfaced immediately after

Ronald Reagan's election to insinuate themselves into the good jobs while the conservatives were still dancing in the streets.

When it came time for all of us to be "woodshedded"—to be interviewed off-the-résumé for the purpose of making sure we wouldn't have to reveal somewhere down the road that we'd had, say, electroshock treatments—it turned out to be Fred Fielding or one of his chief deputies who did the interviewing. I don't know anyone who thought of Fielding or his crew as conservatives. But I wonder if my luncheon companion didn't just hit the nail on the head: one of the main reasons why Fred Fielding has lasted so long in the Reagan administration despite his center-to-left Republican credentials is that he knows so much about so many important people. (For example, he knew the SEC's former head of enforcement was a wife beater long before the story broke.)

Fielding was but one part of an intriguing process that all political appointees must undergo before they get internal clearance. In some cases, such as that of James Watt who was sworn into office on the day after the President, the process moves swiftly. In mine, it did not.

The President's call asking me to be the head of EPA had come on February 20, but the White House did not announce my name until the end of the month. And then it took me until *May 20* to be approved.

I still do not know why it took that long. Whenever I asked, the usual story was that because I had lived out of the country so often it took longer than usual to check my background. I had studied in Mexico City for four summers when I was a grade school and high school student, and I'd spent nine months in India on a Fulbright grant immediately after graduating from law school. But that hardly made me one of the most-traveled appointees.

I never bought that story, and I did not discover the real one. But it was clear that the holdup was not on the part of the Senate; it was in the White House's own internal clearance procedure. The personnel people used to tell me that it was taking that long to talk to "the camel drivers in India and the taxi drivers in Mexico City." I wonder.

All applicants put forward by the White House have to be checked by both the FBI and the IRS. Everyone has to sign a form giving the latter agency the right to inspect his or her tax returns. Some people have great difficulty at this step. I didn't, which should have made the checking even simpler. Fred Fielding's office was the next step.

You had to fill out a form provided by Fielding that included a number of potentially far-reaching questions. He insisted you admit anything in your past that might prove embarrassing to the administration. "Is there any special group that would oppose your nomination?" "Have you ever been involved in anything controversial?" Given my experiences in the Colorado legislature and the many controversies we were involved in, I knew it was going to take me some time to answer that one fully.

Next you had to complete a financial disclosure sheet, listing all sources of income, what you owe and to whom, and whether or not you have any fiduciary relationships, and with whom. That form also has to be filled out for your spouse and children. (That's where Geraldine Ferraro got herself in trouble. She failed for six years to fill out such a form, claiming she had "no interest in" and "received no benefit from" her husband's financial holdings.)

After you'd filled out Fielding's form you were invited in for a little chat to amplify the record and go beyond the printed page (off the record, of course). My talk, with Fielding's aide Richard Hauser rather than with Fielding himself, was relatively brief, as I had no secrets, but a number of people had rather lengthy stays in that office.

At one point in the interview Mr. Hauser, who was very nice throughout, fixed me with a somber look, and said, "Do you know anything about being in a stolen Volkswagen in 1961?"

"My God," I said, startled, "*my* VW was stolen then, but I've never been in a stolen Volkswagen!"

I did volunteer the information that Robert Burford and I were "seeing" one another. As my divorce was not yet final, and Burford was soon to be the Director of the Bureau of Land Management, I thought it was something they might need to know, though I didn't really feel it was any of their business.

It was interesting to speculate on how much people were telling Fielding and his crew. I was not as prescient as my friend with whom I had lunch in early 1985. He recalled, "When I saw all those people trooping in to Fielding's office and baring their souls, I knew we [the conservatives] were in trouble right off the bat."

In my opinion, my interview with that office was just another step in the process. I did, however, have another problem. This one was named Minor, but the trouble he caused me was almost major.

When he phoned me not very long after the President himself, he said his name was Ernie Minor. He said he was the liaison between the White House and EPA, sort of the transitional head, and he promised to take care of everything for me and to smooth the way for me to settle into the job. Something about his manner bothered me, but I couldn't put my finger on it. Nonetheless, my unease increased when I got to the Denver airport and discovered he had booked me in first class (something I never do myself and certainly wouldn't do as a governmental representative, even an unconfirmed one). And he had made a reservation for me at the Hay-Adams Hotel on 16th Street, across LaFayette Park from the White House.

I've since learned that the Hay-Adams has a proud and distinguished history (it occupies the site of what were once the residences of John Adams and Samuel Hay) and it has recently been sold and redone with taste and beauty. But in early 1981 when I came to Washington for the first time as President Reagan's nominee for EPA Administrator, all I knew was that it was just plain dirty, and it was falling apart at its historic seams.

There was an ornate lobby, but once I'd left it I had the increasing feeling that I was ascending higher and higher into a huge firetrap. And when I got to the end of the long narrow hallway, I let myself into a tiny room that faced an unattractive interior open space. The wallpaper was peeling off in long strips, and the room was covered with such a film of dirt that I couldn't even set so much as a lipstick down anywhere. I had to wear the same dress I'd arrived in because I refused to unpack in that room, which was the first time I'd ever had to do that in any country, including Mexico and India.

I spent one night there, and the next morning at the crack of dawn, Mr. Minor or no Mr. Minor, I called the River Inn and booked a room, wailing, "You've got to let me back in!" This was no time to be living in a depressing room. This was supposed to be one of the best times of my life.

Ernie Minor picked me up and drove me to have my official photo taken, then to the Old Executive Office Building and the White House, and finally he took me to the Environmental Pro-

tection Agency. As the day wore on he became increasingly con-
descending, and his manner became imperious, but he reached
new heights when we reached the EPA. Instead of putting me in
the Administrator's office, he put me in the Deputy Administrator's office. Then he began to tell me how we would function in
our respective roles, and it soon became clear that this man envisioned himself as the real head of EPA, with me as a rather
pleasant-looking façade. In effect, he told me I could handle all
the "important stuff," and he would take care of the budget and
personnel.

I felt a tinge of panic. Here was this former advance man for
Spiro Agnew, a guy who had spent almost all of his years of public
service as a public information specialist, telling me that he would
take care of budget and personnel, and I could handle everything
else. After those two items there *isn't* anything else! The only
things that count in an agency are the money and the people. If
you don't control those, you don't control anything. I was insulted
to realize he thought he had such a greenhorn in his sights.

I got on the phone as soon as I could and called a Denver
lawyer I knew who'd had both Washington and EPA experience.

Jim Sanderson was one of the senior partners of a very successful mid-sized law firm that did a lot of environmental and
regulatory work, but he had spent time in Washington in the early
1970s. He had worked on the Hill for Senator Allott—at the same
time as two other bright young men who would be heard from
again, Paul Weyrich and George Will—and had gone to EPA as
a lawyer when the agency was still quite young. The knowledge
he had gained in those positions stood him in good stead when
he entered private practice. Sanderson understood how Washington worked.

"Sanderson," I implored, "get yourself out here right away!"
Thank God, he did.

My next call for help went to Jim Watt. I knew that when he
had said to call him if I needed anything he truly meant it. People
can say what they want about Jim Watt, but his generosity is not
feigned. And he had a coterie of good people who had been
helpful to him during his own preconfirmation period.

Because Watt, like Sanderson, had worked in Washington before (as a lobbyist for the Chamber of Commerce, at the Department of the Interior, and later as an attorney for and then a

Commissioner of the Federal Power Commission) he was able to put together a good staff in a relatively short period of time. And it was all too apparent to me that a staff of my own choosing had to be near the very top of my list of priorities. Jim quickly called together three of his top people, Don Hodel (now Secretary of Interior), Doug Baldwin, who handled press for him, and Stan Hulett, who did his Congressional Affairs. He told them, "I want you to give Annie all the help you can."

Hulett was especially helpful. He called five Washington lawyer friends, men who'd been involved in both Washington and environmental law for some years, plus three nonlawyer women who also had impressive backgrounds and some experience that dovetailed neatly with that of the men. The main purpose of the group was to brief me thoroughly on the important issues that would come up at my Senate confirmation hearings. As things turned out, I could not have asked for a better or a more helpful group.

Each of the eight people had an area of expertise within EPA. Hulett's lawyer-lobbyist friends were John Daniel, Bill Frick, Chick Ables, Mike Glenn, and Ed Warren. The women, all of whom later came to work for me, were Kathleen Bennett, Jacqueline Schaeffer, and Kitty Adams. And the briefing sessions, which were not unlike what the President goes through in preparation for a campaign debate, were held in the living room of Kitty Adams's house in Alexandria, Virginia, just across the Potomac River from Washington, D.C.

For at least six weeks we met several times a week in that living room, and they put me through my paces, covering the basic areas of air, water, solid and hazardous waste, pesticides and toxic substances, and drinking water. By the time we reached the end of April (my hearing had finally been scheduled for May 3) I was not just ready, I was loaded for bear. The hard drill was about to pay off.

Other events of varying degrees of seriousness took place at the same time. One morning in April, while I was in the office that Jim Watt had been kind enough to provide for me within Interior—I felt it would have been not just wrong but also poor politics for me to "office" in EPA prior to confirmation—I got a phone call from the White House. The caller said, "Mrs. Gorsuch, would you please come over right away? There's a special reception and lunch at noon, and we want you to go through the briefing papers before the affair begins."

"Of course," I said, mentally taking note of the fact that I was not as dressed up as I would have been had I planned on attending a White House function. "But what is it?"

"I'm sorry, but all I've been told is to get hold of you and make sure that you get here fast."

I took a cab, and was met at the front entrance of the White House by someone from Elizabeth Dole's White House Liaison office, who ushered me into an anteroom and gave me a small stack of papers. I sat down to read them, and absentmindedly started to finger the amethyst cross I was wearing on my tweed jacket.

I glanced up for a moment and noticed that people were beginning to gather in the large room across the hall. Some looked rather familiar, people whose pictures I might have seen in the papers. Then I started reading the papers, and I froze.

The occasion was a gathering of the country's major Jewish leaders, and the purpose was to introduce them to the Reagan administration's Jewish nominees. And there, plain as day, was my name. Good old Irish Catholic Annie!

I almost screamed. Instead, I rushed to get hold of the person from Dole's office who had greeted me.

"What's with you people?" I said. "I'm not Jewish. You've got to get me out of here, and you've absolutely got to get these papers changed right away. You're going to insult these important guests by this kind of mistake. And, look, I'm wearing a cross! That's as bad as wearing orange on St. Patrick's Day!"

She looked at me blankly. "But isn't Gorsuch a Jewish name? I know we have a Jewish nominee from Colorado, and I just assumed it was you."

As it turned out, the person in question was Phil Winn, who had been named to the Department of Housing and Urban Development. And he is Jewish. As for me, I got my Irish-Catholic-with-a-German-sounding-married-name self out of there, hugging the wall as I moved toward a rear entrance, my hand carefully covering my amethyst cross. It was the first time I saw that the White House staff had not done its homework. It would not be the last.

The Jewish mix-up paralleled the situation that had always prevailed in my electoral district back in Colorado. There were three main contenders for the office: me, a Mr. Fitzpatrick, and the incumbent, whose name was Gaon. The district was heavily populated by three distinct groups, which happened to be Jews, Catholics, and Irish. What made the situation ironic was that many of the Catholics voted for Mr. Fitzpatrick, figuring he was one of them, whereas he was actually a Protestant; a lot of Jews voted for me, thinking Gorsuch was a Jewish name; and, finally, many non-Jews voted for Gaon, apparently thinking he was Italian, when he was in fact Jewish. Later the three of us figured out that all the mistaken vote switching probably evened out in the end.

The next snafu turned out to be more serious, and this time it was the fault of someone at EPA. The affair was to have lasting implications.

Although only the U.S. Senate has confirmation power, and therefore I spent the bulk of my visiting time on the Hill seeing Senators, there were a few Representatives I was advised to see for a variety of reasons, usually because they held important committee posts or had marked and influential views on environmental matters. One such person was James J. Howard of New Jersey, chairman of the Public Works and Transportation Committee, and therefore also a member *ex officio* (by virtue of being Chairman) of its Water Resources subcommittee. When John Daniel, one of the best of my briefing team members and the lawyer I'd talked into coming with me as my chief of staff if I was confirmed, and I paid a courtesy call on Congressman Howard, we got quite a surprise.

"Do I want to meet Anne Gorsuch?" we could hear him shouting from his inner office. "Do I ever! I want to find out why that woman tried to *sabotage* me! Where is she, where is she?"

The Congressman was as angry as anyone I had ever met. He screamed at me, attacked me, and told me I was lower than a snake. And when he was done with me, he turned on John Daniel and berated him for being part of the plot that he clearly felt was an attempt to drive him from office, even though he had just been reelected. He did everything but physically throw us out of his office.

It took some time, but we finally learned what had happened. Representative Howard's defeated opponent was behind it all, and

EPA's main headquarters in Washington was also a culprit, but in truth no one involved had any evil intent.

Howard represents New Jersey's Third District, an area in which a large construction grant proposal was pending at EPA. All during the campaign Howard's opponent had been stressing the issue and promising to get EPA to announce its award to the district.

Characteristically, it was taking forever for the agency to get its act together and make the grant, and election day came and went without an announcement. Representative Howard won, as he has been doing since 1964, and his office continued about its normal business, confident that when and if EPA acted they would find out about it in the regular course of affairs, and they would then let the citizens of the Third District know. What Howard's office discounted was the tenacity of the former opponent, who had adopted the practice of phoning EPA *every day* to ask if anything had happened on the project.

One day, bright and early in the morning, the Construction Grants section of the Water Office of EPA released its decision that the project was going to go forward. Not long after the decision was made, a call came in as usual from the former opponent, who was told, since there was no reason not to tell anyone, "Yes, as a matter of fact that was just granted this morning." There had not even been time to follow the normal procedure and inform Mr. Howard that a construction grant had been made to a facility in his district.

The vanquished opponent then made an announcement to the delighted home folks. On hearing who had let his constituents know of their good fortune, thereby stealing his thunder in the process, Mr. Howard was not, to say the least, thrilled. Indeed, he was furious, almost as furious as he was the day—weeks later— I walked into his office to pay a courtesy call.

The problem was that Mr. Howard blamed me for what he perceived as a screw-up. It made no difference to him that I was not yet in office or that I didn't even use the EPA premises at 4th and M Streets. He saw it as part of a Republican plot to embarrass and defeat him, and he would hear no explanation other than his own. And, as I would find out much later, he would never forget it.

The last significant incident that took place while I was preparing for my confirmation hearing was not just serious, it was tragic. It was mid-afternoon of March 31, and we were gathered once again in Kitty Adams's living room. The day was rainy, still a bit wintry. We had been working steadily and hard—in fact, we had met there so often that Kitty was running out of cover stories to explain to one of her neighbors why this same group of people was showing up at her house with such regularity. Normally she didn't worry about what to tell her neighbors, but this one was different; he was an executive with the Washington *Post*. We were beginning, with the hearing only a few days away, to get a little confident and even a little punchy. We laughed and had a good time, growing secure in the knowledge that the group had prepared me well and that I had fully absorbed their many lessons.

Then someone happened to turn on the radio, and we learned that President Reagan had been shot.

To say that a pall descended doesn't even begin to describe it. At first everyone spoke, then no one did, then everyone again. It was frightening and eerie. We were stunned by the fact that "it" had happened again, another madman had tried to kill another world leader, another American President. And for all we knew at the time, he had succeeded.

I have to admit I also thought of myself. And whether I even wanted to be a part of an administration that was not Ronald Reagan's. He was the man we conservatives had worked so long and so hard to elect. After all that time and work we finally had a man in office who truly reflected our values.

I find my reaction to that terrible day rather strange. I really do not believe in the theory of the irreplaceable man. But as a result of that shooting, I do. Bush is not Reagan, and there isn't anybody else like him whom we could elect. He really *is* irreplaceable. That very sad day I felt, "There he goes."

To appreciate the atmosphere that surrounded my confirmation hearing, it is important to understand what the White House had wrought by its four-month delay in naming an EPA Administrator. First of all, the country had had four months of James Watt. That may sound unkind, but it is a fact. Jim Watt and I are fundamentally different people.

Although I have made a few comments that have produced both headlines and trouble, confrontation is not really my style.

Jim, on the other hand, *loves* to confront his critics. And with the environmentalists, he didn't just confront them, he *baited* them.

In addition to his rather combative comments (some of which were triggered as much by his keen, if not always appreciated, sense of humor as by his political philosophy) there was also his record as the head of the probusiness Mountain States Legal Foundation. In that job Jim Watt never made any bones about siding with business, even if it meant backing the lawsuit of a John Birch Society member who refused to let the Occupational Safety and Health Administration (OSHA) inspect the premises of his heating and plumbing company, or fighting Indians over water rights. And, almost as if he had set out to anger the Eastern liberal press (isn't that redundant?) he had also fought legal battles over issues that brought him in conflict with senior citizens, women, and minorities.

Knowing—and I suspect even enjoying—that he was controversial moved Watt to say, just prior to his own confirmation hearings, "I am bringing a new dimension" to the Department of Interior. The head of one environmental group said it was like "hiring a fox to guard the chickens." And *The Nation* editorialized that it was more like "hiring Robert Vesco to head the Securities and Exchange Commission."

Through it all Jim Watt just laughed. While stormy, his confirmation hearings went well, although there were sixteen votes against him. But his comments—those he made publicly and many he made to small groups that managed to find their way into the newspapers—continued to rankle his opponents, especially the environmentalists.

It should also be rememberd that almost all the environmentalist groups and organizations had gathered in the Rose Garden and endorsed Jimmy Carter in his race against Ronald Reagan. So there was very little chance that they would be happy with the President's choice of Interior Secretary, given the obvious differences in attitude, and no way in the world they would be happy with anyone he chose to run EPA. In fact, at that time I firmly believe they would not even have been satisfied with Bill Ruckelshaus.

In opposing me, the press took its lead from the environmentalists. And initially I could understand that. But I made the mistake of thinking that reporters would do a better job of finding out just what my record had been back home—especially with regard to issues on which I had *opposed* EPA while a state legislator. When I began to see it printed that I had opposed the Colorado Clean Air Act, when I had been the bill's prime sponsor in the House, I realized how wrong that assumption had been.

Putting aside the question of the reporters' responsibility for accuracy, where were the editors? Where were the fact-checkers? Or do they all take a break when the subject of the article is a conservative?

I'd never had what one might call a problem with the press in Colorado. I had been open with reporters, and though there were stories with which I disagreed, I certainly didn't try to stay away from the press. But my exeriences in Washington made me leery from the very beginning.

Looking back I can see that a great deal of the press's dislike for Jim Watt and his policies (or what they perceived as his policies) had spilled over onto me. He'd been needling them for almost four months before I appeared on the scene, and I would have been better off if I had been able to see just how far he had got under their collective skin. I did understand it somewhat, at least to the extent that it was one of the several reasons why I knew I would have to be superbly prepared when I went before the Senate.

In addition to the Watt Factor, there was the political reality of the Reagan election, and what it meant. Ronald Reagan had campaigned on the promise to reduce both federal spending and the size of the federal government. He had said there would be cut-backs almost across the board, and he would completely eliminate some government agencies, such as Education and also the Department of Energy. Clearly, EPA would have to be affected. But what bothered me was the "party line" kind of news story that assumed that because I was also from Colorado and also a conservative (and using an office in Interior lent me by James Watt) my primary mission would be to gut EPA and do away with all the environmental protections. It was a form of guilt by association that we neither liked nor deserved.

If the Watt Factor and the Reagan Agenda were not enough, there was another important element—the Stockman Presence. I had barely heard of the former two-term Congressman from Michigan before I came to Washington, but I certainly heard of him once I arrived. And heard of him and heard of him and heard of him.

As he wasted very little time showing, he was one of the two or three most powerful men in the administration. As head of the Office of Management and Budget, he began by telling the Cabinet and the rest of the agency and department heads (with the initial exception of the military) just how much they would have to spend. And there was to be no arguing with him. His budget figures were not suggestions; they were pronouncements. And the matter-of-fact way he testified on the Hill about the coming slashes in spending did not always sit well with the heads of important committees, many of whom, I would soon learn, would then take out their ire on the official in charge of the about-to-be-slashed agency or department. And if that official were still awaiting confirmation, then look out.

4

CONFIRMATION DAY

As we neared the day of my confirmation hearing, I feared that I might be expected to defend not just the Reagan administration's philosophy of government, but the entire history of the EPA. I might be held accountable for the sins of the past as well as the imagined but uncommitted sins of a conservative present.

There was another matter to take care of before the hearing, a little matter of style.

In the early spring of 1981 I was a happy woman. Not only was I Ronald Reagan's choice to head the EPA, but I was also seriously involved with Robert Burford, once my close political ally as Speaker of the House in Colorado, and now the only person in whom I was interested romantically. The courtship that would lead to marriage was in full bloom.

Shortly before the day of the hearing, Burford (I often affectionately use his last name rather than his first) said to me, "When you walk in that Senate hearing room"—and he had been there himself in early May when the Senate confirmed him as the head of the Bureau of Land Management—"you are going to make a statement just by the way you look. You're a class act, and those guys have never seen class like they're going to see when you walk in for that hearing. Come on."

With that, he took me to Saks Jandel, a very expensive women's clothing store located in the Maza Gallerie, one of several fine places in a posh section of upper Wisconsin Avenue in Northwest Washington. He helped me pick out the most expensive outfit of clothes I'd ever had on in my life. And he paid for it. The purple Yves St. Laurent suit and the deep blue YSL silk blouse cost in the neighborhood of $2,000, which is, as they say, a very nice neighborhood. And Robert was right. My entrance into that hearing room was indeed a class act.

But walking into the room turned out to be a little more difficult than I had anticipated.

The Senate Environment and Public Works Committee has its own hearing room. On the morning of my scheduled appearance the room filled up hours before the hearing was set to begin. Hundreds of people were standing out in the hall wanting to get seats. Senator Stafford, the committee chairman, huddled with a few other committee members, checked with the Rules Committee and the Capitol Police, made a few calls, and then announced that the hearing would be moved to the huge Senate Caucus room on the first floor of the Russell Senate Office Building (which, prior to the construction of the Hart Building, used to be referred to as the "Old Senate Office Building"), the room Senator Sam Ervin's Watergate Committee had made famous.

The move meant a lot of shuffling and scrambling, as the media had to move their equipment as well as themselves, and then get everything reset up. Considering all that had to be done, it is a wonder that it took only an hour, but I was not terribly patient. I really wanted to get going.

Even though I had watched the people stream in, I was still surprised to walk in and encounter the sea of humanity that filled the room. Senate hearing rooms are not unlike courtrooms, with the spectator section in the rear and an open area or "well," between the dais and the witness tables. On the day of my hearing, the well was filled with photographers, all of them turned to face me. Along with the reporters at the side tables, the press numbered around three hundred. I'd had a lot of press coverage so far, but I certainly hadn't expected *this* much attention.

One of the reasons the media were out in such force was that I had refused to talk to the press before my confirmation hearing. I thought it was good politics, and also simple courtesy to the United States Senators who would be questioning me, not to parade my views in the press until the committee members had had their opportunity to quiz me, as the rules of the game dictate.

I had made calls on a number of the committee members, including Republican Senator Stafford, whose staff, I had been told, was extremely hostile to my appointment. Stafford's coming from Vermont meant that he had a number of very vocal environmentalists among his constituency. I had been told that the committee staff wanted him to be very hard on me. My team had prepared me so well, however, that I didn't worry. I would be able to handle it.

As I waited nervously to begin my testimony with a statement, to be followed by the Senator's questions, it flashed through my mind that the White House had given me absolutely no help in my confirmation process. Zero, zip. Wendy Borcherdt and Alex Armendaris had gone to bat for me during the time I was being interviewed by the White House personnel people, and I believe Wendy was instrumental in seeing that I was recognized as a serious contender, but once I had been nominated there was a silence from 1600 Pennsylvania Avenue, except when they wanted to feature my Jewishness.

Jim Watt had come through. And my friend Jim Sanderson had made the learning process fun; when the work day was finished Sanderson insisted on eating and relaxing in style, so I soon came to know all the good restaurants in downtown Washington. We had even managed to get in some sunbathing one day on the roof of the River Inn as we put the finishing touches on the statement I was about to deliver.

Another person who was wonderful was Senator Alan K. Simpson of Wyoming. God bless him. I had lived in his state for only the first eighteen months of my life, yet he insisted on introducing me to the committee and making a statement on my behalf. It was more than generous.

"I am pleased to introduce Anne Gorsuch for Administrator of the Environmental Protection Agency. While she now resides in the neighboring State of Colorado, she is a native of Wyoming. Mrs. Gorsuch is a highly qualified individual. She has fine intellectual and reasoning abilities which are evidenced in her common sense approach to problems. Her wealth of experience in local and state government have made her well aware of the importance of the complexity of environmental issues. . . .

"During her term as the state representative, Anne Gorsuch dealt with such critically important issues as auto emission and high altitude air quality, toxic chemical waste disposal and nuclear waste handling.

"I am very pleased with her past experiences as a very active and dynamic member of the Colorado State Assembly. As a former state legislator myself, I share her frustration and her experiences in assessing the demanding and perplexing position which several states find themselves in in assuming primacy for administration of Federal environmental legislation. . . . Her knowledge of federal-state relationships should enable her to be a very effective administrator.

"So I am confident, Mr. Chairman, that in her role as EPA administrator, Anne Gorsuch will endeavor to strike more for equitable results in the area of state-federal cooperation and begin to extricate this country from this pervasive pattern of paternal environmentalism.

"The preservation of an environment which is beneficial to human life depends not only upon the actions of Congress but upon legislators and governors and also upon the persons selected to be the EPA administrators. I believe that she will be very creatively effective in this position since she has also obtained most considerable experience as a lawyer involved in public policy issues and she will be most capable at understanding and interpreting and enforcing our nation's most intricate environmental laws. . . . Mr. Chairman and members of the committee, I am pleased to commend her to you. Thank you for the courtesy."

I was touched by Senator Simpson's kind remarks. What made them even kinder was the fact that the Republican Senator from my own state, William Armstrong, did not appear on my behalf. I had his support, but he took no active steps to help me become EPA Administrator. In fact, he told one reporter, "I will be happy to support her as long as she doesn't have any skeletons in her closet." Thanks a lot, Senator.

Two others who spoke for me were members of the House of Representatives, Hank Brown and Ken Kramer, both Colorado Republicans.

Hank Brown was kind enough to give the committee a quick and most flattering biographical sketch of me: "Anne is a graduate of the University of Colorado in 1961. She completed her four year undergraduate work there in only two years, plus the summer sessions. In addition to achieving a superb academic record, she was selected for membership in the Mortar Board, which at C.U. honors those who make exceptional contributions to the campus community. At a time when few women entered law school, Anne enrolled in the university's school of law. She completed the three-year program in two and a half years, served as a class officer each year and was selected for the board of editors of the *Law Review*. At the ripe old age of 21, Anne received her bachelor of arts degree, completed law school, passed the Colorado bar exam, and was awarded a Fulbright scholarship."

Hank was followed by my old legislative officemate in the Colorado House, Ken Kramer.

"I served with Anne in the Colorado State House in 1977 and 1978. . . . I had the privilege of spending two years with Anne at that time, and we had an office, not only a seat in the Colorado House, but the same office. . . .

"She was assigned to three committees when I served with her during her tenure in the Colorado State Legislature. Most freshman legislators are given two. She was vice chairman of the judiciary committee the very first year that she got to the House. She also served on the finance and appropriations committee. . . . In the Colorado State Legislature Anne was a prime sponsor of twenty-one bills passed by the general assembly. She was the author of the Colorado presumptive sentencing law, which rewrote the provisions of the Colorado State Criminal Code. . . . Another one of her successful bills repealed over 70 sections of redundant, obsolete, or duplicative Colorado statutes. . . . As a result, she was voted the outstanding freshman legislator of the 1977-78 term. . . . One of the first tasks facing the legislature in 1980 was air pollution legislation. Anne Gorsuch was the prime sponsor of the Air Pollution Inspection and Maintenance Act, which, although amended somewhat in conference, satisfied EPA's requirements.

"In carrying this bill, even though only in her second term, Anne was able to build a coalition that held the basic bill against more than a score of amendments and opponents and which met the core EPA requirements while eliminating the least effective and most costly features suggested by EPA. In her efforts Anne was able to do something which had not been done before, nor since. She was able to pass an environmental bill with support from both the state-rights advocates and the environmentalists.

"The final version of that legislation typified Anne's position on the environment. The bill did as much as possible toward reducing air pollution within the limits of effective technology. It avoided placing unnecessary costs on citizens. And it gave the State of Colorado some share of control in dealing with the problem."

Congressman Kramer was followed by several Senators, including Pete Domenici from New Mexico. Although he had been the prime backer of John Hernandez for the top spot at EPA, Senator Domenici was more than gracious in his remarks about me. And he also made a point that I think surprised a lot of people. He said, "I heard that there were some who thought this nominee was not qualified from the standpoint of experience. I wondered what the qualifications [were] of those we hold in such esteem who occupied this position heretofore, and I am amazed. I would like to submit for the record Mr. Ruckelshaus' background, the first administrator of this agency.

BACKGROUND OF WILLIAM RUCKELSHAUS

1. 1960–62 - Deputy Attorney General assigned to Indiana State Board of Health.
2. 1965–67 - Minority Attorney, Indiana State Senate.
3. 1967–69 - Indiana House of Representatives, Elected Majority Leader.
4. 1968 - Nominated by Indiana Republican Party as nominee for U.S. Senate.
5. 1960–69 - Law firm.
6. 1969–70 - Assistant Attorney General of United States, Civil Division.

"The parallel between this nominee and Mr. Ruckelshaus in terms of experience prior to accepting the role is amazing. In fact, I would think that if one had to put them side-by-side, one would say Mrs. Gorsuch is a far more experienced legislator than he was, and occupied more public positions of trust than he did. Her background is excellent from the standpoint of pure professionalism."

I was particularly gratified to hear the Senator on another point of importance to me. He said, "Another matter raised by those who oppose this nomination is that Mrs. Gorsuch has many friends in the administration. It has been said that she is particularly close to Secretary Watt, and perhaps close to other people in the administration, and somehow that ought to have a damaging effect on her capacity to handle this job.

"Well, I satisfied myself on that, too, in talking to people who have worked with this lady. It seems to me that if someone thinks they can put a lady here to take over this job, who is docile, and who people are going to tell what to do, then the President nominated the wrong person. If Jim Watt thinks that, then he has another think coming. She will be her own person."

The next to last Senator to comment on the record was Frank Murkowski of Alaska. The Senator, who is a Republican, made a point that no one else did, but that I thought truly needed to be made. "And it may just be my observation, but as a Freshman U.S. Senator participating in many hearings, it seems that the first question we don't ask of a man is, What are your administrative skills, but the first question we ask of a woman is, What are your administrative skills? My point being an obvious one, it only takes a short conversation with Anne Gorsuch and you certainly learn that she has outstanding solid administrative skills."

Republican Senator James Abdnor of South Dakota was the final committee member to speak. He did so quite briefly, but he did me a large and very practical favor. He asked the chairman to remove the sea of press photographers that separated me from the committee members before I gave my statement. "She shouldn't have to speak over them," he said, adding, "hasn't it been our practice that they take the pictures and she talks to us instead of the people in between?" Senator Stafford agreed, and had the picture takers moved to the rear of the room.

As I prepared to speak, the short break caused by the logistics of the moving operation gave me a chance to take a few deep breaths.

First of all, I would like to acknowledge and gratefully thank the Senators who chose to introduce me and those who chose to indicate their support, and further those that have chosen the opportunity to give me their views of the function of the Administrator and note their concerns.

Mr. Chairman and members of the Senate Committee on Environment and Public Works:

It is a singular honor and privilege to appear before you as President Reagan's designee for Administrator of the Environmental Protection Agency.

As you may know, the Administrator's postion is one which I actively sought, and I feel that my reasons for so doing are relevant to your deliberations today.

In my opinion, and I am confident that you would agree, the position of Administrator of the Environmental Protection Agency presents one of the most challenging and critical opportunities in Government to formulate and implement significant domestic policy.

In light of the policies of President Reagan, the challenges and opportunities of the position are enhanced. The Administrator must manage one of the largest Federal agencies in America—large both in terms of numbers as well as budget—to implement policies which can achieve the important national objective of enhancing and improving our national environment in a manner that accommodates the objectives of change which are the hallmarks of this administration. The task presents enormous opportunities and challenges.

The President is committed to the preservation and enhancement of environmental values, and that is a commitment I share.

The President is committed to achieving a new federalism in which the decisions and the power to implement those decisions will be shifted from the banks of the Potomac back to the level of government which is closest and most accountable to the people it serves. I share that commitment.

The President is committed to regulatory reform, and here I believe it is important to emphasize that the reform is not limited to withdrawal of unnecessary or overly burdensom singular regulations, but envisions a much broader scope involving the process by which new regulations are formulated and current regulations evaluated. . . .

The challenge of administering the Agency in a manner which will achieve those goals is enormous and intricate—one which I am eager to undertake.

I then went on to delineate what I saw as the requirements for the job, and explained how I thought I met them. I stressed management skills, and pointed out that in all my work, both as an attorney and as a public officeholder, I had been functioning as much as a manager as anything else. I covered the vital statistics of my background and my education, and said proudly, "As a long-term Coloradoan, I come before you with a deep appreciation of the unique beauties which we enjoy in our environment—the majesty and grandeur of the Rocky Mountains, the openness and sense of space of our eastern plains, a climate which enjoys the variety and change afforded by each season of the year. As a Westerner, I come before you with a profound appreciation for the role that water plays in every aspect of our lives, for the necessity of its conservation and beneficial use."

I reminded the committee, which had wrestled with the Superfund bill, the new law aimed at cleaning up the nation's toxic waste sites, that I, too, had experience with touchy issues.

Having labored on Superfund, I am certain you gentlemen understand how fragile such coalitions can be. Difficult decisions and compromises must be made. EPA's decision to reconsider the adequacy of Colorado's inspection and maintenance proposal of 1979, occurring as it did after the legislature was out of session and after contrary prior representations, did not improve State/Federal relations, nor did it provide the healthiest atmosphere for unimpassioned decisionmaking. Nevertheless, there is a positive lesson to be learned from it. The Agency must be cooperative and consistent in its dealings with the States if State cooperation is to be forthcoming. . . .

As directly applicable and important as these experiences are, I would not have been able to absorb so many of the necessary management skills, had I not had the experience of being a working mother. Juggling the roles and responsibilities of being a full-time mother and part-time attorney, legislator and politician is among the ultimate in management challenges.

As Administrator-designate, I recognize three responsibilities of paramount importance: The protection of public health and welfare through restoration, preservation, and enhancement of the quality of our environment; faithful implementation of the intent of Congress as expressed in our environmental protection statutes; and the development of policies that accommodate the national objectives articulated by the President. . . . If confirmed, these will be my primary objectives, and I would expect the American people to judge my performance accordingly. . . .

I closed by making a few promises, restating my philosophy, and explaining why, in my opinion, the President had chosen me to head EPA.

We shall restore the States to their rightful place as partners with the Federal Government in policymaking as well as policy implementation.

In developing and implementing our national environmental program we must understand that its success requires the commitment and investment of the private sector, and that ultimately the cost is paid by each individual citizen. Companies do not pay for these costs. You and I, as consumers, do.

We can and must simplify and streamline the regulatory process. Rules too complex to be understood serve only to alienate the public from the mission of EPA, and that mission is too important to be left solely to the regulated and the regulators. . . .

Much remains to be done and can be done. The public is fully committed to environmental protection, while simultaneously aware of the need to improve our economy and develop affordable domestic energy resources. A delicate balance must emerge.

I believe EPA must take the lead in developing that balance, cognizant of its opportunities and constraints, its potential and limitations, its historic mission and our changing times.

EPA must be non-confrontational in its approach, leading by action and encouragement. I assure you that, if confirmed, this will be my guiding credo.

And then I said something which, certainly in retrospect, it
seemed no one really heard. *"I am confident that President Reagan
did not ask me to serve because of any advocacy position I have taken. I
have not made my living fighting for or against environmental laws and
regulations.* I am convinced that he has asked me to serve because
he believes that my education and experience have trained me to
take the broad overview necessary; that my record in the Colorado
State legislature indicated a strong commitment to hearing all
points of view and forging workable compromises; that the nature
of my public service has made me particularly sensitive to the
elements which make Federal programs so annoying and sometimes even unacceptable to the American people; and that—above
all else—my total efforts and talents will be committed to restoring,
preserving and protecting the environmental heritage that is a
critical, integral part of the legacy our children and grandchildren
must inherit if they are to know the same freedoms, and enjoy
the same choices, that we have known."

I ended my statement by thanking the Senators for their courtesy in listening so intently, and closed by saying, "As I stated
before, the challenge of the position is enormous and intricate,
and one which, with your advice and consent, I am eager to undertake. I will be happy to respond to any questions which members of the committee may have."

I had presented my statement well, in a firm voice and well
paced, without faltering. I was at the top of my form and I knew
it. When it came to the question period, I was, quite frankly, even
better.

At one point Senator Stafford asked what he termed a "multi-
barrelled" question, one that had several parts, and I answered
every one in order without his having to repeat a part. He com-
plimented me, and I mentioned something about having "a good
pencil," but in truth my team had prepared me so well I didn't
need one.

My opponents had hoped that I would trip all over myself,
not know answers, and in general display seeming inadequacy like
Judge William Clark who, in his confirmation hearings to be a

Deputy Secretary of State could not recall the name of Zimbabwe's Prime Minister, but nothing of the sort happened. And even though Senator Stafford had said I could defer answering any questions and submit written responses, I chose to handle all verbal questions on the spot.

That was one of the most enjoyable days of my entire life. At one point I had the opportunity to glance back at Jim Sanderson, John Daniel, and a few others from my prep team who were scattered about the crowded room, and I got a "thumbs-up," which made me feel great.

At the end of the Senators' question period, the chairman thanked me for what he said "must have been a very long day," and then he turned the microphone over to a panel of environmentalists who'd filed statements in response to my nomination (most, though not all of them, in opposition), and had asked for the opportunity to question me. Because it was so late in the day, however, Senator Stafford had the time to let them give only a capsule version of their printed statements.

I had expected their comments to be negative, but I had also expected them to be fair and accurate and based on proper research. Some of them were, but the bulk of them were not. One had me as a very close personal friend of Jim Watt's, and another, Russell W. Peterson of The National Audubon Society wrote that "indeed, as a Colorado state legislator she joined a law suit brought by James Watt's Mountain States Legal Foundation to block Clean Air Act rulings by EPA in her state." How I went from prime House sponsor of the Colorado Clean Air Act to one of Watt's co-plaintiffs in opposition to it was not made clear in Mr. Peterson's statement. His assertion was completely untrue.

Finally Senator Domenici had had enough of the guilt-by-association tactic. "There is a statement in there that they oppose her because there is a possibility she would be unduly influenced by people in this Cabinet who do not favor environmental protection adequately. And I think that is an unfair statement to make about anybody. So she knows Secretary Watt. Big deal. She meets with him, she is his friend. She is probably going to have to work with him on the President's perfectly legal advisory group. I mean, I don't think that is a fair statement. . . . I think that is about the most ridiculous recommendation for turning someone down that

I have heard since I have been a United States Senator, I really do."

The hearing ended at 4:15 P.M., and I wasn't a bit tired. I left with a whole crew of happy celebrants for a reception in a Senate office building that I hosted for over a hundred friends and supporters. After that a number of us went around the corner to The Monocle, a popular little restaurant that has been in the shadow of the Senate office buildings for years. It was a great night.

The Senators would not vote on my nomination until they had brought John Hernandez before them for his confirmation hearing, which was scheduled for three days later. But I had no doubt they'd vote to confirm me.

They confirmed both of us at the same time without a single negative vote.

In response to Senator Stafford's comment that it had been a long day, I said, "It has been my pleasure, and I look forward to many future long days." I would get my wish, but what happened on some of those long days would turn out to be a big surprise to me.

5

ANNE ENTERS WONDERLAND

The first time I saw the Washington headquarters of the Environmental Protection Agency, I said, "Oh, my God. If these people are in charge of keeping my air and water clean, we're *all* in trouble."

I had walked into the lobby of the West Tower, the official entrance to EPA, and had taken a good look at the gigantic fish tank that covered the entire back wall of the reception area. The water was grayish, cloudy and murky, and if there were any fish still alive in it, they had wisely donned a protective invisibility. Even the outside of the tank was dirty, covered with a greasy film. One of my first official acts was to drain the tank and board it up so that no one would have to look at that putrid sight.

Upstairs in the offices that were to be occupied by my yet-to-be-named chief aides it looked as if an occupation army had just pulled out, hurriedly. Boxes of papers were spilled on the floor, and chairs sat atop tables. One man told me that when he arrived as a late addition to the transition team, he kicked over a box in his office and was startled to find a family of mice. The general level of dirt was so high that it could not have accumulated just since the Carter people had moved out; it had to have been building up for some time.

In some hallways, ceiling tiles had fallen, to be followed by dripping water. There were missing floor tiles. In one area papers were stacked so high they reached a desk top, and the storage problem was apparently so acute that boxes of papers were lined up in the halls. I went into one lawyer's office, which measured about 12 feet by 12 feet, and there was a clear path only from the doorway to his desk; the rest of the office was filled with junk.

One of my first appointees was John Horton, the Assistant Administrator for Administration, and he made it a twenty-four-hour-a-day job to clean things up. He had people shipping out garbage around the clock, and he doubled the janitorial staff for the duration. We shipped out tons of paper. *That* was when we could have used a paper shredder. The mountains of paper we threw away must have taken years to accumulate.

One of the real ironies involved a room in the basement off the garage that was used for word-processing training. When I went down there I found the air to be so foul that I had it tested; it turned out to be so filled with carbon monoxide that it was unsafe for human use. In the headquarters of EPA itself! And that was not the only area within the agency where we found dangerously polluted air.

Aside from the damage caused by careless and sloppy people, there was a more fundamental physical problem with the EPA headquarters. It had originally been built as an apartment house complex, not as an office, and the quality of the materials was not such that they could withstand the extra wear and tear that comes with office use. In fact, as well as in hindsight, it was a very bad idea for these particular buildings to have become EPA headquarters.

Some description is in order. First of all, EPA is not near any of the other federal agencies. It is close to the Potomac River in the Southwest sector. What happened, according to the story I was told, is that back in the 1960s a group of developers (which, it is rumored, once included Spiro T. Agnew) took advantage of certain federal guarantee programs and received generous and risk-free financing to build two twelve-story apartment towers connected by a mall that would include shops and offices. They razed the slum dwellings that stood on the former swampland, displacing the poor people who had lived there for generations as renters, and put up the project. But it was like the party to which no one came—they couldn't rent the new apartments. So one of the developers, wise in the ways of Washington, began to negotiate with the federal government, and the result was a twenty-year lease, signed in 1970, turning the majority of the space over to a brand new governmental body with a no-nonsense name—The Environmental Protection Agency. Of course, at the time, no one ever dreamed that EPA would use *all* the space.

It was a very nice deal for the owners, but not, as things would turn out, a very good one for the government, or for the people who had to work there. Located down at the end of 4th Street, S.W., it is near a string of seafood restaurants too expensive for most federal workers. And there's not much else in the area, except for Arena Stage and the end of a freeway.

EPA headquarters' two buildings are located about three football fields apart, connected by a mall containing stores and offices. The Administrator's office is on the top floor of the West Tower. What adds to the strangeness of the arrangement is that the twelfth floor of the West Tower contains the "penthouse" of the original apartment building. The elevators do not go to the twelfth floor, they go only to the eleventh floor; to get to the top one has to use a separate, postage stamp–sized elevator. It is a unique situation; excluding the CIA, of course, there isn't another high-ranking federal administrator whose office is literally so difficult to get to. My location added fuel to the fires of those charging me with isolation. But short of building a new building, there was nothing I could do about it.

Another most unusual situation is that EPA has no cafeteria. The original plans call for one, but it has been missing now for thirteen years. Although the contract between the builders and the General Services Administration (GSA) specifies that there be a cafeteria, it has disappeared into a black hole somewhere, with no trace.

As a result, I rarely ate lunch around the main headquarters. After I'd tried the overpriced restaurants along the river once or twice, I found that despite their semi-interesting view of the Potomac River *channel* (not the river itself, which is just beyond) I was better off with a sandwich from the nearest deli. Being in EPA was not at all like being at, say, the Federal Communications Commission, which, at 1919 M Street, N.W., is within easy walking distance of dozens of good and several of the very best restaurants

Washington has to offer. Fortunately, I had to travel a great deal and frequently went out for luncheon meetings. I've often wondered if the spirit of EPA would be improved simply by moving it to a more pleasant and convenient location.

The second problem was agency morale.

One of the first things Ernie Minor had done when he took over during the transition was to go in and almost wipe out the public information office. In truth, it needed to be done—the office was putting out in excess of sixty-five publications each year, including some in comic book form—but it didn't need to be done quite the way he did it. He was brutal. And he also acted in a cloak-and-dagger fashion, so that throughout the office no one knew if his of her head would be the one to roll come the next morning. He and his staff alienated people unnecessarily, and of course the resentment spread like wildfire throughout the whole agency, where it remained not too far below the surface as I was taking office.

The rampant rumor, enkindled by the environmental community, that President Reagan was antienvironment hardly helped things. It was probably no surprise that at the moment I took over agency morale was about zero.

One of the reasons for the strength of that rumor was that Ronald Reagan, while campaigning against Jimmy Carter, had said a few things that made it sound as if he cared little for and knew little about the environment. One of the most quoted was the line about "killer trees," which his aide James Brady made even more famous by joking about aboard the campaign plane in front of reporters. The other side of that same coin was that Ronald Reagan had always stressed the idea of getting government off peoples' backs. The environmentalists unfairly construed that as calling for deregulation when what he meant was regulatory reform. There is a world of difference between the two terms. The environmentalists had spread the word that Ronald Reagan as President was going to *deregulate* the environment, when that was never the case. Regulatory reform, however, certainly was on the agenda. And anybody who is knowledgeable about environmental affairs knows that there is no riper pasture for regulatory reform than EPA regulations.

This was true in part because of the way Congress had originally intended the law to work. EPA was supposed to set a national standard, and then outline a general framework on how a state, given its particular starting point, was to meet it. Then the agency was to accept each state's plans, allowing for the obvious variations within the framework. In theory EPA was really supposed to be concerned only with whether or not the state met the national standard, and not get involved in *how* that was to be done. But what had happened was that EPA had strayed from that legislative intent, and had given states authority to implement programs only if they, the states, had adopted specific EPA regulations that required them to dot every *i* and cross every *t*. This was the case in all of the major program areas.

Congress had originally envisaged the law as giving enough latitude to adapt to each state's differences, necessary both institutionally and geographically. Very often the environmental issues are affected by geographical or weather conditions—you can't use the same plan in Alaska as you can in Florida.

But EPA had never seen it that way. Instead, over the years the agency had developed horrendously complicated regulations that were simply unnecessary, that nine times out of ten just made states madder than hell, and they couldn't follow. In some instances the regulations were actually counterproductive. Eventually we took water regulations that were six inches thick and got them down to less than half an inch, *without sacrificing any quality*.

Another reason why morale was so bad was the simple fact that the agency had gotten too fat and too ineffective. Democrats and environmentalists don't like to be reminded of that, and the latter group would probably scream in protest, but it's the truth. Prior to my arrival EPA hadn't done anything for four years. From 1976 to 1980 EPA increased in population from about 9,550 full-time people to 11,015. And its annual operating budget rose from $771 million to $1.269 *billion*. EPA had grown in budget by 65 percent and in personnel by 15 percent during the Carter years— *with no discernible output at all*.

And the reason you never heard anything about it was that all the environmental critics were *in* those offices! Jimmy Carter had given them jobs; when he was gone they eventually returned to the organizations from which they'd come. Had they improved things? Hardly.

Another often suggested reason why agency morale was so low was that I had chosen not to use an office at EPA headquarters prior to my confirmation. Columnist Jack Anderson tried repeatedly to make that point by referring to me as "the Ice Queen in Isolation at Interior." I didn't buy it then, and I don't buy it today. I felt it would be a major tactical error to ensconce myself at the agency before the United States Senate had approved me. I did not want to give the Senators the impression I thought my confirmation was a foregone conclusion. What I probably should have realized was the extent of the misimpression people would get based on my accepting Jim Watt's offer of space in the Interior Department, with its hint of his having control over me and my work.

If the physical and the spiritual aspects of EPA left something to be desired, these were small problems in comparison with the third area, the substantive programs themselves. In every major programmatic area—air, water, toxic substances, and hazardous wastes—the agency was not just behind in its work, it was woefully and in some instances scandalously behind.

Take, for example, the programs aimed at improving air quality. State Implementation Plans (SIPS) are to be submitted for "go" or "no-go" decisions by EPA, based on the requirements of the Federal Clean Air Act. When I took office there were *two thousand* of those still unapproved at EPA, the most recent of which was eighteen months old. Not a single one had been acted on, not one had been approved or denied. Some of them had been sitting there for *years*.

The backlog made a farce of the Clean Air Act. You can't get clean air until you make decisions on those types of plans, and here there were plans in-house from every area of the country—all of them unanswered.

Another scandal involved New Source Performance Standards, which have to do with determining a standard for any new source of air pollution. A standard has to be drawn based on the "highest and best technological means" of controlling pollution. For example, in the gravel industry there are a great number of regulations designed to prevent air pollution. When gravel is mined, it is passed along a series of screens, which separate and size the gravel, thereby sending a lot of dust and dirt into the air. Each bed, or screen, was considered under the law a new source for which controls must be adopted.

EPA is charged by statute with developing New Source Performance Standards for all sources of industrial pollution in the country. In the Carter years there was apparently no effort to get those standards written and performance monitored. There were some on the books, but they were so bizarre and unworkable that industry was resisting totally.

The gravel industry felt that writing a performance standard for each individual screen—which is what EPA had mandated—was both impractical and too costly. It felt that the way to solve the problem was to place a bubble over all the screens, and then test the air going out of the screens for the cumulative pollution levels. This was too simple for EPA, which insisted that standards be written for each screen. Industry got its back up, and the situation was at an impasse.

Not surprisingly, there was a great deal of distrust and hard feelings between EPA and industry. Historically there had always been some problems, but nothing like what prevailed when I came to office. When EPA first became an agency in 1970, industry greeted it with skepticism and resistance, mainly because it represented a whole new way of thinking for the companies. They'd never had to "think ecologically" before. To the degree that there was an entrenched resentment of EPA, it continued after the passage of the Clean Air Act. So far-reaching and innovative is the Act that when it was passed, environmentalists who truly knew what was going on in this country said, "We will never need a land use law in America now," referring to legislation that Congress had successfully resisted for decades, "because one aspect of the Clean Air Act gives us all that and more." And they were right. In effect, the Clean Air Act is a federal land use act.

Industry resented that, and it continues to resent it. And, I think, rightfully so.

It is my opinion that during the years when the Republicans were in power (EPA was established midway through Richard Nixon's first term) there was a degree of respect between the agency and industry. There may have been disagreements, but there wasn't hatred and open warfare. Clearly there was resentment, and resistance to the enormous cost of complying with some of the early regulations, and clearly there was some cheating. But in the Carter years the situation became bitterly hostile, mainly because the administration gave no thought whatsoever to costs. Not even when, under the law, they should have.

For instance, in the Water Act it says that EPA should develop the best cost-effective standards. But the agency ignored the word "cost-effective." That action by the Agency resulted in one of the most significant cases—*The American Paper Institute vs. EPA (4th Circuit Court of Appeals)*—in the history of EPA. And the court ruled that EPA had to take the cost to industry—the economics—into consideration.

If one could say that the people then in charge of EPA—with the exception of Douglas Costle who had actually run a statewide environmental protection program in Connecticut before coming to public service on the federal level—were well meaning, that would be one thing. But I cannot give them that. I saw, as a state legislator battling with regional EPA officials, no sign that these were well-meaning people.

In my opinion they are simply anti-industry and anti-business. They want to make controls as costly as possible, purposely, almost as if they think it is somehow possible to go back to nature. They operate on a different program, and it is one the rest of the country knows nothing about. I believe that if they could, they would happily make regulations so costly that they would have the effect of cutting off all economic growth. They would be happy to deindustrialize the United States.

In addition to the backlog problems we encountered in the realm of air quality, there were also horrendous problems in regard to water.

Almost the day after I walked in the door at EPA I had a court order on my desk demanding that the agency release its effluent guidelines, which are the equivalent in the area of water to the new Source Protection Standards in air.

According to laws on the books since 1976, EPA was supposed to set standards, proceeding on an industry-by-industry basis, to govern effluents into water. And, again, the standard was that of "best available, economically achievable." Because it was so far behind in setting these standards, EPA had been sued by one of the environmental groups, and the resulting court order did not just say "Do it by X date," it included an entire calendar specifying how many were to be set and by which dates. That was the order that hit my desk on one of my first days in office.

When the people in the Water Office saw the court order they told me there was no way they could comply with the dates specified in it. So I told our lawyers to go back to court and inform the judge of the problem, and ask for an extension.

"I don't care if that lady just walked in there," thundered the judge when he heard that request. "If this order isn't followed, she's going to jail." Later, after I'd had a chance to look into the history of the matter, I could see that he was absolutely correct. The agency was *so* delinquent in developing these standards. And the problem that created was simple: If you don't have the regulations, then you will never have clean water.

One of the first assignments I gave my newly created management team was to study the decision-making process that took place in the development of these water regulations. I told them to make me a standard flow chart indicating lines of authority and responsibility. They came back with a gigantic chart that had arrows going off the wall in all directions. After I'd studied it briefly I could see only too clearly that using the "system" represented by this chart one could *never* make *any* decisions!

I told them to draw me a new chart, one that contained all the same input from all the same groups but also included time frames for performance. They did, and the judge was finally satisfied. In fact, they've been on schedule ever since, and will be finished by the summer of 1985. Result? Clean water.

Another problem that had gotten disastrously out of hand prior to my taking office involved the amount of money wasted in the sewage treatment construction grants program, a scandal that had made a series of page one stories in the Washington *Post*. This problem, however, had a happy ending, and it is, ironically, one that David Stockman can take full credit for, as he managed to get significant reform legislation passed. The legislation set new standards for plant construction, and included a reduction in funding levels. He had told Congress that unless the grant monies were reduced from $3.4 billion to $1.6 billion, he would see that they were cut out entirely. It was neat bit of gamesmanship that worked.

The result of Stockman's handiwork was Part II of the Clean Water Act, which in my opinion and that of many experts is the most significant environmental legislation passed since 1980.

Eric Eidsness, who ran the Water Office for me, agreed that our most serious backlogs on taking office involved the "Best Available Technology" guideline regulations. "Of the 48,000 regulations, 38,000 would have expired by 1982, and without them, neither the states nor EPA could write permits except 'Best Professional Judgment' permits, which were ad hoc decisions and therefore all over the lot, and really went against the intent of the law."

He also appreciated how serious the problem was with the effluent guidelines:

"No one knew how much industry was discharging, so the implications of not having the guidelines were staggering. There were more pollutants being discharged both directly and indirectly in the water than in any other form. The lack of these guidelines from which permits would be written—and once there was a permit, then an individual company could no longer appeal—was in my opinion a most significant programmatic backlog," he said.

Pesticides and Toxic Substances was the third area in which we met severe problems when we took over. As Dr. John Todhunter, whom I picked to run that office, recalls, "There was not a sense of direction, in either Toxics or Pesticides. The biggest problem in Pesticides was that there was quite a backlog [an understatement if ever I heard one!] of registration petitions. Some 1500 to 1600. Also, the agency lacked the big picture view of how registration fit into the Pesticides Act, and there wasn't a comprehensive picture of what needed to be done to put the statute into an integrated operating mode. And it was the same thing with Toxics."

As a result, very little had been done under FIFRA, the Pesticides Control Act, or TSCA, the Toxic Substances Control Act, which had been on the books since 1976. Basically the act said that EPA had to examine every chemical substance sold or used in the country, and either regulate it, ban it, or say that it didn't need to be regulated. If a printed caution was called for—such as, "Use Only in Well-ventilated Places"—that should be taken care of too.

The act covers something like 65,000 chemicals. Clearly, they couldn't all be regulated at once, so in 1978 a government task force, the Interagency Testing Committee, identified those with the greatest exposure potential in 1978, and came up with a priority list. The agency was supposed to act on those right away. When I took office there were four priority lists, but the EPA had not acted on a single chemical. Dr. Todhunter got his troops rallied and when I left office, all chemicals on the priority lists that had been generated before and during my tenure were addressed.

It might be helpful to consider the options given the big picture. From a waste management standpoint, three approaches can be taken. One, regulate it in usage (TSCA or FIFRA). Two, regulate in disposal (RCRA, of Resource Conservation and Recovery Act). Three, clean up where unregulated disposal is or has been taking place (Superfund). The only one that gets any real media attention is Superfund. But if we don't have one or two in place, we will have a problem with three forever!

The last area of serious problems that I encountered when I took office involved RCRA (pronounced "wreck-rah"). Passed in 1976, the act was designed to control the ongoing disposal of hazardous material so that the nation doesn't have to create any new Superfunds. When RCRA was passed, EPA was given two years to develop its regulations. When I walked in five years later, the only thing on the books was a flimsy interim plan.

This means that for three years, from 1978 to 1981, across the entire country there was uncontrolled disposal of hazardous wastes. For three years we knew what was going on yet continued to create new Superfund sites—and continued to contaminate our ground water. I sometimes wonder if we are ever going to get our ground water cleaned up in this country. As a matter of fact, no single site has ever been totally cleaned up.

I would be remiss while on this topic if I didn't mention the famous "Midnight Regs" that were pushed through by the outgoing administration just as Ronald Reagan and his people were moving into office. In the case of RCRA the new regulations were simply untenable. One that caused a particularly great furor called for *zero* dumping of containerized liquids. The only difficulty with that requirement is that it is physically impossible.

Let's say you have a barrel of sand you want to dump. If you compress that sand you will still get some liquid, no matter how dry it looks. In fact, if you compress *anything* you will get some water. The technicians I was dealing with, both agency and industry people, all knew that the Midnight Regs were going to have to be revised; it had been a set-up job to make the Carter administration look good on the environment despite its poor record. Even though the law read "These regulations will become effective in November of 1981," there wasn't anybody in or out of government who didn't understand that they had to be revised.

Knowing that, my office charged with developing those regulations sent me up a package that contained the regulations and their explanation. This combined document of twenty-five to thirty pages said in effect, it is a terrible thing to do to the American people, but we are going to have to allow some liquid in landfills, where the containers would have to be dumped.

Well, for one thing, it was to be *containerized* liquid, which is somewhat different, though certainly unacceptable in the long run; and for another, nothing was said at the time about *bulk* waste and how much liquid that might contain, which was potentially a far greater problem.

I read the document several times, and sent it back. "This is garbage," I said. "It reads like a roller coaster. It goes up and down, and I get carsick just reading it. It has no logical flow. I don't understand it, so I don't understand what we're doing, so I'm not going to sign it."

That proposed set of regulations crossed my desk twice more as we passed the November and neared the critical February deadline, and twice more I vetoed it. It still read like a roller coaster, and I still could not understand it.

Then I made a mistake. A significant one.

Knowing that we faced an impossible standard—"no containerized liquids"—and knowing that we were going to come up with an environmentally pragmatic solution, and not being a technician or a scientist myself, I assumed that my people would not bring me technically deficient regulations a fourth time. I was wrong.

Adding to our problems was the fact that industry, rather than shipping them to landfills, was holding onto their containers until we cleared up the regulations. The problem here was that after a certain date these companies would no longer be just "generators" of hazardous waste, but would become, by law, "storers" of hazardous waste, which would mean a whole new and different set of forms to fill out and standards to meet.

Late on the night before the deadline, my chief of staff John Daniel, who was as dead-tired and overworked at the moment as I was, brought me the new regulations, and told me the staff had assured him that my concerns had been addressed, and that they were "good regs." So I signed them—without reading them. It was the first and last time I ever did that.

It turned out that they were *terrible* regulations.

What the regulations said in essence was that there could be liquid in landfills, based on "percentage per pit, by volume." All the media could understand was that the Reagan EPA, the Gorsuch EPA, was saying it was now okay to have liquid in landfills. That became the story. And if the press went wild, the environmentalists went absolutely crazy.

What had happened as best I can reconstruct it is that my people had leaned too heavily on the proposals and suggestions of certain industry sources. John Daniel or I should have caught it, but we were tired, and it slipped past us.

It became excruciatingly clear to me that it was finally time for me to come to grips with this problem intellectually.

"What is it," I asked my people, "that we are trying to control here? What's the evil of liquid in containers?"

The answer from my top technical people was that over time the container will not be able to withstand the combination of the presence of the liquid and the pressure of the earth. The container will eventually collapse, leak, and the hazardous material—if that's what it is—will then get into the ground water. That was the evil.

"Oh," I said, somewhat taken aback. "Is that all there is to it?"

"Yes," they said.

"Okay. Next question. What's the problem with the regs pronounced by the Carter administration?"

"Well," someone responded, "if you take, for example, a barrel of kitty litter and compress it, then it has liquid in it."

"Oh," I said again. "Then I have the obvious solution. You write, 'There should be no *visible* liquid in containers!'"

It was then my staff's turn to say, "Oh." In Washington, one tends to forget that solutions *can* be simple.

I sat there thinking, I don't *believe* this. These regs have been in a rewrite for six months, but I sat down and rewrote them at my conference table in ten minutes!

And everybody was happy with the new regulations. Everybody. Industry was happy, even the environmentalists were happy—though they would never admit it.

By the way, there were no follow-up stories in the press explaining how the problem got solved. "Liquid in Landfills!" was too good a story to correct.

One of the things I am proudest of is that the substantive regulations under RCRA were all promulgated during my tenure at EPA. They are tough regulations, and they control the disposal of hazardous materials on land. I hope that ten years from now there will be *no* disposal on land, but for the moment, the regulations we put into effect represent the highest plateau we can now reach.

6

LITTLE KING DAVID

I am proud of the fact that I always stood up to David Stockman.

One of the central differences between my administration and that of all my predecessors at EPA was that I insisted on getting personally involved in the budgetary process. My comptroller, Morgan Kinghorn, an excellent civil servant and a superb comptroller who has seen all of the agency's administators, was initially startled to see me get so involved. But he became a real ally, and he helped me steady my lance as I galloped off for my encounters with David Stockman and his minions at the Office of Management and Budget (OMB).

The way the budget process had worked in the past was that OMB would give the agency a number, and the five major program directors—Air, Water, TOSCA, RCRA, Administration, Enforcement, Research & Development, and Superfund (after 1980)—would sit in a room, and whoever had the biggest stick would come out with the biggest share. In contrast, the buget we constructed for fiscal 1983 (which would be considered by the Congress in January 1982) was the first EPA budget ever to be based on programmatic objectives, needed manpower, and dollars in each programmatic area down to the five-man office level out in the field.

And I held an extensive two-day hearing for each programmatic area. The head of each program had to survive my grilling about the whys and wherefors of his or her proposed allocations. As a result, and to understate it, I knew what that agency was doing.

The whole process of getting my five top people to justify their money and manpower figures turned out to be excellent preparation for my budget hearings on the Hill. By the time I went up there I knew my agency cold, down to the smallest local levels.

A long time before I was in any kind of hot water I learned there was a great deal of sexist hypocrisy in my being called to the Hill so often. Put simply, it didn't take publicity-conscious committee and subcommittee chairmen long to figure out that one of the best ways to get on national television, and therefore local TV, was to call Anne Gorsuch as a witness before his committee.

Let's face it. In 1981 I was the only woman in the Reagan administration in Washington at that level. And I testified on the Hill more than anybody in the Cabinet. Despite what these Congressmen—and they were all men—might say about their deep and passionate concern for the environment, they were not primarily interested in that noble cause.

Talk about sexism. The only other woman in a high post at that time—Margaret Heckler and Elizabeth Dole were not yet in the Cabinet—was U.N. Ambassador Jeane Kirkpatrick in New York. She just did not get the coverage I did.

The only person who could upstage me, in terms of drawing more of a media audience, was David Stockman. Though he claims not to remember this, Jim Watt once asked me, "What's your secret?" I told him it wasn't worth a sex-change operation.

Even today, Secretary of Transportation Elizabeth Dole cannot, for better or worse, draw that same kind of attention. Of course it is important to recognize that one of the unwritten laws of Washington is that whether you are a member of Congress or of the press, you do not attack a Senator's wife, and certainly not the wife of a Senator as popular and powerful and capable of acidic counterattack as Senate Majority Leader Robert Dole.

Be all that as it may, I knew we were in for a battle of the budget with David Stockman because once he burned me the first time, I refused to play the game by his rules. The way it goes is that you play a little charade on the public and the Congress by which you both look good, and King David remains on top of the power heap.

The "dance" began in the spring when Stockman or one of his top aides called and said, "I'm whispering a number in your ear; this is your target." And then you get a budget together that comes very close to that number.

Shortly after I took office I got a call from Stockman's aide Fred Khedouri. He said, "This is your whispered number."

I didn't complain, nor did I, as most of the "players" do, inflate it. I submitted a budget that met that figure, or came very close to it. Of course that meant we could do only some of the things we wanted to do in TOSCA, for example, but that's the way of the world, especially in Washington.

In late summer, by which time we had most of the budget put together, Khedouri called me with a different figure. *Lower.*

Well, there were a few things we could postpone, there was still some fat in the Research and Development budget, so once again I went along. It meant developing an entirely new budget, which is hardly a simple process, but we did it because we thought we were doing the President's bidding. My poor comptroller, Morgan Kinghorn, was going nuts.

We sent our reconstructed budget back to OMB, and it came back in *pieces.* It wasn't cut, it was shredded. And we had been using David Stockman's own revised "bottom line" figure!

They hadn't just lowered the figures, they had made programmatic decisions! They had eliminated offices here, added others there, cut six and a half people in one obscure office, but added ten someplace else, and axed dollar amounts all over the lot. Their alterations represented management and policy decisions, not budgetary decisions.

For example, they eliminated one of the existing offices within the Water area, but added an Office of Federal Compliance, or some such title, which was an attempt (laudatory under other circumstances) to eliminate some of the duplication of environmental regulations that exists among the various federal agencies and departments. That kind of decision was hardly within the scope of OMB's function.

It takes a lot to get me angry, but that did it. I had been twice a team player, at reduced figures; I had required every manager in the agency (myself included) to put forth an incredible amount of energy in order to meet those figures; and then David Stockman was pretending to be me through the budget. I was angry. I decided to appeal.

The appeals process is an interesting example of reduced democracy. If you aren't satisfied with your alloted budget, the first step is to go over to OMB and discuss your differences with Stockman himself, alone. If you aren't able to resolve the differences, you request a hearing before the Budget Appeals Board, which consisted of top presidential aides James Baker and Ed Meese—and David Stockman. Stockman was in the interesting position of being both your prosecutor and your judge. Finally, if the Appeals Board did not satisfy you, you could take the rather bold step of asking to go before President Reagan.

At square one I had a forty-minute meeting with Stockman. I was loaded with facts and figures and even some emotional as well as logical appeals. I made an excellent case, and he listened intently, taking no notes and hardly saying anything. At the end of my presentation he stood up, and said curtly, "Thank you very much. That's the way it's going to be." And he left.

Now that made me *really* angry. I asked to go before the Appeals Board as soon as possible.

That appeal went well too. The panel restored quite a bit of what I wanted. But I was very disappointed on two counts. One, they cut fifty million for Superfund. It made little sense to cut the Superfund totals, that money had been collected in taxes from industry, and was already earmarked, like Social Security, to be spent from that special fund, not from the general fund, which meant it would not add to the federal deficit.

I knew I had to ask for the maximum with Superfund. If I didn't, then I would have had to go before the Congress and explain why I wasn't spending that money. And they and the media would see it as part of a nefarious Reaganite anti-environmental plot.

The other point I felt strongly about involved what I viewed as a credibility issue for the President. In 1981 Stockman had gotten Congress to agree to a $2.4 billion appropriation for Sewage Treatment Plant Construction Grants. Although it hadn't been carved in stone anywhere, there was a general agreement on the Hill that that would be the annual amount appropriated for that purpose for the next four or five years.

This was only the second year of the program, and Stockman wanted to cut that figure to $2 billion. I felt very strongly that not only would the President be hurt, but that even if we did ask for less the Congress was going to appropriate $2.4 billion anyway. So what was the point?

I decided to appeal to the President. And that stunned David Stockman.

The meeting was attended by me, David Stockman, President Reagan, Ed Meese, Jim Baker, Craig Fuller, and Ken Duberstein, the White House congressional affairs person, among others. Thank God for Mr. Duberstein. At one point, after I had made a heartfelt pitch for the Sewage Treatment grant funds, he spoke up and said, "Mr. President, Anne's right. There's a general consensus on the Hill that you agreed to $2.4 billion, not just this year but next year too. And you're going to get it. But you're going to establish a credibility problem for yourself if you ask for less."

The meeting ended, and I went back to my office. Before the day was over the President called me personally to tell me that I had won.

I got substantially everything I asked for. I did not get the amount for Superfund that I wanted, but I got a far greater amount than Stockman or the Budget Appeals Board would have allowed me. And I did get the $2.4 billion for the Sewage Treatment Construction Grants program.

Near the end of our conversation, the President said, "Okay, Anne, that gives you pretty much what you wanted. But you will have to give a bit, too. We have to throw David a bone."

The bone was a slight reduction in the budget for research and development.

The oddest result of the whole process was what happened to my funding request for Superfund. I had asked originally for $275 million; Stockman reduced it to $225 million; the President put it at $230 million; the House gave me $230 million, the Senate $200 million, and the final amount appropriated was $210 million, which, minus pieces of the program we didn't want, came to an effective total of $190 million. And these were the same folks who were always yelling at me for not spending enough money and not spending it fast enough!

My biggest disappointment as a result of the whole budget

brouhaha was that I lost a great deal of respect for David Stockman.

I have enormous respect for David's intellect. I think he is probably the smartest man in the President's Cabinet. He has tremendous intellectual capacity. It was a joy to work with him because he was so bright, and I continued to feel that way even through the budgetary squabble.

And certainly the man had a very tough job. As a matter of fact, when I first came to town I told an interviewer that "I wanted the toughest job in town, but David Stockman already had it, so I took the second toughest."

I truly admired the man. What bothered me the most was that when it was all over, he was *personally angry* that I had won. To me, that indicated a character flaw. Several people have suggested to me that I created a mortal enemy that day.

Some of the people in my camp felt that a story about my fight with Stockman over the budget on the front page of *The New York Times* on the morning of my appeal to the President had more than a little to do with Mr. Reagan's decision in my favor. I don't know. I think it would be better if I let John Daniel, my chief of staff, tell the story himself. After all, he had more than a little to do with it.

"The whole appeals process is stacked against you, because Stockman is always there, along with Meese and Baker, who are worrying about the *world's* problems. And you, the Administrator, have to go in there all alone. Anne couldn't take any of her people along. So you really have very little chance. In fact, at one point, when she was complaining about the large, suffocating cut in the R&D budget, Ed Meese said, 'If we give you all that research money, all you'll do is go out and find more problems that need to be solved.'

"It was soon clear that Anne would have to carry her appeal all the way to the President. When we went to see Stockman to begin the process of appeal, Anne was determined to get every penny of that money restored because she felt those people at OMB had given her the bottom line to begin with, and she was not going to go through all that agony for this kind of treatment. So she prepared an appeal letter to Stockman that was about six to eight pages long, single-spaced, and it was a hard-hitting letter.

"There were only about half a dozen of us who were privy to

the letter. Kinghorn's people had drafted it, Anne of course had seen it, John Hernandez had seen it, I had seen it, and Byron Nelson, our public relations guy, had seen it. And Byron came to me and said, 'John, we're taking such a beating in the press on this budget cut issue, and this letter is *so* good, we've got to make sure it gets out. But I guess, knowing Anne, we don't dare leak it.'

"So we worked on it a few more days prior to Anne's meeting with Stockman, the first step of the budget appeal, and finally I said, 'Okay, let's do it. Let's give it to Shabecoff [Phil Shabecoff, the *New York Times* reporter who covered EPA and the environment].' So one afternoon when we were up on the Hill for a minor hearing, and while Anne was testifying, I slipped out and went down from the Rayburn Building over to the basement of the Longworth Building, and in this dark basement room Byron and I let Shabecoff read the letter. We told him he couldn't have a copy, but he could read it. So he did, and soon he was furiously writing down everything he could.

"Well, the morning of Anne's meeting with Dave Stockman, there appeared in *The New York Times* the best article ever written about Anne. It was on page one, column one, and it had Shabecoff's by-line, and it outlined her appeal to Stockman.

"So that day we went to see Stockman, and he was livid! He kept asking Anne if she knew anything about it, and she kept saying, 'No, I don't.' And he asked if she knew who did it, and she said, 'No, I don't know.' Finally, because Stockman was reacting so strongly she said to Morgan Kinghorn, 'Do you know who did this?' And Morgan said, 'No.'

"Later, we're walking down the hall, Joe Cannon, and Anne, and me. And by this time Anne had narrowed down the list of suspects. So she turned to Joe Cannon, her appointee and Kinghorn's boss, and said, 'Did you do it?'

"And he said no, and started protesting, and then she just turned and looked at me.

" 'I did it,' I said.

"She didn't say a word for a while, just kept on walking, and then she said, 'Don't ever do that again. We do not leak stories. We are going to deal with these matters head-on, and within the team.'

"And I said, 'Fine.' And I never did it again. That was the only story I ever leaked, and the only background story I ever gave, or anything like that, during all the time I worked for Anne."

From the very beginning, I could feel OMB's breath on EPA's neck. Early on, while Jim Sanderson was still under consideration for my number-three job but was encountering media and environmental opposition, Boyden Gray of the Vice President's office and Christopher DeMuth, who was the head of OMB's regulatory side, came in to see me, unbidden. Their mission was to advise me to get rid of Sanderson because of all the allegations against him, which they said were "embarrassing." I told them in no uncertain terms that I did not turn on my people because of unproven allegations. I also told them that the internal affairs of EPA were certainly none of their business. But I never forgot their visit.

Then there was the matter of Mr. Jim Tozzi, an intriguing gentleman, a genuine character given to dark suits and thin-lipped locutions, a man to whom a limo was never a limo but always a "stretch." Talking with him was always an experience in jargon-building. Tozzi, who has since left the government for the greener pastures of lobbying (when he left, he opened his closets to reveal enough free booze to give a huge going-away party, which he did, and which rated a story in the *Washington Post*) had the slot just under Chris DeMuth at OMB, and it was generally believed that he was the one who did all OMB's regulatory reform work.

I first met Tozzi when he came in to interview for the job as my regulatory reform head. I never could figure out why he would have wanted that job when the one he had already was far more important. Later I concluded that he was really interested in getting a look at me and my shop for his general information and use. He was that kind of guy.

About halfway through my time at EPA we found ourselves in a real crunch. We were under a court order to release some pollutant guidelines for pharmaceutical manufacturers. We had done our work, and then submitted the guidelines to OMB for their review as required. The manufacturers had put on a lot of pressure for certain changes, which we had resisted, but the court deadline was swiftly approaching, and there was still no word from OMB. Finally, they told us that they weren't approved, though OMB would not put it in writing, as required by the Executive Order, which might have allowed us to buy some time from the judge. This despite the fact that an Executive Order said that if OMB held anything past a certain length of time, they had to put their objections in writing.

All Tozzi would tell us was, "They're not approved." That continued to be OMB's response right up to the last minute. It was the night before the deadline, my last day to obey the court order and sign and release the regs. It got so dark in my office that we could see the moon outside. Finally, John Daniel said, "Anne, I recommend you sign the regs without OMB's approval."

We called OMB to tell them what we were going to do. I called Stockman, who had surprisingly little to say, and John called Tozzi. Tozzi didn't say anything for a few moments after he'd heard the news. Then he said, in a quiet voice, "Daniel, I hope you people know that there's a price to pay for this, and you've only begun to pay."

John Daniel was so startled that he asked Tozzi to repeat it so he could write it down, and when he had, he said to Tozzi, "Thank you very much. I'll give this to the Administrator right away." He did, I signed them anyway, and we all had a good laugh, because it was such typical Tozzi. But now, looking back, maybe we should not have been laughing.

My third David Stockman story is one that I am still thinking about very hard. And I will continue to think about it for a very long time. It is a story I didn't hear until early in 1985 while doing the research for this book. I wish I could tell you that I find it hard to believe, but I am afraid that I have to believe it. It makes too much sense.

Dr. John Hernandez, who became my Deputy Administrator, had been considered for the post of Administrator, and had gone through the interview process shortly before I did. Unlike me, however, he was also interviewed by two men from David Stockman's office. I will let him tell the story himself.

"My meeting was with Glenn Schleede, the number three man at OMB, and Fred Khedouri, OMB's budget director for EPA. I went into that interview very cautiously because I knew that these people wanted to make a lot of major cuts at EPA. So I was quite reluctant to say anything that

I didn't believe in, in way of philosophy or approach. I was absolutely terrified of becoming the head of EPA and all that mess it was in, so it was in the forefront of my mind all during that meeting that anything I said to those guys I would have to live with if I became the Administrator.

And, finally, at one point, Fred Khedouri leaned over in his chair, and kind of quiet like, but dead serious, asked 'Would you be willing to bring EPA to its knees?'

"I was so startled that I kind of just laughed, as if I couldn't believe he said that. But he had said it, and I just demurred.

"And when Anne was selected as head of EPA instead of me, I was very much relieved."

John Hernandez never asked me if I had been asked that same question. I wish he had. I had not been asked the question. It would have been helpful to me to know that Stockman's people had asked it of him. Had I known, I would have gone to the President and demanded Stockman's resignation. But as Hernandez later told someone, he simply didn't want to know the answer—in case it was yes.

I have thought about this startling and sickening bit of information a lot since learning of it, and I am convinced that this attitude toward EPA, and therefore toward the environment, was behind a lot of the problems I encountered. But knowing the question was asked, and knowing who asked it, and knowing whom he worked for helps me to understand some of the things that happened to me and my people in the years that followed.

Part II

THUNDERHEADS OVER THE POTOMAC

7

The Ice Queen Cometh

It took me no time at all to realize that given the mess I had inherited, I would have little or no chance for success unless I made drastic changes in the way things had been done *and* found the very best people to help me, both outside and inside EPA.

I had already found several of my top people within the crew that had so ably briefed me for my confirmation hearings. I already had Jim Sanderson, the Denver lawyer who'd worked in Washington ten years ago, on board as a consultant to handle a myriad of duties, especially some of the unpleasant ones, and that was a big plus.

I'd wanted Jim to come to Washington and work full time for me, which would have meant taking a leave of absence from his busy law practice in Denver. I almost succeeded in getting him, but we ran into a number of problems, not the least of which was an overeager and inaccurate press that tried to create a conflict-of-interest situation where there was none.

What I had in mind for Jim was a brand new position, one that would have been, in effect, the number-three job in the agency, after those of myself and John Hernandez. The position would be a mini-OMB within EPA, sort of my own Office of Management and Budget.

I sometimes wonder if I would have gotten into the trouble I

did if I'd had Jim Sanderson around all the time to advise me.
There is something about Sanderson that likes a brawl. And he's
fiercely loyal.

I had also asked John Daniel to join. John, a lawyer with a
strong background in environmental issues, had worked for the
State of Ohio—kind of an odd home for an Alabama native, but
legal specialities have a way of uprooting people—and in private
industry for The Paper Institute, and was Johns Manville's Washington counsel at the time he volunteered to help me get ready
for confirmation. In fact, although he had to remind me of it,
when my name first surfaced in the press as a possible candidate
for the EPA post, John had called me out in Denver and introduced himself, offering to help me find my way around Washington if I got the job. As it turned out, he was one of the lawyers
whom Stan Hulett called, at Jim Watt's request, to help me when
I arrived as the Administrator-designate.

That John Daniel was a Democrat bothered me not at all. I
liked him and his style—low key, Southern, and bright as hell—
right away, and we worked well together from the start. John is
not a table-pounder (indeed he has the demeanor of a choir boy,
and a face and smile to match), but he has an underlying steeliness
and loyalty that won't quit. He would become my chief of staff
and true right hand.

Just as I had been found as a candidate for Administrator by
the personnel troops who labored during transition, any number
of others were also being looked at and evaluated and interviewed
for all sorts of other jobs. The names of several people I chose as
top-level assistant administrators had come up that way.

John Todhunter was a Ph.D. biochemist on the faculty of Catholic University in Washington, and he also did quite a bit of con-
sulting and was a member of a panel of scientific advisors with
headquarters in New York State. He too, coincidentally, was a
Democrat. I chose him to head the Toxics Office. Kathleen Bennett was an industry lobbyist and analyst for The Paper Institute
(where she and John Daniel had known one another) who knew
the Clean Air Act and its requirements inside and out. She had
never been an administrator before, but I felt she had both the
smarts and the temperament. I was right.

Another person who'd been rather directly involved in the
campaign was John Horton. He had raised funds for Raymond

Donovan, the ill-starred former Secretary of Labor. I put Horton in charge of Administration within the agency, a post that covered the agency's operational aspects, such as personnel, space management, mail handling, computers, and all other plant management matters.

My able and loyal head of the Water Division, Eric Eidsness, had a background in water management on the local government level. At the end, when things went all wrong, Eric Eidsness would be treated very badly, and not just by the administration; he was promised a job and didn't get one.

The person in charge of the Waste Office, Rita Lavelle, was not my choice. She came to us somewhat late in the game from the White House personnel office. And when they sent her over the first time, I refused to hire her on the grounds that she lacked the background for this highly important, high-profile job. But somehow she was sent back, and this time I said yes.

John Daniel told me that when he talked to Rita for the first time about working for EPA he showed her the new organization chart, and pointed with his pencil to a slot on the midlevel, saying, "This is where we're thinking you might be useful." But she took his pencil, and pointed higher, saying, "But what about *these* slots up here?"—indicating the Assistant Administrator level, which is where she eventually landed.

The Waste Office consisted of two very important subdivisions, RCRA and Superfund. For the former, I named a civil servant, John Skinner, a Ph.D. in Aeronautical Engineering, as head. And William Hedeman, a superb public servant who'd been with EPA since the late 1970s, was my choice to head Superfund.

One of the central management problems of the Environmental Protection Agency under my predecessors was that the Enforcement division had been allowed to take on a far greater, almost autonomous, role than the original legislative designers had in mind. Indeed, it was a tail-wags-the-dog situation. Historically and theoretically the Enforcement office had been a step above the substantive program areas of Air, Water, Toxics, and Waste Management, but was supposed to do the job of enforcing their orders, rules, and regulations. Unfortunately, the way things had developed over the years, the internal parts of EPA were not working together according to the original blueprint.

Far too often, as I had seen back in Colorado, a business whose representatives initially came to the regional office in good faith, asking for guidance, received conflicting information. The people in Air, for example, might say, "Here are the rules you have to follow when you construct your rubber plant so that you won't pollute the air." The company would follow those guidelines, and then, when the plant was up and operating, someone from Enforcement would come along and say, "We interpret these guidelines differently, and you are in violation of EPA regs governing air quality."

Determined to put an end to what I viewed as an inexcusable situation, I changed the status of the Enforcement Office. And in so doing I touched off a firestorm of criticism, the thrust of which was that I had defanged, perhaps even emasculated, the infamous enforcers. All of which, of course, was what the press had been presenting all along as par for the course for the Reagan-Watt-Gorsuch axis that was determined to despoil the environment. (One day, fairly early on, Kathleen Bennett came to me and said, ruefully but with sincere disappointment, "Every morning I read in the *Washington Post* how we are pillaging and plundering the environment, and then I come to work and you keep shouting at me, 'Make sure your office is in compliance with the Act and make sure your regs are issued promptly.' Somebody out there is not getting the right message.")

I said at the beginning that I had made some mistakes. The way I handled the reorganization of the Enforcement Division was one of them. I'm not saying that the reorganization itself was a mistake; it wasn't. But I allowed a misperception to arise and fester, a misperception that EPA under Anne Gorsuch was not interested in enforcing the environmental laws of the land.

I viewed the public-relations aspect as something that could wait until we had worked out the bugs. As I had done before, I believed that there was an element of trust involved—that the media would wait until the results of the change were in before making up their minds about what the reorganization really meant.

It was another time when I would learn that in the Wonderland of Washington, perception—especially *mis*perception—is all. Reality is quite a few paces behind.

As I viewed our responsibilities under the various environmental acts, the Enforcement division was supposed to be serving the regional aspects of the various programmatic areas. If someone out in a regional office had a problem with toxic chemicals, for example, he or she should be able to refer that problem to the lawyers in Enforcement with the feeling that they were all working toward the same goals. Instead there was confusion, distrust, and perpetual second-guessing. So to solve the problem I took all the lawyers out of Enforcement and put them into a new office one step on the agency ladder *above* the programmatic areas. I folded the old office of General Counsel into the new one, and called the result the Office of Legal Enforcement and General Counsel.

The furor erupted immediately. I was suddenly the public environmental enemy number one. According to the press I had *eliminated* the enforcement function. The implied reason, of course, was that I was doing the bidding of those unseen forces within the Reagan administration that were so probusiness that they didn't want *any* enforcement of EPA regulations, and certainly no new cases developed for legal prosecution.

As damaging as the headlines were to the general public's perception of what I was trying to do, what we all were trying so hard to do, they were also very damaging to internal EPA morale. First of all, a number of Enforcement division lawyers were unhappy with the switch because they were used to a degree of autonomy (and, yes, power) under the old arrangement, and did not take kindly to being bossed by the top legal officer—and they carried that attitude into their new offices. A few of them were actually disruptive.

Second, I had a number of EPA employees, lawyers and non-lawyers alike, who simply believed what they read in the newspapers and thought they no longer had to be very concerned about enforcement.

I still believe it was a necessary change, one that if left untouched would in the long run turn out to be truly beneficial. I can see now, however, that when viewed from the outside, and even from the inside, it appeared that there was a major problem with enforcement. Clearly there was the normal disruption that goes along with any big change in an organization, and there were malcontents who fought the change, and finally there were those on the inside who thought they'd been given a signal by the new administration to go slow on enforcement, if not to disregard it entirely.

So I did have a significant problem with Enforcement—the office, not the concept—and it was probably my biggest problem until Rita Lavelle and Superfund.

The other major innovation of my reorganization was the establishing of my own mini-OMB, minus a mini-David Stockman, thank God. With this office on one side of the chart, and the Office of Legal Enforcement and General Counsel on the other, the lines of force and authority were now clear.

Below these two offices were the basic programmatic areas, plus Research and Development, and Administration, and above them were only the top three posts: Administrator, Deputy Administrator, and Chief of Staff (me, John Hernandez, and John Daniel). There were also several other important slots and offices on the chart—the Administrative Law Judges, the Office of Civil Rights, and the Office of Legislative Affairs and Public Affairs—but these all reported directly to me. It was a good plan, and even though some parts of it were badly misunderstood and the intentions behind them badly reported, I think it has helped the agency, and made it a more efficient part of the federal government.

In the Carter years the regulations controlling disposal of hazardous wastes had finally been sent out in late 1979 and throughout 1980, but when we took office it fell to us to bring all those regulations to fruition and the actual light of day. We soon found out that couldn't be done with the decision-making structure then in place. There was a process of iteration upon iteration that sent the ball from one office to another and then back again, so anyone in-house who opposed the regulations knew all it took to keep them from becoming functional was to send it back. You could veto anything to death, because there was no way to break out of the system and get the regulations issued.

Under the system I devised we still had a review process, and all the people who needed to see a set of proposed regulations got a shot at them, but we had a dispute resolution process that helped, rather than hindered. And no longer was the objection of a single office or part of the agency sufficient to sound the death knell.

Under the old process there was no way for the originating office to break out of the circle and get a final answer. The Policy Office under the Carter people had become a dog that chased its own tail, and the person who ran the Policy Office was in effect running the agency. And at that time that person was a fascinating man named Bill Drayton.

They were telling William Astor Drayton stories when I got to EPA, and they were still telling them years later. An indefatigable worker, Bill Drayton kept three full-time secretarial shifts going all day and all night, so that if he felt like getting a letter out at 11:00 P.M. or 1:00 A.M. he could do it. As one might suspect, he was the bane of his staff, often holding staff meetings in the middle of the night at his apartment across the Potomac River in Virginia. He was really the one who ran the agency because he ran the Policy Office, within which he had Budget, Finance, Contracts, and Personnel. He had control of all the buttons to make the agency run.

Doug Costle, my predecessor, was satisfied with the old arrangement whereby he and Barbara Blum, his Deputy Administrator, were making all the contacts, while Drayton stayed behind and ran the agency on a day-to-day basis. This was the same arrangement that Bill Ruckelshaus had when he was the original Administrator. And Russell Train, Costle's predecessor, handled things the same way.

In my case, recognizing that the true challenge of the job was one of management, and because the agency was in such a mess when we came in, I decided to be a real hands-on Administrator and get to know the agency from the inside out. And I did. By mid-1982 I felt I could spend more time on the road, making speeches and trying to reach out to some of the agency's constituencies, and then I let John Daniel handle a lot of the day-to-day administration. But basically I had a different way of running EPA from the very beginning.

One of my first acts was to break up the Policy Office, Bill Drayton's old shop, and restructure it so that there were no more bottlenecks, and decisions could get made. If there was a dispute, it was my job to resolve it; the buck definitely stopped with me. Unlike the arrangement under Drayton, I put policies and budget in one office, and in another there were personnel, administration, contracts, and the general financial affairs of the agency. This way no individual could again have all that power. Even though the EPA organization chart had listed a number of people who were structurally speaking equal, one of them was actually *primus inter pares*. That did not strike me as a very efficient or sensible system, and it was one of the first things I changed.

Ironically, at least from my point of view, while I was accomplishing all of these internal improvements, I was taking a beating from Congress and the press.

I didn't know it then, but now I can see that one of the best ways to get in trouble with Congress is to *do* something. Then they will look at it, and eventually make a fuss. But if you don't do anything, the Congress just lies there like a dormant giant. They had been after Jim Watt for months when I was nominated, and it didn't take them long to transfer, or extend, their interest in him to me. Like so many others, most of the members of Congress seemed to believe that Watt was calling the shots for me. (To this day, when I give a speech, I ask the audience to indicate how many of them think I used to work for James Watt, and a surprising number of hands go up.) That belief, and the fact that I was doing things within the agency, along with all the hysteria over the rumored budget cuts, caused Congress to take an active interest in me.

It also did not help that the day after my nomination was announced by the White House, the Washington *Post* ran a long and basically unflattering article about me, which stressed all the negatives the reporter could find. It was written by a Joanne Omang, in whose mouth butter had not melted when she had called me several times from Washington after my name had first come up as a possible Administrator.

It is interesting to me that I remembered this article as being worse than it really was. When I reread it I was surprised to find that it was not as inaccurate as I'd recalled. But it was a very good example of how a reporter can put a negative slant on a story. For example, the second paragraph identifies me as "a corporate attorney for Mountain Bell," which I was, and then continues, "reportedly was recommended for the EPA job by another Denver attorney, Interior Secretary James Watt. With her nomination, the government's top two environmental posts will be in the hands of conservative Colorado lawyers."

I find little to object to there. But the next paragraph read in its entirety: "Gorsuch, 38, is known to Colorado environmentalists largely from her controversial work last summer chairing a state legislative committee on a possible measure to control toxic wastes. She opposed any state role and was instrumental in killing the proposal."

While the next two paragraphs softened the impact of paragraph three somewhat, if it is true as is so often said that few readers go beyond the third paragraph of any newspaper story, then the damage had already been done. In addition, several paragraphs later the reporter quoted me as saying that I "absolutely" thought that "cost-benefit analysis should apply to standards for pollution emissions."

The phrase "cost-benefit analysis" would return—not just to haunt me, but to *plague* me on Capitol Hill. It was read by those who wouldn't take the time to find out the facts for themselves, or even read the briefing papers I supplied the various committees and subcommittees, as a code word for raping the environment as a favor to business. Over and over, both in my confirmation hearing and before committees, I would be asked about my "pledge" to bring "a cost-benefit" approach to my entire agency. They always made it sound as if I had suggested some combination of euthanasia and infanticide.

The problem with the statement in the article was that it was all-encompassing to the point of misleading the reader: While some federal environmental laws do require cost analysis (a fact often ignored by the Carterites), others, such as the Clean Air Act, strictly prohibit it.

The whole article ran four six-inch columns (on page four of the main section of the paper), and contained nineteen paragraphs. It wasn't until the end of paragraph seventeen that the reporter mentioned that I had been "named outstanding freshman legislator in 1976."

All in all, the article made me sound like a person to be wary of as far the environment and its protection were concerned. It is interesting to see how much can be suggested by a clever use of placement; *where* you say what you say can make quite a difference in the impression that is left with the reader.

I was also bothered by the reporter's statement that my decision not to run for reelection in 1978 was not based on the reasons I had given—that I had done the things I'd wanted to do in office, and wanted to spend more time with my children and get back to practicing law. Instead, she wrote: "Gorsuch decided not to run for a third term last year, saying she wanted to spend more time with her husband David, an attorney whose firm usually represents mining companies [nice little gratuitous dig there] and their three children. The couple has since filed for divorce. But there was some question as to whether she could have been reelected from her heavily Jewish, middle-income east Denver district, partly because of controversy over her legislation specifying minimum jail sentences for convicted criminals, according to Colorado political insiders."

The trouble with that paragraph was not only that the reporter misstated the point of the sentencing bill, but also, more importantly, that while the legislation had been controversial, it had all happened in my *first term*, and I'd already survived a reelection campaign. So the point is simply wrong.

It was after reading that article in the Washington *Post*, the paper that every United States Senator has on his or her doorstep each morning, that I decided not to talk to any member of the press until I had been confirmed.

That article pretty much set the tone for all the coverage I got while in office. John Daniel and some of the others have said we got much fairer coverage from *The New York Times*, in particular from Phil Shabecoff, but I don't recall any of them being all that fair or accurate. Unlike the press coverage I had received back in Denver, my Washington coverage began on an unfavorable note— and built to a nasty crescendo.

When I arrived in Washington the press was critical, by which I mean generally negative, but after a while it turned and became downright hostile.

If the reporters had fun at my expense, the editorial cartoonists had a field day. One of the most offensive appeared in the Los Angeles *Times* on the day I was to meet with that paper's editorial board. It depicted a cheap-looking woman in a slip, standing in a doorway. She had answered the knock of a policeman who had "Environmentalist" written on his uniform. The view through the doorway revealed a sleazy-looking man climbing out of the window, and on his back it said, "Industry." The caption read: "Oh, no, officer, there's nothing like *that* going on in here!" When I saw that cartoon, I called off the meeting.

I've always found it rather ironic that in 1982–83 I received an award for "producing more newsprint than anyone else." I'm still not sure if that was really a distinction. I found the award a bit disturbing because it meant that I had received more coverage than the Secretary of State, and the environment had accounted for more column inches than the budget! The truly sad thing was that out of all that coverage, if you took out what was irrelevant, you would be left with about half of the total; and if you asked how much of that half was *accurate*, again it would be about half.

There were countless stories about the "great number" of people who were going to be "fired" at EPA. The only person I ever fired was Rita Lavelle. When we countered the charge about the firings, the critics then charged that an inordinate number of people were resigning, apparently in protest against me and my policies, or what they perceived as my policies. So I had the comptroller go back and check the records to see what the attrition rate was. He reported that it was about 1 percent a month, or exactly the same as it had been during the four Carter years, 12 percent annually. Next they charged "Brain Drain"—I was driving away our best and brightest civil servants—so I had the comptroller check according to GS class and grade, the government's ranking system, and, sure enough, the biggest turnover was in the lower ranks, among the clerical people for the most part, which is traditional.

Readers, however, never got to see the answer to the volley, only the initial serve. Facts that correct a mistaken headline are apparently not considered newsworthy.

The press, like the Congress itself, seemed always to be preoccupied with how many people the agency had, not with the quality of the job we were doing. And this was despite the fact that the Reagan administration had the widely proclaimed goal of reducing unnecessary federal programs and manpower. The Washington-based press cares only for how many people you have and how much money you have—the size of your turf. Forget about results.

It was my experience throughout my time at EPA that the press did not know the issues and was not particularly interested in learning them. Instead of doing substantive research in order to find where the water regulations were, for example, and how soon the agency planned to get them out, they simply read somebody else's old clips, and based their story on that. And personal interviews rarely touched on issues; invariably they began with a question like, "How do you respond to Jack Anderson's charge that you are an 'Ice Queen'?" I read more crap about why I wore a purple suit (I did it: "so it would match her eyes") than what I was doing when I wore it. Reporters never came in to talk about the water regulations or the changes in the Air Act, or the pros and cons of those changes. That sounds like quite a large generalization, but if pressed to name the exceptions, the only person I can think of is Phil Shabecoff of *The New York Times*, who has been reporting on the environment for some ten years, and understands the issues. But often even he got sucked in along with all the others, courtesy of whoever wrote the headlines for his stories.

Did any environmentalists ever come in and display a genuine interest in getting at the truth of what I was doing at EPA? Absolutely none.

When I had my first meeting as EPA Administrator with a group of environmentalists, I was naïve enough to think that we were going to discuss the issues and perhaps debate our differing points of view. They began the meeting by saying, "We want prenotification of any agency action," a privilege I was told my predecessor had granted them.

I said, "We don't run this agency like that. I wouldn't give prenotification to my mother or the Pope. There is going to be no favored nation clause in the way I'm going to administer this agency." And that was the end of that meeting. We never discussed issues at all.

In my experience with Washington-based environmental lobbyists, their main concern is seeing how much money they can raise for their organizations by scaring the American public half to death. The truth about the vast majority of them is that they are not interested in the environment at all. They are interested in power, political power, and the environment is just a platform for them.

We scared those environmentalists who had preceded us in office because we were getting things done. In doing nothing, they created a vacuum, and we began to fill it with results, and that just scared them silly. Because once you put a regulation on the books, it is unlikely that anyone will be able to change it. They could see their whole platform disappearing before their eyes. They were never going to be able to establish water regulations, for example, because we were going to do it. They could see this whole page of unwritten laws being filled, and once they're written, you don't undo them. All the real substantive power was slipping away from them.

They had left us more power than we deserved, because they left agendas of inaction that we filled. What we inherited from them was a legacy of inaction, of decisional voids. We started filling those voids. And they could see all of those substantive areas slipping away from them.

I will bet that we produced more regulations in the twenty-two months of my tenure than were produced in the entire four years under President Carter. How's that for being the "De-regulator of the Environment"?

8

SUPERFUND

One of the most pressing needs when I took office was to find good people. Contrary to what has been written, I did not begin the job with the attitude that I would *not* find any top-notch people already working for EPA. I can see how people might have thought that I had that attitude because I preferred to let my top people name their own aides from the Civil Service. And when I had the Assistant Administrators (AAs) in place and didn't name any office directors, that must have added to the sense that I didn't care about career civil service people.

But quite the opposite was true. In fact, I sent Jim Sanderson out right away on what amounted to an executive search within the agency itself. One of his very best finds, perhaps his very best was William Hedeman. A lawyer who had only been with EPA for about a year Hedeman was working in the Office of Federal Relations, an office that had been relatively important during the Carter years, but one that I was in the process of downgrading as part of my reorganization. What made him an obvious choice to head the Superfund part of the Waste Office was that he had worked for the Corps of Engineers for a number of years, and had the sort of legal background and legal mind that would fit neatly into Superfund needs. We elevated him, gave him a chance to do more, and he made us look like prophets.

101

Hedeman, who continues to run Superfund today, deserves great praise for what he has done. It is estimated that there are between fifteen thousand and twenty thousand hazardous waste sites in this country today. The Toxic Substance Control Act called for an almost immediate ranking, based on priorities, of at least the four hundred worst sites, and it fell to Bill Hedeman to establish the decision-making mechanism. He devised what is now called the Mitre Hazard Ranking system, a system that has withstood the toughest kind of criticism from all sides and all points of view.

The central question was, How do you judge "most hazardous"? The matrix Hedeman came up with rests on rather simple criteria: What is the degree of exposure to human population? How does that exposure pose the greatest danger? Obviously pollution in the drinking water is the greatest danger; air pollution is relatively limited, but once something dangerous gets in the drinking water, it's gone. So Mr. Hedeman had his work cut out for him. But when he'd finished, no one could fault him.

When Bill Ruckelshaus came in, despite his promises he decimated the ranks of my appointees in a gesture that was as hollow in meaning as it was harmful to the individuals and their families involved. But Hedeman survived, because he was a civil servant *and* because he was so clearly the best man for the job.

After I'd left office I did not see Bill Hedeman for over a year; it was simply too much for me to see him, or any of the others I'd had so much respect for, in light of what had happened. Early in 1985 we met for lunch, and had a very good visit. I asked him if he would be willing to give me, for the purposes of this book, some of his observations of the history of Superfund. A short time later he did so, in a taped conversation with John Greenya.

"The Superfund law had been passed in December of 1980, and Congress had not appropriated any money to run the program until August of 1981. So, because of Congress's slowness, one year of the program had been lost. However, during that first eight-month time frame, much of which Anne had not been associated with because she had not yet arrived at the agency, the staff began to prepare a rewrite of the National Contingency Plan, which had a number of recommended directions in which the program could go.

"It went up to her prior to my arrival in September of 1981, and in talking with John Daniel I'm advised that Anne reviewed the plan—it was some four hundred typewritten pages in length—and concluded that since it would be a regulation it was much too long and it was also much too rigid in terms of how the program should be run. So that in the interests of flexibility and such, she, John Daniel, John Hernandez, and, I believe, Bill Sullivan, who was enforcement counsel at the time, personally rewrote the plan.

"You do not have any Administrator in the history of the agency who has done that. Instead of sending it back to the career people, the plan was personally rewritten. And when I arrived, on October 27, 1981, Anne presented me with the plan and said, 'Here's the rewrite; I want you to go through whatever has to be done to get it dispersed in the Federal Register.'

"The plan was proposed, as I recall, in February of 1982 in the Federal Register. And we took public comment, and were able to promulgate it in final form, in July of 1982. The Environmental Defense Fund promptly brought a lawsuit against it, and the agency in the end had to settle that lawsuit. They argued that the plan was so flexible that it wasn't a plan of any sort; [that] it completely eliminated any public involvement in agency decision-making; it had no standards on how clean is clean or the direction that the agency should go in cleaning up sites; and it prohibited the listing of federal facilities on the national priority list, among other things. We settled that lawsuit and agreed to make changes in the plan, and a new plan will be proposed in the Federal Register on February 11, 1985. . . .

"It was also at a time in which those who were advocating the legislation were saying that there were somewhere between thirty-five thousand and fifty thousand sites in this country that had this problem, and that they had to be addressed.

"I think Anne's inclination at that point was to come up with a regulation that gave the greatest amount of flexibility to EPA as possible so that it, one, would not be entrenched in any particular direction at the end of five years; two, it avoided manipulation by the public in the sense of involvement in decision-making; and, three, it did not commit in any way to final clean-ups, in terms of "how clean is clean," but allowed the flexibility to proceed in a way in which the agency could operate and maneuver without being held to any particular direction.

"An irony to this is that those who opposed Anne and the

Reagan administration could obviously get their best shot at an infant program because it is the most vulnerable. We did not know when she came in how many sites existed out there that presented a problem, [but] we also knew that whatever we were dealing with would take an awful long time to fix. When Anne left EPA we had cleaned up 6 sites on the national priority list—out of 405. The list has grown to 812, and we have still only cleaned up 6 sites.

"It illustrates the point that these abandoned hazardous waste sites are a bear to deal with, highly controversial, technically impossible to deal with at once in any clear fashion, and if you really wanted to pick a program to attack, Superfund was the most logical because it had not become entrenched, it had not had a direction, the resources needed to run it had not even been appropriated by the Congress until August of 1981, and it was very unclear where everybody wanted it to go. . . .

"Her motives were honorable in the sense that she had a direction she wanted to go in, and the direction was to get the states directly and actively and perhaps exclusively involved in this problem within this five-year period of time. [But] the overall effect of all this was to slow the program down. . . .

"The Administration had no perception whatsoever of the national public hysteria over the problems of the nation's hazardous wastes. Instead, the approach was tempered with an overzealousness towards turning the environmental programs back to the States, getting the federal government out of the picture, and moving to reduce taxes and deficit programs. No one stepped back to look at the big picture as it really was perceived by the public.

"By so doing, they walked into a trap that had been laid by their enemies. They played right into their enemy's hands.

"I could never say that Anne was insensitive to the problems of hazardous waste in this country. In her mind, the issue was more, 'Who should be responsible for dealing with the issue in the long term?', not that there was a problem—in contrast to Rita Lavelle, who constantly came in and said, 'I don't think there's a problem at this site. We shouldn't spend the money.' I never saw that attitude coming out of Anne. If the professional people would go to her and identify a problem, she would go ahead and fund it. But her concern was where the direction of the Superfund program was going.

"I always felt that Lavelle had a perception that man and toxic waste could live coequally, that risk was largely exaggerated, that sites that presented problems really weren't problems. I did not have the feeling that Anne felt that way.

"I also felt that Lavelle was a friend of business. She was advocating the approach that from the standpoint of risk, and in particular risk management, one had to live with risk. Probably the most glaring example of that was a case we had in which the State of Arkansas was asking for Superfund money to clean up a site that was heavily contaminated with a high concentration of PCBs, and Lavelle's response in a letter back to the Congressman was that for the risk to be of concern, a pica child (a child that eats dirt) would have to eat the equivalent of three candy bars a day worth of dirt.

"Now, aside from the poor analogy, she demonstrated an insensitivity to the concerns of the public in the vicinities of these sites who felt that their public health problems and the effects on their children and others were being adversely affected by these sites. Anne didn't feel that way.

"That is essentially what overshadowed the Superfund program, that fundamental policy call that Anne had made.

"Did she change? No, I don't think she did change, because I don't think she had time to change. The question that has no answer, because the chapter was never written to conclusion, was whether she would have changed, given the controversy surrounding the program, had she remained as Administrator."

While I take issue with some of Bill Hedeman's interpretations and observations, I nonetheless am moved by his careful, honest, and complimentary statement. Once again I find myself wishing that I had had the nerve to give him the job that went to Rita Lavelle.

I think it's important, just as Hedeman said, to keep in mind some of the history of the Superfund program, especially since it now barely resembles the program I met in 1981. For one thing, there was so much dissension in Congress itself that it could not decide which agency should administer the bill. It solved the problem by giving all the power to the President, who in turn delegated most of the power by Executive Order to EPA in the summer of 1981, shortly after I had been sworn in as Administrator.

Another point to remember is that EPA does not have sole authority over Superfund matters. Various other agencies all over Washington have a piece of the Superfund responsibility, including the Department of Interior and the Department of Health and Human Services, which has always felt it should conduct health studies at *every* Superfund site. People tend to forget this, but Superfund is a public works measure (the Senate committee with principal Superfund oversight is the Committee on Environment and Public Works) and is therefore looked at as "found money"— funds with great pork barrel potential.

My main point is that everyone in town soon knew three things: Superfund was the only game in town, the only new source of money; it was likely to be the only new source of money for the next four years; and it was an enormously popular program with the American public. So they all wanted their share of the pie. And, oh, what a big pie you have, Grandma!

As Hedeman mentioned, my philosophy was to conserve the fund, to make it go as far as it could with that five-year revenue. Also, we wanted to get more state money in instead of relying solely on the fund itself for cleanup. Our goal was to get as much money as possible into the ground as soon as possible, minimizing the federal contribution. And within the context of the legislation that made sense.

What changed things was that Congress realized that it had accidentally invented a combination of sliced bread and the wheel. The public *loves* Superfund, and the taxpayers don't have to pay for it! Nineteen eighty-five was supposed to be the last year of the fund.

Just how much has the fund grown, and how large will it become? Consider this statistic: The law requires that there be a minimum of 400 sites on the Superfund list; as of early 1985 there were 769, and someone who follows the law closely told me that eventually there will be *at least* 2,000 sites. Everybody on the Hill is going to be figuring out how to increase the fund. They are going to cast the net of that tax on mining, on everybody who makes breakfast cereals, and vitamins. Everybody will be vying over how to make that fund bigger.

Some of the folks at EPA would tell you—if they dared—that

one of their greatest fears is that they will get too much money in that fund too fast. And because of all the temptations that will follow, the result could well be the same kind of scandal that we saw earlier involving construction grants for sewage treatment plants.

The Superfund figures have essentially doubled every year for five years, and when you have that kind of exponential growth it becomes very, very difficult to manage or control the situation, much like a runaway horse.

An aspect of the Superfund Act that always kind of tickled me was that it says, though not quite so bluntly, "By the way, while you're at it, try to find a Superfund site in every Congressional district." Congress knew it had all the earmarks of a classic pork-barrel opportunity. And, putting aside for the moment the question of the very real dangers to humans that are involved, it has not failed to live up to that opportunity.

Like Bill Hedeman, John Skinner, whom we tapped to run RCRA, was another internal find. He too was a bright, aggressive guy ready to handle more responsibility. I gave him a new mandate, and he knew just what to do with it. The real work of the RCRA office had been badly neglected. Passed in 1976, the Resource Conservation and Recovery Act called for its regulations to be on the books by 1978, but when I got there nothing had been done. Skinner took that situation from the nothing we inherited in 1980 to the point that in January 1983 we had the regulations for disposal of hazardous wastes in the ground on the books and ready for the implementation of what are termed Part B licenses (which apply the regulations, and which landfills must qualify for or go out of business).

Now, unfortunately, that program is going terribly slowly. I don't think John Skinner is getting the kind of support I would be giving him were I still there. And that is sad. If these landfills go out of business there is the very great danger that they will become the Superfund sites of tomorrow, because they will have closed down without ever having been properly regulated, and are adding to the level of contamination. Every day that EPA doesn't go like gangbusters on Part B licensing, it is creating new Superfund sites in this country. You can talk about Superfund all you want, but as long as RCRA is neglected, it's like pushing stuff through a sieve.

Consider this: 2 percent of the generators of hazardous wastes in this country are responsible for 98 percent of the waste. Stage one of RCRA was designed to regulate the majority of the problem, with the fewest number of people. Under the reauthorization of RCRA that took place last year the Congress put in the remaining 2 percent of waste, and thereby increased the number of regulated people by 98 percent. And that may put John Skinner under, because he doesn't have the first part done yet. It's noble to say we want to control 100 percent of the waste generators, but we can't do that until we take care of the 98 percent of the problem.

It may be all well and good to regulate all the dry cleaners in the country, to choose a group that will now come under the eye of EPA for the first time, but if you don't have the basic regulations in place and applied, where are you? What's the good of having them on the books unless you have them applied through licensing?

In terms of national publicity, you hardly ever hear of RCRA, at least not in comparison with Superfund, but in terms of the challenges given to Skinner and Hedeman, theirs were comparable efforts.

It may sound strange, but once I had Hedeman and Skinner in office, I was a lot less concerned with who would be their boss. Until then I had been spending about half my time doing the job of the Assistant Administrator for Solid Waste and Emergency Response (running Superfund and RCRA) and it was wearing on me. So it was with great relief that I saw these two able men launched in their federal posts. I was anxious to turn my attention back to various other priorities, and I agreed to reinterview a young woman we had already turned down once for the job of Hedeman and Skinner's boss, a woman who both times had been sent to us—or so we were led to believe—by the White House, a woman named Rita Lavelle.

Before beginning the story of Rita—not an easy one for me to relate—perhaps it would be instructive to describe the process by which we sought to find the PAS's, the Presidentially-Appointed, Senate-Confirmed high-level managers.

The agency I took over in the spring of 1981 had become so big and so complex and so important that it barely resembled that of William the First. When Ruckelshaus was in charge as the first EPA Administrator, the agency had jurisdiction over only air and water and drinking water—that was it! No toxics, no hazardous wastes, no pesticides, none of the subject areas that have proved to be so difficult and newsworthy.

The months prior to my taking office were taken up with planning the reorganization of the agency, and trying to find people to staff it. In that latter job, Jim Sanderson, Joe Ryan of the White House personnel office, and I spent entire days pouring through résumés and holding interviews in Ryan's OEOB office. It was a laborious process, but there was really no way to streamline it. We had to find the best people, and that took time.

My obvious aim was to hire someone as Skinner and Hedeman's boss who was at least as good as they were. In retrospect, it probably would have been smart to have made Hedeman his own boss, but that would have meant finding someone else to run Superfund, and I was too happy with him where he was. We looked and looked, and we interviewed every candidate we could find. I think my standards began to slip a bit as I saw how long it was going to take to get someone better than Skinner and Hedeman, and since they were doing so well I became less convinced that I absolutely had to have a top-notch person in that slot. What's more, I had been spending so much time doing the job myself that I was in effect monitoring both programs.

That last task was very much worth doing, because Superfund was a brand new program about which the Administrator needed to know a great deal. And RCRA, because so little had been done in it, might as well have been a brand new program too.

I remember sitting in my office with Jim Sanderson and Joe Ryan doing our usual three-on-one interview with an applicant who looked like not just a good candidate, but an excellent one. He was great on paper, and every bit as good in person. In his fifties, he had a very impressive background, including management posts of real responsibility, and fantastic credentials as a chemist. He was almost too good to be true.

Toward the end of the interview Joe asked his usual question about "Do you support the President and his objectives, and if you disagree, where do you disagree?" and there was no problem. Then Sanderson said something I don't think he'd ever said before in a similar interview.

"How'd you vote in the last election?"

The man got a sort of odd look on his face, and replied, "I didn't vote."

"You didn't? Why not?"

"I'm not a citizen."

The three of us all but fell out of our chairs.

"No," he continued. "I'm a Canadian. But I don't see any reason why that should keep your Senate from confirming me."

He may not have seen any reason, but unfortunately the Constitution does; only American citizens can hold the type of presidential appointment for which U.S. Senate confirmation is mandatory. How the applicant had gotten so far along in the interview process we never did learn. But that was, unfortunately, the last we saw of him.

By now I'd all but despaired of finding anybody for that slot. But it didn't cause me any sleepless nights because I was so pleased with the quality of the men who were running the two substantive programs.

9

EDUCATED BY RITA

So along came Rita. The first time around Sanderson interviewed her, and issued an immediate "forget it." She simply didn't have the experience for a job of that stature. But she must have had some friend or friends in high places, because not long after that word came down from the White House personnel office that we should see her again. This time John Daniel interviewed her.

There was a rumor, and it made it into print more than once, that Rita Lavelle came to Washington originally to lobby for her employer, Aerojet General, in regard to Superfund, and that while she was here she discovered that the job of Superfund Director was vacant, and made up her mind to get it. Later she said that she didn't even know her former employer had any Superfund sites but one of the articles that quoted her was used to trip her up.

When Rita came back for her second interview, John Daniel was still not impressed, but Joe Ryan, who is one of those people whose persuasiveness is nine parts persistence, kept going on about how "She has all this public relations experience, and since the office is basically being run by the program directors, then it wouldn't hurt to have someone with this kind of P.R. background"—which was all true, as far as it went—"and that while she doesn't really have all the management experience in the world or the proper educational background, she really wants the job, and if desire counts for anything, then" blah-blah-blah. It was like water dripping on a stone. Joe wore me down.

He said Rita had confessed that she had not "interviewed well" the first time, and that he had advised her to come back and give it her best shot, this time before me.

As his clincher, he said, "And, Anne, you know how it is for women; they're frequently not given opportunities to grow, and so it becomes one of those Catch-22 situations: You don't have the management experience because you've never been given the opportunity for management experience, so therefore you're in this ever-downward cycle, and you as a woman should be sympathetic to that, and certainly you have been before. . . ." So, finally, and in part because of a fear that he would never stop, I relented and told Ryan to bring her in. I must add, lest it sound like I am trying to blame Joe Ryan for Rita Lavelle's being at EPA and in charge of Superfund, that Joe and I worked together very well. We almost always reached an amicable compromise, even if he did at times overplay his persistence; working with him was always a pleasure.

John Daniel, whom I should stress also admired Joe Ryan and enjoyed working with him, has a vivid memory of one statement Ryan made that day. "Anne and I had both been complaining that even though we had been looking for a long time, we thought we should keep looking, and suddenly Joe said, *This* is your candidate.' I never did learn why he said that."

That is, he didn't learn why until the writing of this book. John Greenya went to see Joe Ryan, who has left the White House and now runs an executive search agency, and asked him if he recalled making that statement. "Yes, I said that," replied Ryan without hesitation, "and I'll tell you *why* I said it. I said it because one day at a meeting in the White House personnel office, my boss handed me a résumé and said, 'This is your Superfund candidate.' It was the résumé of Rita Lavelle."

Joe Ryan's boss was John Herrington, today the Secretary of Energy.

When I first saw Rita Lavelle, I was not favorably impressed. That may sound cruel, but it is the truth. The woman does not make a favorable physical impression. She is overweight, an unnatural blonde, and her appearance is blowsy.

On the plus side, and offsetting her lack of managerial experience, she did seem to have fairly wide experience within Aerojet General. According to her representations, within that very diversified company she had worked not for any one division, but rather had performed public relations tasks for the various segments of the company as they came to her with their perceived needs. I liked that. And I also liked the idea that she would be bringing public relations awareness to a program office that people needed to be informed about.

For the most part, however, and using hindsight, I have to say about the prospect of hiring Rita Lavelle that I just didn't care. Or, to put it in a way that sounds less callous, I felt that she couldn't do any harm. So much for prescience.

At the time I didn't think she was as dumb as she turned out to be. And I also didn't perceive how recalcitrant she was or how much she thought she knew. I didn't see the pitfalls in advancing someone who on paper lacked the credentials for the job. I felt that if she had any real holes, we could fill them.

I was tired of looking, and the White House seemed to want her in the job. As for the strength and importance of her White House contacts, all I knew was that she obviously had them, or we wouldn't be talking to her again. She was the only person sent over by the White House whom we were asked to reconsider after refusing her initially.

To this day, it isn't clear who sent her back. She had claimed a great friendship with Meese (who swore her in), and she knew Deaver's secretary very well. But you don't come out bluntly and say, "Who are your friends over there and just how important are they?" We did know that she had worked for the Reagan gubernatorial team in Sacramento when she was quite young, and had worked to improve her position from one job to another over several years.

The problem is that none of those high-level contacts turned out to be as great and good friends of hers as Rita led us to believe.

So I gave in and agreed to hire Rita Lavelle. She being such an unknown quantity, and Superfund being a brand new program that the Congress was most anxious to see succeed, she had little trouble getting approved by the Senate. I attended her swearing-in ceremony, and was impressed by the fact that Presidential Counsel Ed Meese was also there. That certainly looked like proof of her "Meese connection," which Rita had stressed at her interview.

Almost from the begining Rita was fighting over her turf, mainly trying to expand it, as opposed to being on the defensive. And she had a penchant for unhesitatingly bringing her problems right to me. Her favorite opponent seemed to be Bob Perry, my general counsel, who, under my reorganized EPA setup, also had the main enforcement responsibility. I should not have been involved so often in their squabbles, but I did so in part because the two of them had such different personalities and used such different approaches.

Perry is such a sweet guy and a natural peacemaker, unless you knew him you wouldn't even think there was a dispute. He would come in, almost apologetically, and say, in his quiet, sincere, low-key way, "Anne, there's this small thing that I thought I should perhaps bring to your attention." But Rita Lavelle, talking about the same thing, would storm in, all but pound my desk with her shoe, and say, "Dammit, Perry's screwing up my program again!"

It was my job as Administrator to resolve those kinds of programmatic conflicts, but not at the rate—or the *crescendo*—at which they were occurring in that program. Inherently there is a jurisdictional dispute, and institutionally there has to be friction between Rita and Bob because the program's not only an administrative program, it's also an enforcement program. Those things overlap—not only are you trying to go forward with cleanup, you are trying to negotiate with the several responsible parties to enforce their liability. And when the administrative part of the program overlaps with the enforcement part, it inevitably comes to the question of who's in charge.

Rita did not want Perry running any part of the program, period. I could understand her initial objections, given the overlap, but for her to say, as she frequently did, that Perry had no jurisdiction at all over her programs was plain wrong.

There was one area in which I agreed with Rita. My decision did not win me any friends internally, and, to the extent they knew about it, probably made me more enemies on the outside, especially among the environmentalists. Nonetheless, I thought my agreeing with her was justified at the time. It involved what EPA calls "emergency response monies." These are funds that are designed for use in crisis, as opposed to chronic situations—say, a thirty-drum spill in the Platte River, or a train derailment, rather than a dump site where hazardous wastes are constantly leaking. Superfund contains emergency response monies to cover these things.

Ideally you have a well-understood list of what constitutes an emergency response, and how much money can be spent for each type, to the extent that would be possible. And then the Regional Administrators can be told how much they can spend on these emergencies without having to ask for approval from headquarters. Rita wanted to keep the amount spent very small; the Regional Administrators (RAs) wanted a hell of a lot more latitude. It was a natural institutional problem.

I agreed with Rita for two reasons. One, I was concerned about fund conservation; two, I was worried about precedents. I was particularly aware that because Superfund was a brand new program, every decision to spend money established a precedent for future expenditures.

I thought it would be wiser to play these situations by ear for a year or two, and then, with some experience under our belt, we could more realistically assess what kind of funds to allocate. We might decide that for a certain type of spill, a $25,000 limit would be enough, but another kind would call for $100,000. And these funds could be spent without headquarters' approval because we would have real figures as to what it cost to deal with these various emergencies.

The RAs were not at all happy with my decision, but that displeasure was small compared to their reaction to how Rita handled their requests for additional emergency response funds. She simply wouldn't give them any. And this was the beginning of the RAs' attitude toward Rita that was nothing short of true animosity.

At first I took the position that these were only natural in-house differences of opinion and approach. But then I began to notice that Rita had what you might call a problem with facts. For example, early on Rita told me that Sonia Crowe, my Administrator for Region IX, wanted an increased authorization to deal with a spill of angel dust (phencyclidine, a drug that can cause disorientation and hallucinations), on a mountainside in California.

I was scheduled to go to California for my regular reporting session with Sonia, and Rita told me that Sonia had been very angry about her refusal to allow her to exceed the spending limit "by a lot" for what Rita described as a rather insignificant spill. Based on that representation, I told Rita I agreed with her.

When I arrived in California I got a much different story. Sonia Crowe said, "Anne, I'm very, very concerned. There was a significant spill on this mountain, and it's right above a drinking water supply. If that gets into the drinking water, we will have a major problem."

In fairness, Rita may not have known that the spill was near a drinking water supply. But she should have; it was her *job* to know. I began to get more and more leery about Rita Lavelle. I began to wonder if I were getting *all* the facts. And how good was the judgment she was applying to the situations?

As the months passed I began to hear a different sort of rumor. I began to hear that Rita was reporting, frequently, to the powers that be in the White House about internal EPA matters. Initially I was ambivalent about this development, if that's truly what was happening. I didn't know who the hell she was talking to or what the hell she was saying, but I figured if she was keeping somebody in daily touch about her programs, maybe all the better. At least, if she were talking to someone, he or she would have a real good idea of what we were doing in Superfund. And I'd had the feeling all along that no one at the White House had any knowledge of what programmatic decisions were being made at EPA, notwithstanding my several efforts to keep them informed.

On the other hand, the rest of the Assistant Administrators, Rita's colleagues, all looked to me as the boss, and they went through me, as they should have, not to some shadowy figure or figures in the White House. If they hadn't I would have considered it an act of disloyalty. With Rita I wasn't sure exactly what I thought. It *was* a huge program, and "education" is a good thing, so if she was keeping someone informed, fine.

What never even occurred to me was the possibility that she might be taking some *direction* from the White House.

Originally, I thought she was simply trying to elevate herself, just enhancing the status of Rita Lavelle. After doing the research for this book, I've come to believe that she was keeping someone informed and receiving direction from the White House.

How good were her White House contacts? To this day, I do not know. When I was called before the grand jury prior to her indictment and trial, I was asked about a few names that meant nothing to me then. But I found out later they were the White House people she had spoken to on more than one occasion, or so it was alleged. But I have no firsthand information as to the extent or frequency or nature of those contacts, or even if they actually took place.

As I mentioned earlier, with two solid program directors (Bill Hedeman and John Skinner) in place, eventually I didn't have to monitor Rita as closely as I would have had to without them. Nonetheless, in our meetings in the early months it soon became clear that I would have to give her a good deal of visible support because the career people were not impressed with either her background or her performance.

By mid-1982 I could see that when I wanted to get things done in either Superfund or RCRA, I had to go to Bill or John directly. Toward the end of 1982, a couple of things happened that indicated to me just how big a problem Rita Lavelle was. In November, she wrote her famous "candy bar" letter, the one that exhibited such insensitivity to children's health that John Dingell became so furious at her—and all of us, indirectly—that he hauled us up on the Hill for a lengthy and laborious hearing.

The hearing did not go well for Rita. As Bill Hedeman told me much later, "I found myself, sitting next to her, having to bail her out on questions for which she had no comprehension of either the most fundamental aspects of the problem or program, including the difference between a remedial action and a removal action. It was an embarrassment."

Over the Thanksgiving holiday, I had a chance to review the C-Span (the cable system that televises Congressional sessions and selected hearings) tapes of Rita before Dingell's committee. Hedeman was right; it *was* an embarrassment. For the first time I could see just how big a problem I had.

By the time I held my administrator's review of Rita's program in the middle of January, 1983, I was all but totally ignoring her whenever I had substantive questions.

Hedeman recalls that meeting vividly. "It was such a bizarre meeting. After we left it, even Rita seemed a bit concerned by its tone, but then she passed it off lightly, saying that Anne must have been in a bad mood. She promised to 'straighten it out,' but she never mentioned it again.

"There were other Rita problems. For example, Rita was supposed to attend a national conference on hazardous spills in Milwaukee, Wisconsin, and was to be the keynote speaker. She was asked to testify before some committee that morning [but] still wanted to make that keynote speech, so she went ahead and arranged to be flown out by means of a private jet to the conference. At the last possible minute, Anne found out about this, and terminated that effort. I received a call in Milwaukee, saying that Anne was going to send John Horton, the Assistant Administrator for Administration, in Rita's place, and that Rita would not be coming by any private jet. But Rita lived in these illusions of grandeur, even to the point of asking that we arrange a police escort to get her from the airport to the place to speak. And I think Anne kept hearing about this, and I've always had the sense that she came to realize the problems that she had with Rita upon reviewing those tapes of the Dingell committee hearing. Or at least that was a major "two-by-four" type signal that came to her like a bolt from the sky.

"However, shortly after that Anne became ill—she had the first of several kidney stone problems. In December of 1982 Anne went on vacation over the Christmas holidays, and while there became very ill. She did not return until about the middle of January 1983. When she returned she set about to have major program reviews from all the Assistant Administrators and their Office Directors to find out where things were going; these were scheduled to go for about three to four hours.

"Ours was slated for somewhere around the middle of January 1983. It was very peculiar. The three Office Directors present were myself for Superfund, Gene Lucero for the Enforcement Office of hazardous waste, and John Skinner, who headed RCRA. John Daniel also was present, and, of course, Rita and Anne. And Anne was openly . . . I wouldn't say 'hostile' to Rita, but in the presence of the three people who worked for her [Rita] came close to virtually ignoring anything Rita said or did.

"Instead, she carried on a very intense conversation with each one of us three Office Directors on each of our programs. She kept saying, 'the whole truth, and nothing but the truth, no matter how unpleasant it may seem.'

"The meeting had such an impact on me, however, that I said to my wife when I got home that night—and I rarely discussed the job at home—that I didn't feel Rita would be around much longer. The vibrations at that meeting were that intense."

10

GRABBING THE REINS

Before I took office, Vice-President Bush on instructions from the President headed an administration-wide effort called the Task Force on Regulatory Reform. He wrote to state and local governments, as well as to industry, asking everyone to identify the regulations that were of greatest concern to them from the standpoint of duplication or redundancy, or simply because they involved too much processing or red tape. Interestingly, more than half of the regulations specified by the respondents were EPA regulations. As a result, I would tell people that when I started to work it was like coming into an office with a three-room in box.

As I confidently told a crowd at San Francisco's Commonwealth Club, regulatory reform "will be an ongoing initiative for this Administration and one that will occupy a great deal of our time and attention."

That statement, I was most displeased to learn, would turn out to be dead wrong. In a matter of weeks after I made that boast, the administration announced that it had won the war on regulatory reform. And General Bush withdrew his troops from the battlefield. It was a very strange move, of which this Captain, for one, was not advised.

To say we had won the war on regulatory reform in less than one presidential term is simply a joke. One early critic of America's effort in Viet Nam used to say that we should just declare victory and pull out. It's possible there was an element of that attitude in

121

the White House's thinking, and it's also possible that the Vice-President's heart really wasn't in the regulatory reform fight from the beginning. Nor was he in much of a position to do much.

I don't mean to demean Mr. Bush, who was always very good to me. Because President Reagan had said the effort needed a high profile and a continuing presence, Bush became the natural choice to head the task force. But I think he had so many other highly important things to worry about that he eventually lost interest. He must also have tired rather soon of the charge levied by the environmentalists and picked up by the press that the Reagan administration's true aim in the environmental area was *deregulation.* So much more remains to be done—certainly at EPA—that for anyone to declare victory in the area of regulatory reform is nonsense. It is abdication in the face of the enemy. In a sense it was easier for us than many other departments and agencies because we didn't need Congressional action in order to implement New Federalism; all of our main laws, with the exception of TOSCA, had been enacted by Congress in the mode of New Federalism.

Based on my legislative experience I came to the EPA believing that the budget was *the* tool of management, and through it one controlled policy direction. Through the mini-OMB we set up a three-fold system: (1) control of policy through effective budgetmaking; (2) rationalization of any anomalies among the programs (because each one functions under a different statute, and what you're doing in, say, Waste may conflict with an Air regulation; (3) a management system.

As for the management system that I devised and put into operation, I still find it embarrassing to stand up before an audience and say that one of the things I'm proudest of is my EPA management system. It required each manager to negotiate with my own internal OMB for a certain set of goals on a quarterly basis, and for five quarters in advance. Naturally we would build the budget to meet those goals, and we would allocate both dollars and people so that the program could meet management objectives. The first step in the process was to examine the relevant statute to see what it required, and if there were any Congressional deadlines that had to be considered. Simple. And it's still there, still in place, the best thing that ever happened to that agency. Probably the main reason I call it my proudest accomplishment is that it is the longest lasting, it will continue to be used to monitor progress—and to make sure there *is* progress—by whoever is Administrator.

There was a further overall objective, to improve the quality or credibility of the science. The scientific information is the predicate of everything EPA does. Love Canal is a notorious example of what can only be called sloppy science. It was a Doug Costle–Carter administration undertaking that they hurried out the door. Once the details of that scientific study became known throughout academic circles, it was roundly rejected as being very, very weak.

The *problem* at Love Canal was admittedly horrendous. But the work the agency did in examining the site was terribly sloppy. While it may have been good enough to show that there was a problem, from a technical, scientific point of view it was so incredibly poor that you couldn't rely on it to fashion a solution. And then, of course, the situation became politicized. So when the President said, "I want the scientific credibility of that agency reestablished," I heard him loud and clear.

This next point may be a small example, but it invariably gets loud applause when I mention it in speeches: After I had reorganized EPA I had more people with scientific backgrounds in top management posts than I had lawyers! Another first.

When it came to the area of personnel, the cartoonists had a field day, usually depicting career civil servants hanging from EPA window ledges by their fingernails. Gary Trudeau was especially fond of this imagery. The truth of the matter was something quite different. We *did* reduce the size of the agency, but solely by attrition.

By virtue of this reduction-by-attrition, the personnel were reduced by 19 percent and the operating budget was reduced by 22 percent. Interestingly, the question that was always asked was how we could get along with fewer people. The question that was never asked but which should have been was: "What kind of *results* are you getting from the Agency?"

Unfortunately, the only criterion for success in Washington seems to be how many dollars and warm bodies you control. No one ever asked about results. The fact that we were doing things faster and better with fewer people and less money was looked upon as irrelevant.

Some critics claimed that was merely a cosmetic change, but

they were wrong. It went much deeper than that. From an internal perspective it had a big impact. It said we were finally going to start paying more attention to the scientific, as opposed to the political, direction. No longer would the scientific area be politicized.

Love Canal was politicized, from beginning to end.

Another major objective was regulatory reform. Looking back, I would have to say that the only progress we made in that area was getting the Water regulations in shape—but that was substantial. And I give John Hernandez credit for that.

One area in which we did not do much regulatory reform was in Air. But there was a good reason for that: Air was up for reauthorization before the Congress, and it didn't make any sense to rewrite the regulations while Congress was rewriting the laws. If we had, we might have ended up doing it twice, or else we'd chance sending Congress the wrong signal. So we purposely didn't do anything in that area.

And I admit that there were other areas where we just didn't really get off the ground as far as regulatory reform was concerned. There is still plenty of room for regulatory reform within EPA. When you get right down to it, by mid-1982 we could justifiably claim that EPA was the only government agency that was actually practicing what Ronald Reagan had preached—the only agency practicing regulatory reform, more results for fewer dollars, more credible science, and New Federalism.

If the purpose of New Federalism was the attempt to delegate as much responsibility as possible to the states and local governments and still maintain credibility and satisfy the intent of Congress, we were the ideal agency. Congress had said as far back as the early 1970s with the Clean Air Act that EPA was to establish the national standards, and then set up a framework of regulations so that the states could comply with those standards, and eventually to delegate the responsibility for running those programs to the states themselves.

In many ways it was rather amazing that Congress had been that far-sighted, because while there is certainly a continuing need for a federal presence in environmental protection, the state and local level is where the problems can be solved. At least that is the view of the agency's role I have always held, and which I am certain the President still holds; but if the rest of his administration still feels that way, they have a funny way of showing it. EPA—and in particular the Federal presence in Superfund—is getting so big one would think the Democrats were in office!

Delegation to the states runs contrary to one of the most fundamental aspects of Washington life—protecting one's turf. That's the main reason none of the other EPA Administrators, Republicans and Democrats alike, was able to accomplish in this area what Congress had intended. Once you say, "50 percent or more of the Air programs are being run by the states," it's hard to say with a straight face that you still need the same budget and the same number of people to run the Air program from Washington.

When you get right down to it, nobody at the White House really knew what we were doing on the substantive levels. They may have had their spies telling them who was doing what to whom, and how so-and-so was doing with his or her private agenda, but as far as knowledge of the real work is concerned, they had little or none. And that did not serve the President. Nor, when push came to shove, did it help me.

Some of you may doubt it, but my time in office was fun. I had the agency jumpin'; the people were *working*. And quite a few of us actually enjoyed it, even if reading the Washington *Post* every morning was like walking through a minefield.

In the midst of all this I was traveling and speaking at an increasing rate, trying to get the actual word directly to people. I had all but despaired of getting accurate press coverage. Here are only some of my speaking engagements from 1982:

May 20, New York City:	McGraw-Hill publications luncheon
June 11, Sun Valley:	Western Regional Council
June 16, Jackson Hole:	Wyoming Mining Association
June 25, Chapel Hill:	University of North Carolina, Business–Higher Education Forum
July 14, Denver:	Colorado Association of Commerce & Industry
July 28–30, San Francisco:	Commonwealth Club Bay Area Council Crown Zellerbach

July 30, New Orleans:	Private dinner
August 10, San Francisco:	American Bar Association
August 28, Saint Paul:	3M CEO dinner
September 13, Colorado Springs:	Colorado Petroleum Marketers Association
Boise:	Fund raiser for Congressman Craig
September 14, Sun Valley:	Northwest Electric Light & Power Association
September 17, Wilmington:	E. I. DuPont de Nemours and Company executive committee luncheon
September 27, Minneapolis:	Cargill Grain Industry
Saint Paul:	Minnesota Power & Light Commission dinner meeting
September 29, Des Moines:	Iowa Development Commission
	Iowa Manufacturers Association
October 4, St. Louis:	Montsanto Company CEO dinner
October 5, Pittsburgh:	U.S. Steel Corporation dinner
October 6, St. Louis:	Water Pollution Control Federation 55th annual conference
October 7, Charleston:	Contractors Association of West Virginia
October 11, Phoenix:	National Association of Water Companies
October 13, Seattle:	Private dinner
November 10, New York City:	NAM Roundtable
November 10–11, Rochester:	New York Center for Environmental Information
	Gannett editorial board interview
December 8, Denver:	Colorado Farm Bureau
December 9, Spokane:	Northwest Mining Association

December 10, Los Angeles: Western Oil and Gas Association

In 1983, an unexpectedly brief year, it was more of the same. Beginning in Washington, D.C., with a luncheon talk to the Washington Business Roundtable, and ending in Denver with a talk to Colorado Federation of Republican Women (where some remarks displeased the Reagan Palace Guard), I spoke in Dallas, Oklahoma City, Washington again, Boca Raton, Cheyenne, Tempe, San Francisco, and New Orleans.

At almost every one of those stops, and sometimes several times a day, I was met at the airport (coming or going) by a flock of reporters plus camera crews, all asking questions that showed little or no understanding of the issues involved. As per usual, they were covering me, not the issues.

My public relations people were always after me to spend more time on what might be termed a "defensive p.r." effort, but I wasn't interested. In fact, I got so used to being attacked that I posted Abraham Lincoln's quotation on the door outside my office: "If I were to try to read, much less answer, all the attacks made on me, this shop might as well be closed for any other business."

What annoyed me was that the media kept making basic mistakes. They continued to report that we were "slashing the budget," but they never made the distinction between Superfund (most of which was paid for by the special tax on the petrochemical industry) which was growing, and the agency's operating budget (which came from the general fund, i.e., the taxpayers) thus adding to the federal deficit. I firmly believe that in some instances the distinction was purposely blurred. Another example had to do with the fact that OMB wanted us to repeal the rule limiting lead in gasoline, but the way the story came out, *EPA* wanted to repeal the rule.

And then there was the case of the Thriftway Refinery in New Mexico. The headlines read, "Burford Tells Refiner Okay to Violate Lead Content Rules." The truth was somewhat different. What happened was that Thriftway, a small refiner, was having a hard time financially, and they came to EPA with a petition to suspend the application of the regulations governing them. I had the staff study it, and it looked like a legitimate hardship case, but they weren't asking for the right remedy.

I met with several company officials and their Washington lawyers in my office, along with some of my staff, including my General Counsel. I told them that because the regulations in question were in the process of being revised—indeed, the revised regulations were at that moment being reviewed at OMB—and because we would probably be exempting operations such as theirs in situations such as theirs under the new regulations, we were certainly not going to put them out of business by strictly applying the rules that still happened to be in effect. And a procedure was already on the books to mitigate the fines in case of financial hardship. I told them they had "the word of the Administrator" that they would not be fined out of business for violation of the regulations while they were being revised.

I don't know how it happened, but someone leaked the results of that meeting to one of the Congressmen most opposed to me and my stewardship of EPA. He notified the Inspector General of EPA, and demanded an investigation. It was done, and the IG asked a prestigious Washington law firm to study the question and give an opinion. The report exonerated me completely, and the Justice Department declined to take action. The story of my exoneration went unreported.

As far as press coverage and all the charges they made were concerned, nobody could have been as wrong as often as I was supposed to have been. Anything we did, the environmentalists went nuts. *Anything*. At one point I told someone that if I really believed all the negatives they were writing and saying about me, I wouldn't be able to live with myself.

And when I did have press conferences in an attempt to get some of the facts straight, the questions were always confrontational. No one ever asked for information or clarification. Everybody was an antagonist. I could never understand why *I* was the news, not what we were doing.

One of the best examples of that kind of treatment was my sole appearance on "Nightline" with Ted Koppel. I say "sole," because after what happened to me only a masochist would have gone back a second time.

When I was asked originally, they wanted me to be on the show live, which apparently is their policy, but I said no, telling them that I didn't work that late—11:30 P.M. So that, I thought (and hoped) was that. But when they found out that I was going to be on the West Coast, and repeated their request, pointing out that the three-hour time difference should make it easy for me. My public relations officer Byron Nelson III urged me to do it, so I relented. But unfortunately he agreed to allow a camera crew to follow me around *all day.*

I had a rough day planned, with air trips to three cities, and here I was with people following me everywhere I went, including the ladies' room! The day began in Denver, including a lunch in Colorado Springs, and ended with a cocktail party in Oregon at which I was to be the guest of honor. And in between all the functions I had substantive business to take care of that included a planned meeting with my Regional Administrator for that area, Steve Durham. There were so many people hanging all over me that I finally had to scrub my meeting with Steve.

I was angry at Byron Nelson, and let him know it. But he said the TV people claimed they needed all that "footage" for the lead-in portion of the show. I tried to be understanding, but when I got off the plane in Oregon at 6:00 P.M., and the "Nightline" people said I had to come with them, I put my foot down.

"No, I'm to be the guest of honor at a cocktail party being held from six-thirty to eight. I'll be at your ABC affiliate's studio at eight. You just have your driver pick me up in time."

They reluctantly agreed, and come 8:30 I was sitting in the studio, listening to the lead-in to the show, which, incidentally, featured none of the footage they'd taken that day, as I was virtually characterized as being personally responsible for every barrel of waste in the country. The show lasts thirty minutes, with my part about twenty, and there is simply no way you can counter all of those kinds of charges in that length of time. Koppel painted me as an antienvironmental ogre who had filled every drum of toxic waste with my own two hands.

In order to have been wrong that often, I would have had to stay up nights figuring out new ways to be evil. After that experience I put an end to my own career as a friendly and cooperative guest on so-called "news" shows.

I realize that, for most people, hearing about the internal workings of a scientific, technically oriented agency like EPA is about as exciting as reading an auto-parts catalogue. For that reason, I have placed my detailed account of what happened during my tenure as head of EPA as an appendix at the end of the book. I urge everyone to read it—especially my critics—because it is the proof of my claim that my people and I *did* accomplish quite a bit in the area of environmental protection during our time at EPA.

In addition to traveling around the United States I represented the U.S. on a number of foreign trips. As this country's top environmental "officer," I journeyed to Mexico City, Canada, Nairobi, and Paris.

Mexico presents a number of truly serious international problems, such as the sewage problem on the West Coast, which is almost critical, as opposed to chronic; Tijuana's uncollected and uncleansed sewage is discharged off the coast and ends up on the Southern California beaches. And there are equally serious air pollution problems all along the border, especially in the El Paso area.

The Mexican Minister of Environmental Affairs wanted to set up a meeting, and I asked John Hernandez to check it out. He reported that the preliminary agreements had been reached, and only formal ratification was needed. I got ready to go to Mexico City, a place I have known and loved since I was in grade school and spent my summers there studying Spanish.

Shortly after I arrived I ran into something that would have been funny if it weren't potentially so serious. It involved John Gavin, the former actor who is our Ambassador to Mexico (and a very good one). I found out that he had asked my staff for air-monitoring equipment to place on top of the American Embassy in Mexico City. He wanted to prove that the air was as bad as he suspected it was (it is) so that he could get the Department of State to designate Mexico City as a hardship post, which would mean extra pay for his people, or, failing that, get the Embassy relocated outside the city, perhaps someplace closer to Cuernavaca up in the mountains.

My staff had promised to get him the equipment, but as soon as I heard about it I said no. I was afraid it might cause a revolution, as an unwarranted intrusion into foreign affairs. If the Mexican people learned from us how bad their air really was, who knows what they might have done. Also, I offered some serious technical reasons for quashing the idea: The monitoring equipment has to be in place for a while, and then if you don't maintain it correctly, and if you don't have the trained personnel to run it, you won't get accurate readings. We couldn't spare any of ours from Washington, and so on and so on. And that way we deflected Ambassador Gavin's attention, which is a nice way of saying we put him off. I was convinced that idea would have been more trouble than it was worth.

When we got to the meeting, instead of the paper I expected, I was handed something that stated the United States agrees to this and this and this—all very specific actions that we had not been warned about, and not one of them an action I was willing to take without a whole lot of study and consultation back in Washington.

I was so upset with my staff I could hardly see straight, but I managed, by calling on some reserve of diplomacy and grace, to get us out of there without causing a diplomatic incident.

Our "graceful exit" was eased somewhat by the unexpected— one high-ranking official decided he was smitten with me. I got the whole treatment, flowers, flowers, and more flowers in my room, and repeated invitations to dinner. It got to be a little embarrassing.

I have been going to Mexico since the fifth grade, and I noticed a long time ago that Mexicans tend to be attracted to anybody who has blue eyes. With no false modesty I state that I had a string of men standing outside my door every summer I went down there, so I wasn't entirely surprised when it became clear that this official was showing more than a "diplomatic" interest in me. Indeed, it was a heavy crush. My room soon began to resemble a funeral parlor. And when I asked him politely not to send me any more flowers, he sent a book. It was a pictorial essay type of book on Old Mexico, which meant that it was within the bounds of propriety. I don't know what I would have done if he had sent romantic Spanish poetry!

The longer we stayed, the more I realized that Ambassador Gavin was right about the terrible air quality. I have always loved Mexico City, but I found myself vowing never to return. The air was that vile. The air in Denver is bad, in large part because of Denver's wall of mountains, but Mexico City has a *ring* of mountains and it has tens of thousands of old clunkers with zero emission controls that seriously compound the problem. As a matter of fact, another time when I was there in winter, when it's worse, the newspaper headlines said that said 50 percent of the population suffered from bronchial problems.

To illustrate the degree of the problem, I washed my hair every morning, and when I came home to get ready for dinner I combed my hair and the comb was black with dirt. After wearing a dress only one day, the white hem was black. That has never happened to me anywhere else. Mr. Gavin is undoubtedly right, which is a terrible shame, because it is such a beautiful and charming city. But the population is enormous, perhaps double what it was when I first visited there, and the cars and all the increased industrial activity have produced an almost untenable situation.

Among the items included on the Mexican's agenda for the meeting were more money for the Bilateral Commission; more money to study water problems between the two countries; and a request for various pieces of equipment. In addition to the equipment, they wanted us to send them people to teach them how to use it. I explained that these were matters I had to study, matters that would require consultation with and approval of people back in Washington, not matters I could agree to on the spot. Once the Mexicans got the picture, they were gracious, especially the Enamored One, who said he wanted to see me in Nairobi where we were both scheduled to take part in a United Nations conference on the environment.

Another important trip was the one I made to Canada in May 1982 to speak at an international symposium on asbestos, which is a major Canadian industry. The Canadians were worried about the U.S. position on asbestos, which can cause great misery in humans who have been exposed to too much of it, a form of illness that makes life all but unlivable for years until it kills you. As the Administrator of EPA, I could have banned asbestos, a very sexy stand that would have earned me points with the environmentalists and all sorts of other people who had been opposing me. But I have problems with banning, as much from a philosophical point of view as anything else. I think banning is like trying to scrap technology. It is a recognition that something nonhuman can take on the characteristics of good or evil, and I don't buy that. I believe rather that it is the use to which a substance is put that has moral implications.

So I was not about to ban asbestos. I gave a very reasoned

speech about the need for limiting its use, one that took the U.S. position and that of the Canadians into consideration. Indeed, I was more than fair to them. And, frankly, I expected some thanks from my hosts, because if I had decided to ban asbestos that would have caused them some serious industrial problems. In my naïveté I thought their thanks might take the form of reciprocation, say, a more reasonable attitude on their part regarding acid rain. No such luck.

In fact, the Canadians' general attitude was rather unpleasant. To put it plainly, they were the biggest bunch of overbearing bastards I'd ever had the misfortune to deal with. They were tablepounders who seemed to enjoy playing the tough-guy role.

The acid rain problem has become an even bigger issue since I was in office. Putting aside for the moment that it has become the scare issue of the day—remember a few years back when the big news was fluorocarbons that supposedly threatened the ozone layer?—acid rain does represent a serious environmental as opposed to a health hazard.

It is by now fairly well accepted that the sulphur dioxide from coal-fired power plants and the nitrous oxide from auto exhausts are the primary causes of what is known as acid deposition. And while acid deposition comes in both liquid and dry forms, all you hear of is acid "rain." Clearly it is a harmful phenomenon, though it can be neutralized to a great extent if it falls on a basic receptor, such as the ocean.

In the United States over the last fourteen years we have reduced the levels of both sulphur dioxide and nitrous oxide. We have done so by controlling emissions from coal-burning industrial and power plants and from automobiles. So logic dictates that whatever acid rain problem we have must have decreased over the last fourteen years.

The Canadians, however, maintain that it has *increased.*

The best statistics that I'm aware of on acid rain are those of the United States Geological Survey (USGS), but because they are not EPA statistics, they have not been taken seriously. Nonetheless, the USGS measurements, which have been taken for twenty years, show that there has been a decreasing problem in the Northeast and an increasing one elsewhere in the country. The USGS measurements should be taken into consideration, but to the best of my knowledge they have not been.

Our standards are tough. And compared with those of other nations, they are *very* tough. Canada has none in effect. The Clean Air Act requires that SO_2 and nitrous oxide levels be reduced to a point that is protective of the health of the frailest little old lady in the U.S., or the sickest little child. That's the law's standard. What's more, once you get to that level, the law requires that you go below it for "an adequate margin of safety." In almost every area we now have substantial compliance with that standard.

This means that we are not really talking about a health issue here. And we could reduce the level further; we have the technology to reduce it to zero. But it would be incredibly costly, and it would show up on your utility bill and on the price tag of every product that is produced by electricity.

Even so, I don't know of anyone who says that if we reduced all the way to zero, we could save two more fish. There's as yet no way to prove a direct causal connection. But the Canadians wanted the U.S., through me, to agree to a reduction of an additional 50 percent of the sulfur dioxide emissions.

That struck me as insanity. Given that logic, why not go all the way to zero? There is no logic to a two-thousand-ton reduction.

Yet the proposal that Ruckelshaus's second EPA came out with, which was a modification of what the Canadians wanted, would have cost every customer in Ohio somewhere in the neighborhood of $400 more each year. The point remains: You have to know if you're really buying anything. It *could* be worth it, but you don't know for sure. The figures aren't reliable.

The next logical question is: Why are the Canadians so hot on this issue? Well, at the risk of sounding cynical, let me ask another question: Who do you think would like to make coal-fired power too expensive, so that we would have to buy nuclear and hydro-electric power? If you said the Canadians, go to the head of the class.

What about the image of Canadians as big altruistic environmentalists? Well, in all of Canada there is only *one* industrial smokestack scrubber, and it was put in as the result of an international court order. Another interesting fact is that the largest man-made emitter of sulphur dioxide in the Northern Hemisphere is the Sudbury smelter in Sudbury, Ontario.

When you bring that up the Canadians say, "But we reduced emission." To which the proper response is, "That's true only because you also reduced production." But under our laws shutting off the machine would not be an acceptable solution; in the U.S. intermittent controls are not sufficient. You have to have continuous operational control.

Canada has no Clean Air Act. Nor does it have effective emission-control devices in cars. What it does have is a terrific lobby in Washington, whose wining and dining is the envy of their American counterparts.

Clearly we have to deal with the problem of acid rain. But in my opinion it is nowhere near as great a problem as it has been made out to be. At least not as great as the Canadians have made it out to be. Tests do show that some lakes have an abnormally high concentration of metals, which may be linked to the acidification of the lake. And that obviously has health repercussions in terms of the possible effect on drinking water and contamination of fish. But I think the link is tenuous at best, and that we are not talking about primary, but rather about secondary effects. (All of EPA's statutes distinguish between primary and secondary effects. The primary are those which are directly health-related, whereas the secondary are welfare-related, for example, does it hurt the trees or the crops, or does it look bad?) So far I've seen no proof that acid rain is a problem with primary effects.

Until someone can convince me otherwise, I will continue to believe that the Canadians' main interest is in selling us more nuclear and hydroelectric power. If they were truly concerned about the risk of acid rain, they would do something about reducing their own level of emissions.

For whatever it is worth, consider the growth in acid rain–related research funding. In fiscal year 1981, it was about $7.2 million; today, if Congress approves, it will be in the neighborhood of $60 million.

If my trips to Canada were frustrating and annoying, my trip to Nairobi for the United Nations Environmental Protection Agency [UNEP] was exhilarating and exhausting. To begin with, we literally flew halfway around the world. I was in Miami, and had to fly to Newark to catch an overseas flight to London, where John Horton had arranged to have a former business partner show me and Denise Mitstifer, my personal assistant, the town. That was a very nice thing for him and them to do, but by the time we arrived I was so beat that all I could think about being shown was a room with a bed. Horton's friend and his driver took us to a very expensive hotel in downtown London, and then politely waited while we arranged for accommodations.

I had said we wanted two rooms, but when I heard they were $150 a night each, I asked Denise if she minded sharing. She said fine. When I told the woman behind the desk that we would take only one room, she seemed startled. It was only then I realized that John Horton's former partner and his driver were standing right behind us. It appeared I was asking for a single room for the four of us! We all had a good laugh, and after a very quick nightcap I hit the hay.

The flight to Nairobi the next morning was horrendous, something like sixteen hours. We arrived red-eyed, only to be met by the blundering American Ambassador who wanted us to go to the conference immediately and sign up, as if the badges and name tags would not wait for us.

Being in Africa was really quite a jolt. It *is* a different world, and I found it both exciting and somewhat disorienting. The conference itself was rather dull, except for the bombs I threw. I had been instructed to tell the UNEP people that instead of the larger share of their operating budget that the U.S. had been providing for a decade, we would now be paying only 40 percent. They were definitely not going to enjoy hearing that news.

Before we'd left there had been disagreements among the various staffs as to who should "lead" the delegation, me or former Senator James Buckley (brother of William F.) whose position at the State Department was the Undersecretary of State for Security Assistance, Science and Technology. As I recall the decision was Solomon-like: we split it.

The international press had taken its cues from the American press, and the prevailing assumption was that the Reagan administration's commitment to the environment was zero. It didn't help matters that my main message was to be, "Sorry, but our commitment isn't going to be 110 percent. If there is a worldwide commitment to environmental protection, then why are we the only one shouldering the burden? It's time for you to show your commitment, and the way to do that is with dollars."

The third world looked to UNEP as being tantamount to an aid to their own construction agencies, say, for the building of sewage systems in Kenya, but the Reagan administration took a different view, seeing any joint effort as a form of technology-sharing, but not as a construction or a public works program. And I was the one who had to give them that message.

Typically, although the push for cutting in UNEP's budget came from the State Department, the press laid it right at the feet of EPA. I took the black eye for the whole thing.

When the resolution on the substance of the conference came up for a vote, and we won, I almost fainted. We would be bringing home the bacon, a claim the U.S. can rarely make in dealing with the U.N.

One particularly interesting part of that trip was meeting my counterparts from other nations. The Japanese were incredibly gracious, and they were supportive of our position that if there was truly a worldwide commitment to the environment, then it was time the *world* shouldered some of the burden.

As for the Enamored One, he made good on his dinner invitation, and to protect myself I had Denise accompany us. The American Ambassador gave us a car and a driver, but the latter was almost worthless; he ended up driving us all over Nairobi's red-light district to get to a restaurant that turned out to be about a block and a half from the Embassy. When we finally got to the restaurant, Denise promptly fell asleep, right at the table. Some protection. But by that time I was (though in a different sense) as interested in my friend as he was in me—I needed his vote. The dinner was pleasant, I managed to elude his grasp, and then fate stepped in. His government replaced him with a woman who took a decidedly third-world point of view. So much for romantic diplomacy.

Before I left I had a curious experience. The Russian delegate asked for a private meeting with me. So again I dragged Denise along. We held the meeting on the terrace of the U.N. Building where he apparently felt we were safe from bugging devices. I wasn't worried about any bugging devices, as I planned to do nothing but listen. As it turned out, he wanted to talk about the possibility of resuming exchanges of scientific information, which had been curtailed in the early days of the Reagan administration in response to the Afghan invasion. He wanted me to use my "good offices" to get them resumed. That was all he wanted. I promised to relay his message. Under Ruckelshaus, they were partially resumed at a low level.

Our Ambassador gave a reception for me just before we left, but instead of giving it at the Embassy or at his official residence, he gave it at a downtown hotel, which did not impress me as a classy thing to do. And once again he gave us a driver who was in the wrong line of work. We left the meeting site, and gave him the name of the hotel. He whisked us there, and we went in, chatting all the while, only to discover it was the wrong hotel. We hurried outside to find him gone! So we, conspicuously American, walked through the streets of Kenya at dusk until we found the right hotel.

At first I wondered if my problems with the Ambassador had anything to do with the fact I had been getting such bad press back home, or if it was simply that he was such a cold fish. I concluded that the press had nothing to do with it. I did get to visit his home before we left, because he gave a luncheon there for Jimmy Stewart, who was in the country to receive an environmental award (and whose daughter lives there). Meeting Mr. and Mrs. Stewart was a pleasure. What was not a pleasure was to see the Ambassador a few days later roll out the red carpet when Jim Buckley, his *State Department* superior, arrived. But then, as President Carter once put it, whoever said life was supposed to be fair?

We made one nonbusiness side trip that thrilled me, and I am sure the rest of our group too. We were flown in a small plane from Kenya to the foot of Mount Kilimanjaro where we took part in a photo safari. The day was clear, and we could see the snowcaps in the distance, and the animals darting in and out of the trees. It was beautiful. And elemental. And not a bad way to say goodbye to Africa.

On the way back we had enough time in London to do some shopping. I bought china, and even got to Harrods to buy some smoked salmon. But that was a whole different world after seeing Kilimanjaro, and on the plane home, remembering my Hemingway, I looked out the window and imagined I saw leopards in the snow.

The final foreign trip that stands out vividly in my mind was to Paris in the fall of 1982. I remember Paris mainly because we worked so hard and got something done.

The occasion was a special meeting of the Organization for

Economic Cooperation and Development (OECD), which was to deal with a number of issues, (for agreement and subsequent OECD Council approval), one of which presented a touchy problem—the extent to which chemicals should be tested before any country says they can be marketed. To put it as simply as possible, there are two methods of dealing with this issue internationally. One is the requirement for minimum premarketing test data (MPD), and the other is a premanufacturing notification (PMN). The latter, PMN, happens to be the United States position, and is part of the TSCA law.

Theoretically the purpose of adopting either one was to co-ordinate the economic unity represented by Western Europe, the USA, Canada, and Japan so that we don't impose nontariff barriers on one another's products, but do provide the necessary regulation of hazardous substances. The premise of the meeting was that just as there is a community interest in economic development, there is a community interest in proper regulation.

I was faced, however, with a most interesting problem. Douglas Costle, President Carter's EPA head, had told the international community on at least two occasions that he would support MPD. Unfortunately for that point of view, he was no longer in power at EPA. But that did not stop him—with the sub rosa help of certain Carter holdovers within EPA—from trying to accomplish that same end.

My view on the matter was that if we wanted to change positions, fine, but we couldn't do it in the face of existing U.S. domestic law. Indeed, there were several legal strictures that said just that, plain as day. To put it simply, if we wanted to adopt MPD, it was for the Congress, not a United States delegation to an international forum, to make that decision.

Also, it should be pointed out that the USA had six years of experience with PMN, while none of the other countries had any experience with MPD. How did we know if it would even work?

Costle's proposal, which he had made at the group's last meeting, which had taken place while Carter was still in office, was still before the group. Because it would have effected a unilateral legislative change in TSCA, the proposal represented an "end run" around Congress. Because if OECD adopted the proposal, it would be a binding resolution on all the member countries, and

Costle and the people he represented could go to Capitol Hill and say, "You have to change TSCA to get in line with the rest of the world." It was a very clever ploy.

As I sat in the airplane on the way to the meeting in Paris, I read the briefing papers that had been prepared for me, and I soon realized, with a sinking feeling, that there was no cohesive statement of policy. Various conflicting positions were represented, some advocating the positions of the previous administration. I could detect a strange odor; the papers were nothing but a bunch of junk.

And not only did I realize this, but so did Mr. Abraham Katz, the U.S. Ambassador to the OECD. I didn't know him, and he didn't know me, but when I gave him my opinion of the briefing papers, of which he had a copy, he looked at me with great relief. He held the same opinion, but didn't know how to raise the point.

Katz asked, "What are you going to do about it?"

Without any hestiation, I replied, "I'm going to call my whole delegation together as soon as I arrive, and get to work!"

"Well," he said, in a statement that endeared him to me instantly, "just tell me what you want me to do."

The briefing papers were so murky that neither of us could tell from reading them what the important issues were. So as soon as I was checked in I called our delegation together—it included primarily representatives from the Department of State, the Food and Drug Administration, and EPA—and asked, "What exactly is the problem, and what is our solution?"

After we hashed things around for a while I was relieved to see that the differences of opinion were not great. We started from scratch and redrafted the U.S. statement.

The pretest protocol put forward by the Costle group was based on a schedule of different seriatim tests, all of which had to be performed on each chemical before it could be introduced into the marketplace. The burden of all of these tests could be economic ruin. But TSCA, the operative U.S. law, didn't happen to work that way.

So my job was to go in and try to reverse gears, 100 percent by saying, "Sorry, we like TSCA. TSCA works. And it is the legislation of the United States. I don't have the authority to adopt a scheme that is contrary to our current legislation, especially when I feel, and when our delegation feels, that the alternative isn't necessary, and that it flies in the face of Congressional intent." By working day and night—I did take time out for a dash through the Louvre and Mass at Notre Dame, but I nixed a boatride on the Seine!—we got it straightened out. We pulled together as a team, and I don't feel immodest saying that it was my leadership that made it work. But I couldn't have done it without Ambassador Katz.

He told me later that he had never been so worried about a meeting in his entire life. But Mr. Katz displayed some fancy footwork himself, especially in the way he engineered a luncheon meeting at the home of one of the members of the delegation, during which he did some adroit juggling, and not a little bit of cold-eyed bluffing, to make our international "partners" see the wisdom of the TSCA way. And in so doing he saved the Reagan administration from a major international embarrassment.

Cristy Bach, an EPA liaison person who made the trip, said, "For all the sight-seeing we did and all the fun we had, we could have been in Pittsburgh."

And that's how I remember Paris.

Part III

DOWNPOUR

11

EXECUTIVE PRIVILEGE

I was the first to go in the executive-privilege, contempt-of-Congress battle. Like Anne, I was a loyalist to the President, personally and philosophically loyal to him.

The Department of Justice people made a case, which seemed plausible and acceptable to me, that certain documents that were developed for the use of Cabinet Council should be protected. I was an enthusiastic supporter of the Cabinet Council process, and therefore felt that the working papers developed for it should have the same protection that papers for the Cabinet work should have. So I was a willing activist in the Department of Justice's efforts to extend the executive privilege to cover the work product of Cabinet Council materials.

Being a loyalist, I had a personally signed letter from the President ordering me to defend the issue. It was given to me by Fred Fielding; the President didn't hand it to me personally. The letter from President Reagan directed me not to give certain documents to the Committee. And I took that to John Dingell (Congressman John D. Dingell, Democrat from Michigan, Chairman of the Subcommittee on Oversight and Investigations of the House Committee on Energy and Commerce) when I was called before his committee and threatened with contempt of Congress.

Chairman Dingell was very professional, very honest, and very

145

fair. I have no criticism of him. He understood what we were doing. Some of the other members of his committee were men without integrity, men who only sought to abuse and get headlines. They were fed information by the liberal special interest groups that had no regard for the truth or integrity of the issues at hand. They were smart enough, hopefully, to know what the issues were, but intentionally distorted the issues for political purposes.

The media, the leftist media, intentionally distorted this issue against me, so that it was Watt challenging the Congress, Watt being arrogant and defiant against the Congress of the United States which was only seeking information.

That was not the issue. John Dingell framed it properly. There is not room for criticism of John Dingell, but there is lots of room for criticism of the Democratic members of his committee. It was crystal clear what I was doing. John Dingell developed with me a perfect record of what the facts were, what the legal issues were, and what the Constitutional principles were. But the leftist media teamed up with the special interest groups, and manipulated the members of Congress to make an ugly scene. They portrayed me as arrogant, defiant, and uncooperative rather than as a person portraying a Constitutional issue.

And that was intentionally done. The environmental groups—the Sierra Club, Wilderness Society, Friends of the Earth, Audubon Society, etc., intentionally, with knowledge and with clear understanding, distorted the facts for their selfish gain. And then the liberal establishment intentionally and maliciously abused Anne. Her case history is a carbon copy of what happened to me. The same actors, the same players, most of whom simply have no integrity.

I had been cited for contempt by the Dingell committee for refusing to turn over the papers from Cabinet Council. Not long after that, I had a hallway conversation in the White House with Fred Fielding. I asked him, "How are we coming in resolving my contempt of Congress issue?" He said, "We may have a breakthrough. I just came from a meeting with Chairman Dingell, and we have reached a compromise that may be of value to us."

I said, "What did that relate to?"

He said, "The General got into a situation similar to the one you are in, and we didn't want to create any embarrassment for the general, so we gave them the paperwork."

I said, "What General?"

Fred Fielding, with a scowl on his face like I was stupid, said, "The *Attorney* General."

I said, *"Fred Fielding*! You're telling me that the Attorney General had a case similar to mine, and the principle for which you marched me to the end of the plank is not important enough for him to stand on? But it's important enough for me to stand on and get abused like I've been abused?"

And he said, "That's the way it goes, Jim."

I said, "You get me out within twenty-four hours or I'm going to the Congress personally and hand deliver those papers—because I will not be abused by the White House or the Department of Justice. If the principle is not strong enough for the Attorney General of the United States to fight for, I'm not going to let you guys use me any longer."

They'd had the President sign a letter directing me to fight for this principle, but they wouldn't have the President sign one for the *General*! I was furious. And within hours they surrendered the papers to Dingell, because they knew I would be true to my promise. I was fighting for a principle because I was loyal to the President of the United States, and they were playing games with personalities. They just wanted a test case they could have fun with, and they didn't care what it did to people.

But one night, while my fight was still going on, my wife and I were in the receiving line at the White House, and the President said to my wife, "I appreciate what your husband is doing for me on this Congressional issue, and I want you to know that I will visit him every Thursday night if he goes to jail." We had a big laugh about it. It was funny. I had a commitment: if the President wants me to do this, I'll walk the plank. But when they sold the principle down the river for the "General," I would not tolerate it anymore.

If the President asked me to walk the plank, I would have done it just like Anne did it. But the President wasn't being briefed on the truth of the whole situation.

—James Watt
February, 1985

Throughout my fight with Congress Jim Watt was very helpful. At a time when other so-called "friends" were suddenly dropping out of sight, he was always there. And from the beginning he warned me not to let happen to me what almost happened to him. I did not listen as closely as I obviously should have, mainly because I simply didn't think it *could* happen to me. But I did not know about his hallway conversation with Fred Fielding regarding the fact that Attorney General William French Smith had been given a special dispensation when it came to the executive privilege fight.

If I had known that, would I have done anything differently? Yes. I would have felt much the way Jim did. Principle does not rest on personality. But it is something I should have known, and it is also something that Fred Fielding and the people at the Justice Department who so eagerly enlisted my participation should have told me.

This is how it all began. The folks at the Justice Department and, apparently, the White House Counsel's office, went to Jim Watt and said, we've got this wonderful case for executive privilege, and we need a horse, in effect, to ride to bring it before the Supreme Court. And, they also said, we have this wonderful piece of paper that we don't think Congress should see because it's pertinent to an internal decision regarding whether or not reciprocity should be extended to Canada. And Jim agreed.

Well, as he explained, it didn't work out. For one thing, and this was long before he had his confrontation with Fielding, the whole matter was taking up too much of his time. At one point he went to Jim Baker, the White House Chief of Staff, and told him that the people at Justice were, "draining me of all my energy, they are consuming all of my time. They don't just have me riding this horse to the Supreme Court, they've got me working as a full-time employee!"

So when Watt told the Justice Department to leave him alone, they looked around for another worthy candidate to put forth their great cause of executive privilege. (Executive privilege is the Constitutional theory by which the President or his designate tells Congress that there is something it, Congress, may not see. To allow Congress to see it, so the theory goes, would prohibit the President from fulfilling his oath to execute faithfully the laws of the country.)

At about this same time there was a staffer from Representative Levitas's subcommittee who had been routinely as part of the

Congressional oversight function going through various of our files, with our help and blessing, if not exactly our encouragement. Basically he was "just lookin'." He went up to the Boston regional office where he was also allowed access to whatever it was he wanted to look at. When he got to New York, however, the picture changed.

The people in New York called Bob Perry, our General Counsel, to check out the request, and Perry in turn called John Daniel, who said, "Let him see whatever he wants to see." But Perry then called the Justice Department, and there he got contrary instructions. Perry communicated these instructions.

I believe that even though it was not in EPA's (or my) best interests, Bob Perry had had prior conversations with the Justice Department in which the topic of conversation was whether Superfund papers might be the next horse to ride, as far as the doctrine of executive privilege was concerned, to the Supreme Court.

The people at Justice behind the push for executive privilege were all presidential appointees who, to be blunt, shared several characteristics: (1) they didn't have enough to do; (2) they weren't, in my opinion, very good lawyers; and (3) they had tremendous egos. They wanted to make a name for themselves in Washington, and one way to do that while they were at Justice was to have their names on a Supreme Court case. That's my theory.

Another theory, which I call the Conspiracy Theory, holds that there were some people in the administration who wanted to get rid of whichever conservatives they could, and that's why they went to Jim first and me second. Another part of the Conspiracy Theory holds that they figured Jim would probably eventually do himself in, and thus I was a better candidate for the executive privilege ploy. And, interestingly, the people who advanced the Conspiracy Theory also believe my theory. I guess the two are not incompatible.

However, back to the frustrated Hill staffer up in New York City. When he got the word that Perry had said no, he called John Daniel, who instructed the office to allow him access to the papers. Not long after, I got a visit from the unholy trinity of Justice Department lawyers and White House counsel who were so enamored of executive privilege—Teddy Olson, Carol Dinkins, and

Richard Hauser (for Fred Fielding). For a while it seemed that they were there every time I turned around, asking me if I would do the executive privilege fight.

This took place in the fall of 1982, and Jim Watt, who had been down the same road the previous spring, warned me not to get involved. "This isn't an EPA issue, Anne, and, besides that, they will take up all of your time if you let them. Remember, they're not particularly bright." And I *was* wary of them.

In the meantime all the administration received an executive order that said that whenever executive privilege is to be raised, it must be done by the department or agency head.

That worried me a lot. So I called Jim Baker, who was as close to the President as anyone, and said, "I feel very strongly that this is, A., bad policy, and B., bad law. I don't know who the President consulted on this, but what you're doing is putting a guy out as conductor of the railroad when it's really the caboose that's running the train. Why put me, or my counterparts in the other agencies and departments, out front when we're not really in charge?"

I continued, "That's no way to run a railroad, much less a government. And from a legal point of view you're going to get into some real ethical problems, because who is the Justice Department going to be representing—the President, or the agency head acting on his behalf? Because those two people are not always going to have identical interests."

I concluded by telling Jim Baker, "I feel very strongly about this, and I want my views made known to the President."

His answer stunned me. "Anne, are you going to be a prima donna about this?"

And that chauvinistic response to, very frankly, a well-reasoned argument, was his only remark.

Prior to that conservation I'd had many meetings and talks with Jim Baker, and, as a result, I knew that his understanding of environmental law was neither wide nor deep. He is supposed to be the great legislative strategist, but I can recall any number of times during discussions of the Clean Air Act when his eyes glazed over repeatedly and came up peaches and oranges like a slot machine. (Eventually he shunted me off to an aide, Frank Hodsell, for which I was actually quite grateful because Frank not only knew the law, he was interested in it.) None of my many meetings with Jim Baker was satisfactory. And certainly this conversation wasn't.

I attempted to keep Baker informed about EPA issues, but the man simply didn't understand them. Mr. Baker is *not* ignorant or ineducable. But as far as the environment was concerned, he didn't put forth any effort. It is clearly a secondary issue with him.

Looking back, I had a priority while in office that may not have worked out to my advantage. I tried to keep the White House informed of what was going on. I was the one who initiated it. They didn't have to come to me and say, "Hey, what the hell's going on around here?" I tried to keep them informed not only of what we were doing, but also where political ramifications might be involved. I am quite sure this effort was amost totally wasted, because Baker didn't understand it. He didn't have the time to understand it, or he didn't want to take the time to understand it. So it was a relief to deal with Hodsell, because I thought someone in the White House really ought to know what we were doing at EPA. And at least Frank understood.

Another point in Hodsell's favor was that not only did he understand, he also seemed to care about environmental matters. Unfortunately, I did not deal with him on legislative matters. Those sessions were held with Baker, Michael Deaver, and Richard Darman, and they ended up doing little more than putting sand in the engine of our efforts. They did not care, or we would have had a new Clean Air Act. And toward the end, Boyden Gray of the Vice-President's office appeared on the scene to help throw sand. (Boyden Gray did, however, have a very sharp aide named Frank Blake. Frank was the brains behind Boyden. Boyden's specialty was holding meetings. I went to more meetings at his office where nothing was ever accomplished. It used to drive John Daniel crazy. Finally he got to the point where if he got through a meeting without saying anything, he considered it a successful—no, a *victorious*—day. They were meetings for meetings' sake.)

In any event, as a result of Bob Perry's dealings with the Justice Department, we were getting into a very confused situation. He was saying no to requests for documents, and I was saying give them anything they want and give it to them in triplicate if that'll make them happy. My attitude was based on my experience as a legislator: I believe in the legislative process, and it has to be an informed process; and if you want to fight somebody who wants a paper, deluge him with paper!

So there came a day when the Justice Department lawyers came to me to press the idea of the confrontation over executive privilege. "Okay," I said, "this is getting silly. I want to know three things. One, I'm a hell of a good lawyer. I'm an especially good environmental lawyer. I am not, however, a Constitutional lawyer. What kind of case do you have?"

"Anne," they said immediately, "this is a superb case. This case is going all the way to the Supreme Court."

"Okay," I said, "that brings up the second point. Have you negotiated this as far as you can with the Congress of the United States?"

"Absolutely. We will not negotiate any further. There is nothing more we can negotiate."

"All right. Now, the third thing I want to know is, does the President *really* want me to do this?"

"Yes," they all said, "the President really wants you to do this."

So I said, "Okay, I'll do it."

Because of that answer, I was satisfied that the Justice Department lawyers had somehow communicated with the President and received the assurance they had just passed on to me. It was not an unimportant issue. Months later, the timing of that information would turn out to be of great interest to John Dingell's subcommittee. Unfortunately, I could not swear precisely when the meeting took place.

What the terrible trio from Justice and the White House did was to prepare a lengthy memorandum, attached to which was an introductory memo that appeared to be for the President to sign; the last line of the introductory memo read, "And the Administrator of EPA concurs." That's what the committee was so interested in, and that's what I can't recall unequivocally—whether at that point I had actually agreed. In either case, it was a misrepresentation of what I really felt, because there did indeed come a time when, based on those three assurances, I gave up. Or, rather, I gave in. But for them to say that I "concurred" is a misrepresentation, no matter when it happened. The committee inferred that this memorandum had been written to the President *prior to the time that I gave in.* Fortunately for Justice, the committee couldn't prove it.

The next step in the drama was to serve a subpoena on us from Representative Levitas's subcommittee. They tried to make the delivery very dramatic, but succeeded only in making it corny. I got to work one morning and found a matched set of staff investigators, one for the majority and one for the minority, sitting outside my office waiting to give me the subpoena personally, even though it would have been perfectly legal, and more customary, to deliver it to EPA's General Counsel. But they were intent on making a grandiose entrance, so I asked them both in, and, with John Daniel present, I told them exactly how I felt.

"If it were up to me," I said, "you would have everything you want. But it isn't up to me. It's no longer something within my control."

They said they understood, and away they went, leaving the subpoena behind. The document gave me a few days in which to respond, but unfortunately the Thanksgiving holiday fell within those dates, and I was faced with the possibility of canceling Thanksgiving for all the people in my office and the Office of General Counsel and Enforcement in order to work on our response. But I decided against it, preserving at least *some* friends.

John Daniel, who is a fine lawyer, then sat down to read the subpoena. He discovered that it was defective!

It was defective because it said something like "Produce all the documents that have been generated pursuant to Public Law XYZ," a section of Superfund. But *no* documents had been produced pursuant to that law because the process for Superfund had not yet been completed. In fact, a whole procedure in that law still has not been completed. So, technically speaking, because there could be no such documents, the subpoena was defective on its face.

Notwithstanding that, I told my people that, "consistent with the President's Executive Order, we are going to make every effort to comply with the order." Considering the time we were given, they put forth a substantial effort; we delivered two huge file drawers of documents, which the committee refused to accept because we "reserved" twenty-three pieces of paper as being "enforcement-sensitive," the stricture put on us by the Justice Department in its famous memo, and the subsequent executive order.

In the meantime it was becoming obvious that Perry, *my* General Counsel, was working more for the Justice Department than for me. What's more, certain things had not been done, such as setting up a procedure for determining what is or is not an "enforcement-sensitive" document. I was having to set up the procedure myself, a job which I, as Administrator, should have been able to delegate.

"Here's what we're going to do," I said. "We're going to have a high-career civil servant *and* a political appointee in the three following areas sign off on anything deemed 'enforcement-sensitive,' plus Richard Hauser of Fred Fielding's office of White House Counsel, and if one of these seven signatures is missing, then boom, off it goes to the Hill: the EPA General Counsel; Teddy Olson's operation, which is Justice's Office of Legal Counsel and Enforcement; and Carol Dinkins's operation, which is Land and Natural Resources."

I got that procedure approved by the lawyers at the Justice Department, but not without severe kicking and screaming, especially where Teddy Olson was concerned. "I don't want to be involved," he whined, "in determining what is 'enforcement-sensitive' or not."

"Hell yes, you will be! Your name is going to be on the bottom of that piece of paper, or it's going to go straight to the Hill." I was damn tired of the personal reluctance of those lawyers who were so eager to get *me* in a fight!

Still, Olson managed to avoid standing entirely on his own two feet. He agreed to a "caveatic endorsement"—he would base his endorsement on that of his fellow Justice Department lawyer, Carol Dinkins. This whole fight was his big case, and here he was standing back. My opinion was that his "caveatic endorsement" was cowardly, and I told him so.

The whole idea of raising the test case with Congress by refusing to release "enforcement-sensitive" documents had come from Justice Department lawyers in the first place, yet this one was resisting the idea that he go on the record as one of the people who verified that the document in question fell into that prescribed category. I had some trouble believing what I was hearing.

There was an exception to the "enforcement-sensitive" ranking, and that was "any document that could be interpreted as being evidence of wrongdoing." Congress was getting increasingly annoyed over the fact that while these documents were being handled by paralegals and by outside contractors, we wouldn't let members of Congress see them! And it was true. (But, my God, we were talking about hundreds of thousands of pieces of paper; and, as EPA increased its enforcement work, that figure could run into the millions!) So, clearly, we had to have a system for classifying these documents, securing them, and determining if they could be interpreted as evidence of wrongdoing.

I thought the system was workable, and also that it was working. But as I was about to learn, not everyone agreed with me.

On December 2, 1982, I went before Mr. Levitas's subcommittee for what seemed like my ten thousandth appearance on the Hill. I was giving testimony before the subcommittee when at exactly quarter to four the whole left side of the committee room filled up! Like magic, or something from a movie.

Norman Mineta of California rose, and said, "I move to hold the EPA Administrator in contempt for failing to comply with the subpoena." His motion almost passed by a voice vote! The Republicans looked to be in shock.

My own reaction was rather curious. I was actually impressed with Mr. Levitas's efficiency. *That* was the way to run a committee! Get your ducks in a row and just go. Bam, bam, too bad, ma'am. In fact, I later said to Levitas, "You do good work." Not only were there Congressmen there whom I'd never met, but I'd never even *seen* some of the faces before. And I had been before that particular bunch dozens of times. In a sense it was almost funny.

Following the vote to hold me in contempt, I went back to EPA supremely confident that the clock would run out on that session of Congress before the full House could vote on the contempt resolution. So much for my prognosticative powers.

In any event, I was still facing an earlier subpoena, the one from John Dingell. And, as we'd expected, John Dingell had done it right. His subpoena was very limited; it pertained only to something like five Superfund sites, whereas Levitas's subpoena asked for everything, everywhere, and I think any court in the country would have thrown it out as being overly broad. Dingell, who had started down this road long before Levitas had, had narrowed his subpoena, which of course made it so much harder to resist.

John Dingell was not after me. He was after William French Smith. I was only a small fish on the way to a big fry. And John

Dingell and I understood precisely what he was doing. In fact, when I received his subpoena before the session was over, I felt it was probably a trial run. So when I got the Levitas subpoena, I called Dingell, and said, "John, if you are going after this as a publicity issue, you'd better hurry, because Levitas is about to beat you to it."

No, said Dingell, he was not after anything "quick and dirty," and "Mr. Levitas is perfectly free to have the publicity." But he added, a bit ominously, "I'm going to get done what I want done."

John Dingell is a smart man. And we had quite a good working relationship, even if he was, in a sense, "after" me. The relationship had started off badly: the first time I met him I thought he was one of the most overbearing, pompous people on earth. I had come to his office as a courtesy call, and there he was yelling at me across his desk as if I were one of his staff members who had done something wrong. When I finished my cigarette, I stood up and said, "Thank you very much. Good-bye."

When we got out of there, his staffer said to me, "That didn't go very well, did it?"

I said, "I don't have to sit there and be abused by your boss. He's entitled to do what he feels he has to do, but I'm not going to sit there and take personal abuse."

Perhaps my abrupt departure made its point, because after that John Dingell was a very different person. Later, he told me, "You have always been a lady. We might disagree, but you have always conducted yourself as a lady, and that is your biggest weapon in front of my committee. As long as you conduct yourself that way, they won't dare treat you differently."

I went back to work under the very wrong impression that Levitas would not be able to get his subcommittee's contempt resolution passed by the full House. But on December 16, 1982, it came up for a vote. I had been out of my office, and I returned to discover everyone clustered around the lone television set, watching the proceedings on the closed-circuit public TV service that broadcasts live from the House floor.

Also in attendance was Robert Burford. Burford is a very smart man; he is also a very funny man. That day he chose to evidence the latter quality by taking bets as to the size of the vote *against* me! While I was quaking in my boots, Burford was making book, as if it were a damn horse race.

Actually, I was not really quaking, because I felt that if worst came to worst and I was cited for contempt by the full House of Representatives—something that had never happened to a Cabinet or immediate sub-Cabinet official in all of American history—I was protected by the quality and merit of the legal case that the Justice Department was at that very moment putting together. Nonetheless, it was a curious and unpleasant feeling to watch the debate, even from the relative privacy of my twelfth-floor office at EPA.

And cite me for contempt they did, by a vote of 259 to 105. (Charlotte Englert, my personal assistant and the *least* political person present, won the pool that Burford set up.)

Eventually there would be enough conflicts of interest to keep several law firms busy, and one of the earliest took root the moment the vote was over. According to the procedure, once the contempt resolution has been passed, the Speaker of the House is directed to "certify" a piece of paper to the Clerk of the House, who then directs the United States Attorney for the District of Columbia to bring the contempt charges.

But all U.S. Attorneys are employees of the Department of Justice, which had talked me into getting involved in the first place, and who were supposed to be preparing my legal defense at that very moment! So the plot began to thicken quite early—the very people who were supposed to be prosecuting me were my legal counsel.

As the weeks wore on I found it harder and harder to deal with "my" lawyers from the Justice Department. Teddy Olson in particular was wearing on my nerves. I have a problem with pomposity, and he was decidedly a pompous person. What's more, while I was being increasingly distracted from my normal heavy EPA workload by all the subpoena-related activities, he seemed to be occupying himself with minutiae. I remember clearly that just before I was to testify in front of Levitas we had a strategy session scheduled, and Mr. Olson kept running around asking everyone if they knew when the testimony was scheduled and just which room it was to be held in. Finally I blew up. "That's staff work, and it's already been done! What's the matter with you?"

Not long after that, in preparing for a session before Levitas's committee, he startled me by saying, "You know, I'll probably be doing most of the testifying."

I was astounded by his lack of understanding. "No, you won't. That's not how they run Congress. The committee's rules are quite strict. I am the witness and you are my counsel; you're there only to counsel me on legal matters. If you try to say too much, John Dingell will slap you down."

I don't think Teddy Olson believed me. In any event, he found out the hard way. Word began to come down, with some frequency, that Chairman Dingell had less than a favorable impression of Mr. Olson. And at one point during a subsequent hearing when Olson leaned over and began to whisper to me during a lapse in my testimony, Dingell banged the gavel so hard it sounded like a gun shot!

He gave Olson a sharp-tongued lecture that clearly defined the limits of his role, and its effect was to make the Justice Department lawyer actually hesitate to accompany me the next time I had to go before Dingell.

I have always felt that we could have beaten the loose subpoena from the Levitas committee, that is, if the Justice Department had been able to represent me properly (or even adequately), as I will later show. But Mr. Dingell was another matter.

His subpoena was concise and to the point. It called for

Copies of all books, records, and correspondence, legal and other memoranda, papers and documents relative to the Tar Creek, Oklahoma; Stringfellow Acid Pits, California; and Berlin and Farro, Michigan, hazardous waste sites, excepting shipping records, contractor reports and other technical documents.

I knew as soon as I read his subpoena that there would be no defeating it on technical grounds. Even though the end of the year, which was almost upon us, would coincide with the end of the 97th Congress, and therefore the subpoenas *and* the contempt citation would be old and unresolved business, the public would never stand for us trying to squirm out that way. And especially not when the media were running "Scandal at EPA" stories almost every day. What's more, the prevailing legal opinion was that a citation for contempt, once returned, would carry over into the new Congress.

One touch of class occurred when John Dingell's subcommittee voted to hold me in contempt. Originally that committee had been ready with its subpoena but had deferred issuing it until I could return from a speaking trip, and then, as things worked out, they gave me a week's extension. So it would have been understandable, given the ways of Congress and the value of publicity, if Mr. Dingell's subcommittee had made a big splash with its contempt vote. Instead it took its vote in executive session.

I have other reasons for remembering Congressman Dingell with respect and admiration, not the least of which has to do with a conversation we had in late December 1982. It took place in an empty committee room in the Capitol.

I had gone to see him in an attempt to talk him out of moving against me for contempt.

I said, "Don't do this, John. Please don't. Levitas is one thing. We can beat Levitas, but we can't beat you. If you do this, it's going to end up like a Greek tragedy." I didn't know *what* would happen, but I could foresee the end result.

"Anne, you're right," said Dingell. "It is going to be tragic. You know I'm not after you. You're just in the way. What you need to do is to figure out who your friends are—whether they're up here, or at the other end of Pennsylvania Avenue."

"I had to make that decision a long time ago," I said, "and I can't reverse it now."

And he said, "Well, then you'll have to live with the consequences."

12

CONTEMPT

It was quite a Christmas in 1982. On December 16, one day before the contempt citation was certified to the U.S. Attorney for the District of Columbia "for presentment to the grand jury," the full House cited me for contempt of Congress. *Minutes* later, in a dramatically timed gesture, the Department of Justice filed its lawsuit:

UNITED STATES
  OF AMERICA,
     and
ANNE M. GORSUCH,

               Plaintiffs

v. -   Civil Action
                               No. 82-3583

THE HOUSE OF REPRE-
SENTATIVES OF THE
UNITED STATES; THE
COMMITTEE ON PUBLIC
WORKS AND TRANSPOR-
TATION OF THE HOUSE
OF REPRESENTATIVES;

THE HONORABLE JAMES J.
HOWARD, CHAIRMAN OF
THE COMMITTEE ON PUB-
LIC WORKS AND TRANS-
PORTATION OF THE
HOUSE OF REPRESENTA-
TIVES; THE HONORABLE
ELLIOTT J. LEVITAS,
CHAIRMAN OF THE SUB-
COMMITTEE ON INVESTI-
GATIONS AND
OVERSIGHT OF THE COM-
MITTEE ON PUBLIC
WORKS AND TRANSPOR-
TATION OF THE HOUSE
OF REPRESENTATIVES;
THE HONORABLE
THOMAS P. O'NEILL,
SPEAKER OF THE HOUSE
OF REPRESENTATIVES;
EDMUND L. HENSHAW, JR.,
THE CLERK OF THE
HOUSE OF REPRESENTA-
TIVES; JACK RUSS, SER-
GEANT AT ARMS OF THE
HOUSE OF REPRESENTA-
TIVES; JAMES T. MOLLOY,
THE DOORKEEPER OF THE
HOUSE OF REPRESENTA-
TIVES.

Defendants

As lawyers like to say, the issue had finally been joined. This great case that was to be such a pure test of the Constitutional principle of executive privilege was finally in the courts. The point that the Justice Department felt was so important that it first tried to enlist James Watt on its behalf (and, unbeknownst to me, Attorney General William French Smith) was finally ready to be adjudicated. It should have been a great day. Unfortunately, it was not.

The lawsuit brought by the Justice Department on behalf of the doctrine of executive privilege—and also, not incidentally, me—was, in my opinion, the sloppiest piece of legal work I had seen in twenty years of being a lawyer.

I had feared for quite some time that the Justice Department brief was going to be less than a quality piece of work, but I had been holding out hope that something a fleet of the government's best attorneys had been working on for more than three months would at least turn out to be respectable. For weeks I had been questioning their announced strategy, and finally my questions turned into complaints, so that by the end we were barely on speaking, much less civil, terms.

How many legal precedents and other cases on the same point of law might one expect the Department of Justice to cite in support of this fiercely held principle? Dozens? Scores? Hundreds? The brief relied heavily on the notoriously unsuccessful case of President Richard Nixon *vs.* the House Judiciary Committee in 1974! And, astoundingly, the legal arguments they quoted from that case were *dicta*, judicial opinion that is not central to the legal point determined by the case.

It was just plain sloppy work. It was disorganized, it had simple facts wrong, and it even contained misspellings. There were also fundamental mistakes. The Justice Department's lawyers refused to raise any of the available *factual* defenses, a tactic over which we had had arguments. For example, they refused to raise the defense that the original (Levitas) subpoena was defective, or that it was overly broad, and that, given the time, we had substantially complied with it—all standard defenses available to us within the facts of the case.

There were two other legal arguments they could have used, one of which is somewhat technical, but nonetheless valid. Under the Superfund law, all power to act is given to the President, who in turn delegated a good bit of it to the EPA Administrator, and then after that there was a executive order involved; so the argument can be made that because he had thereby withdrawn, or "redrawn," some of that power to himself, the subpoena was misdirected.

The Justice Department lawyers did not want to raise the first three defenses because, as they put it, they didn't want the court to be sidetracked from the Constitutional issue. Their reason for not raising the fourth defense was somewhat less academic: They feared that if it were accepted, the House might then just turn around and subpoena the President himself!

The Justice Department lawyers might say that they were representing the President. But if that is so, who was representing me?

The other point that infuriated me then and now is that the Justice Department lawyers wanted me to go on the suit personally in my capacity as a private citizen! We had extremely heated arguments over that.

"Why in the world would you want me to go on in my personal capacity?" I screamed.

"We think it would give the Court a more justiciable issue."

"Are you nuts? If I hadn't been acting in an official capacity there wouldn't be any issue. I didn't *do* anything in my personal capacity, I have no defenses in my personal capacity, and I refuse to allow you to put me on there as anything *but* the Administrator of EPA."

As we got closer and closer to the filing date, the Justice Department lawyers kept putting more and more pressure on me to allow them to amend the suit to put me on it personally. In turn, I would say, amend the damn thing to include some of the factual defenses. No, they would say, and we'd end up screaming at one another again. The only way I kept from getting added to that lawsuit personally was by screaming—I screamed in Washington, and I screamed over the phone from out of town, and finally it worked. But by the end we were barely speaking to one another. And these were *my* lawyers, so to speak.

At Jim Watt's suggestion, I even called the government's top appellate lawyer, U.S. Solicitor General Rex Lee. He listened politely, but said there was nothing he could do until the case had been tried. He said he could not go down and get into it at the trial stage. But if you don't, I said, we won't be able to go back and introduce any of these defenses and there will be nothing left to appeal. It will be all over, and there won't be a thing you can do (which is precisely what happened).

The kids and I celebrated Christmas of 1982 at Disney World, a great two-week respite. But just like everything else that was going on at the time, things did not work out the way we wanted them to.

About two months earlier I'd had a good scare. I woke one morning in such pain I thought it was terminal. I had intense low stomach pain, plus severe dizziness, and such weakness I couldn't get dressed. I had to call my government driver and have him come and get me (which he did only on mornings I had a meeting or was going out of town); he took me straight to a doctor's office, a gynecologist. "Honest to God," I told him, "I feel like I'm dying."

He examined me, and said, "You have one of two things. Either you have a bladder infection, in which case it should respond almost immediately to antibiotics, or you have a kidney stone, and if that's what you have, you'll be crawling on your hands and knees by dusk."

Of course, by that point the pain had stopped as quickly as it had begun. I took the antibiotics, and the pain stayed away. I thought I was fine.

On New Year's Day, in Florida, the pain struck again, and this time was worse. I called the doctor I'd seen in Washington and asked if he could prescribe some more of the same antibiotics, quick.

"No, I can't. But I don't think they would do any good, anyway. It sounds to me as if you really do have kidney stones. You had better get yourself to an emergency room right away."

I needed no prodding. By this time the pain was so bad that I was vomiting every fifteen minutes, even though I had nothing on my stomach. I got to the emergency room posthaste. The hospital must have been Kidney Stone Heaven, because they recognized the symptoms right away, and lost no time giving me morphine. For the next two weeks I had to have a shot of morphine every three to four hours. (I realized that I would never become an addict. The drug kills the pain, but it never gives you any real rest; and even when I was able to sleep I hallucinated all the time.)

Things went from bad to worse. They pumped me full of all sorts of things, and stuck IV tubes into me, all the while hoping the damn stone would move. And then we learned I had one in each kidney, which meant there was complete blockage, which meant I was developing uremic poisoning. I was swiftly turning yellow.

When the doctor explained that the operation, if one had to be done, would lay me up for as long as six weeks, I decided to

get back to D.C. By that point I was having fairly long periods of
no pain, so the doctor thought I could probably make it home by
taking oral pain killers. Encouraged, I went back to the condo to
pack, and while I was putting away my unused beach clothes, the
pain returned. And it was very rough. I took the pills, and immediately regurgitated them.

Now I had a real dilemma. How could I fly home on a commercial airliner? A shot wouldn't last long enough, and I couldn't
keep the pills down.

I called Burford in D.C., "You've got to get me out of here."
He began to make the arrangements, including the staggering
expense of a hospital plane. But then John Daniel suggested that
maybe the time had come to ask the White House for help; after
all, one of its team members was seriously ill. He contacted Craig
Fuller, the secretary of the Cabinet Council (who'd been in on the
executive privilege flap). Fuller okayed the use of a Coast Guard
plane with a doctor and nurse on board, and that's how I—knocked
out for the entire trip—got back to Washington.

Of course the hospital in Washington refused to accept any of
the tests done in Florida, and insisted on running their own. Not
only are the tests painful, but they also necessitate your being shot
full of iodine, and I developed an iodine reaction similar to a bad
case of hives. I was, however, fortunate on two counts: My friend
Frieda Poundstone was in town, and she came right over to the
hospital and took charge; she gave the staff what-for if they even
thought of neglecting me. The retesting of course delayed the
operation, and during that period of delay the stones, for reasons
known only to themselves, decided to start moving.

Both stones ended up in a position the doctor could reach
manually, rather than surgically, with a little device shaped like a
basket that he uses to crush them. The stones were then small
enough to pass (Burford told close friends I'd passed "a six-carat
stone").

Another advantage was that while I was recuperating Frieda
and I did all the planning for my wedding to Robert! He and I
had both been divorced for quite a while, but he had estate matters
to work out, and also he'd insisted on signing a prenuptial agreement (which my lawyer termed the most generous he'd ever seen).
But in early 1983 the way was clear for us to marry, and Robert

was about to make the announcement, so Frieda and I took advantage of my few wide-awake and cogent moments.

One of the most amazing things about kidney stones is that you can be at death's door one minute, but when they pass you feel absolutely well. One moment I felt like dying, and an hour later I was demanding lunch.

As if I hadn't enough trouble, while I was in the hospital Fred Fielding called Bob Perry, and told him to fire the private lawyers I'd hired to advise me on the Constitutional issues.

"Fred," I demanded, "where do you get off telling Perry what to do?"

His response floored me. He said in an aggrieved tone, "You know I would never *tell* Bob Perry to do anything. I merely suggested that it would be a good idea."

What crap. It *was* a good idea, but not for the reasons Fred Fielding had in mind. I had made a mistake in my choice of counsel. I had met and been impressed by a gentleman, and the fact that he represented the Republican National Committee (RNC) made me think he'd be a fierce partisan on my behalf. It appeared to me, though, that he kept his fierceness in reserve in dealing with his friends in high Republican legal circles. It turned out that he and William French Smith belonged to many of the same clubs, literally and figuratively. Neither he nor his associates were ever comfortable with the idea of bucking the Justice Department. So I didn't cry to see them gone. And I made a mental note that the next time I went looking for lawyers to make sure the list contained the names of a few Democrats.

When I finally got back to work, I discovered that my situation had not changed, except to get worse. The Hill was angry; they were mad enough about not getting the documents they wanted, but they got even madder when they saw the way the Department of Justice had captioned its lawsuit: The United States of America and Anne M. Gorsuch *v.* The House of Representatives (et al.). They very much minded the implication that somehow they were not also part of "The United States of America." And I can't say I blamed them.

On February 3, 1983 the United States District Court for the District of Columbia Circuit handed down its decision in the case of U.S.A. and Anne M. Gorsuch *v.* The House of Representatives

et al. Cases of importance are rarely blocked by defendants without even getting to trial, but this case—the great legal work of the
Justice Department—was an embarrassing exception. Federal Judge
John Lewis Smith granted the defendants' motion to dismiss the
case.

Actually, he did it in such a way—and it was a rather clever
way—that he avoided having to rule while still retaining jurisdiction if we couldn't work things out ourselves.

> The gravamen of plaintiffs' complaint is that executive
> privilege is a valid defense to congressional demands for
> sensitive law enforcement information from the EPA.
> Plaintiffs have, thus, raised this executive privilege defense
> as a basis for affirmative relief. Judicial resolution of this
> constitutional claim, however, will never become necessary
> unless Administrator Gorsuch becomes a defendant in ei-
> ther a criminal contempt proceeding or other legal action
> taken by Congress. . . . The difficulties apparent in prose-
> cuting Administrator Gorsuch for contempt of Congress
> should encourage the two branches to settle their differ-
> ences without further judicial involvement. Compromise
> and cooperation, rather than confrontation, should be the
> aim of the parties.

As decisions go, this one was clearly above average, perhaps
even Solomon-like. What's more, it was a clear statement that
Judge Lewis knew his politics as well as he knew his law, neither
of which could be said for the crack lawyers from Justice who
drew up the suit.

I had been out of town on the day Judge Lewis's order came
out, but as I was being driven back from the airport I got a call
on the car phone. It was John Daniel. He gave me the news, which
hardly surprised me (though I smiled to realize that Judge Lewis,
an Eisenhower appointee, did not take the pro–Executive Branch
point of view that the Justice Department lawyers, who had been
so happy to hear he'd been assigned the case, were convinced he
would).

What did surprise me was what John said next. "Anne, do you
know what *your* lawyers are doing right now? The same lawyers

who insisted you get into this fight and insisted you refuse to compromise, the same lawyers who wanted you to go on the suit personally? They are meeting with Levitas and his staff right now, and they are *negotiating* a settlement on your behalf."

John Daniel had been through Hades and back with me in the last few months, and had gotten to know me very well in the almost two years we had worked so closely together, but I think he was still startled by my response. I burst out laughing. Indeed, I laughed so hard I all but fell off the car seat. Maybe it was a hysterical reaction, but the situation was beginning to sound downright comical.

These were the same people, the same *lawyers*, who had assured me that they had this great Constitutional case and they had already negotiated as far as they could possibly negotiate with Congress. And first they file what was, in my opinion, the worst piece of legal work I've ever seen, and then they go off and negotiate with the other side before the ink is dry on the judge's order.

Then it hit me: EPA was not even represented at these negotiations! We were neither consulted nor informed. I feel that is unethical. Again, they may have felt they were representing the President. But who was representing EPA?

The next day, I went to the White House and raised a stink. I didn't care what they called me; I was going to holler until I got the mess straightened out.

I talked to Ed Meese and Fred Fielding, and I told them in no uncertain terms what I thought of what was going on. Both of these men can be very abrupt, but this time they listened with something resembling patience. Frankly, I think they might have sensed I was pretty close to the edge, that my nerves had been rubbed almost raw, and my sense of ethics completely insulted. They told me I would receive a call from Ed Schmults, the number-two man in the Department of Justice. Fine, I said, wondering if I should hold my breath.

To my surprise Schmults called that afternoon, informing me that both he and Carol Dinkins would be in my office later that day to bring me up to date on what was taking place on the Hill. They came in and everybody shook hands and they began to talk, but it was all generalities.

"We're very close to a tenable agreement," they said.

"Great. What is it?"

"Well, we can't tell you that."

"You can't? Why not?"

"It's too sensitive."

I thought I had lost my capacity for being amazed, but they'd certainly revived it!

"You're so full of it, I can't believe it! EPA is your *client.* You are supposed to be negotiating on our behalf. But you sit there and tell me you can't reveal the substance of the negotiations? That's an absolute crock!"

At that point—and I laugh every time I recall this—the phone rang, and it was for Ed Schmults. I told him to go ahead and take it at my desk, and he did, pulling out a piece of paper on which to make some quick notes or take a number. Then he left, Dinkins having preceded him. As he was heading down the hall, I noticed that he had left the piece of paper, which was folded several times, on my desk.

I called to Charlotte Englert, my secretary, to see if she could stop him, but John Daniel, who had a decidedly sly grin on his face, asked me to wait a minute. He had the paper in his hands and was already opening it. There were several sheets, and as he read them, the grin on his face widened.

"Well, what do you know about that?"

"What is is, John?"

He handed me the papers—it was the Department of Justice's negotiating position! And the Committee's!

These highly secretive documents that he'd had no intention of sharing with his client had been left by Schmults smack in the middle of the client's desk. John and I both burst out laughing. What irony!

But we stopped laughing when we read the documents. The Justice Department was giving away the farm. They were agreeing almost entirely with the Levitas subcommittee. I don't know why they bothered to call the talks "negotiations," seeing as how they had given in to almost all of the subcommittee's demands. They were giving Congress carte blanche.

One of the strangest suggestions that Justice had come up with was that EPA produce the documents in a "redacted" form. I know the English language fairly well, but that was a new one on me. I had to look it up to learn that it meant, in this context, "white it out." Justice was saying we could give Congress all the documents, but that anything sensitive would be "whited out." Not too surprisingly, the subcommittee didn't buy that one, so the lawyers countered by saying, "Well, then you can have the documents to look at, but not to keep."

One thing clear about the law on privilege is that if you let someone see *any* part of what he is after, then you have lost the privilege. It's like being a little bit pregnant. There is no such thing.

Finally Justice told Levitas and his people that if they weren't satisfied with that deal, then they could make a *copy* of what they wanted! What would be preserved? Absolutely nothing.

Next on the list Mr. Schmults had left behind was the suggestion that each Regional Administrator would certify for Congress that he or she had produced every single relevant piece of paper. Well, that would simply have put the head of each RA—all of whom are political appointees—right smack on the chopping block. Because the minute you say you have produced everything, some yo-yo always stands up and says, "Ha, here's a piece of paper I just found." Every one of my top regional people would be in jeopardy. It was senseless.

The situation was very strange. Here the Justice Department lawyers, very recent converts to compromise, were busily negotiating with Congress on these very important constitutional issues while I was getting creamed every day in the media for the alleged sins of EPA. But did these "negotiators," or what they were doing, ever get in the papers? Not a line.

What was making me so angry was that I had actually been to see the President himself, and had come *that* close to getting him to agree that we should give Congress whatever it wanted.

I got a meeting with the President, never a simple thing to do. The meeting took place in the Oval Office on February 2, but first I had a rather testy meeting with Ed Meese in his office. I told him that no real executive privilege was being preserved, and that the whole affair was beginning to look very bad to the public.

Meese kept telling me how good the legal case looked, and I answered that even though Justice had finally given me a legal memorandum outlining the case and their supporting documents (though without revealing their negotiating position) I had more than a few doubts about the strength of it. Finally we began to squabble, and Meese got angry.

"This is the *President's* case, and Fred Fielding is handling it. You and I will not argue about it. Fred is going to make the decisions. I won't have you going before the President and making a legal argument."

"Ed," I pleaded, "it isn't a legal argument, it's a policy argument. I deserve to have my day in court, my say."

"No," he said adamantly. "I won't have it." He cut off all further discussion. His manner wasn't just cold, it was icy.

The President, on the other hand, when we got to see him, was almost the opposite. Even though he was surrounded by all the men who had been responsible for this scenario—Fielding, Craig Fuller, Meese, and others—he listened and appeared sympathetic to the situation as I described it.

"Mr. President," I said, "this is not just a legal issue. At least not anymore. It has become a political issue. Indeed, because there is a Superfund site in every Congressional district, we have a *prime* political issue, and one which we have hand-selected, gift-wrapped, and bow-tied for any interested political opponent! The issue is one which plays on the very real emotional concerns of people in this country. To the extent it ever was strictly a legal issue, that aspect of it has been systematically bargained and negotiated away. It is now a policy issue, pure and simple.

"And you are being misserved, Mr. President, by the people who are counseling you on this matter. Withholding the papers makes it look like we have something to hide, and is eroding public support for the program."

I could tell I had the President's attention, so I continued, "Sir, there's nothing in those papers that's wrong, so if you ordered me to release them—*ordered* me—you would look like a hero. As far as the media are concerned, I'd still be the big bad witch of the West, but by ordering me to turn them loose, you would be a hero!"

At just that point Fred Fielding interjected, saying, "But, Mr. President, we're *so* close to concluding these negotiations, so close to reaching an agreement with Congressman Levitas."

Had I been quick-witted enough, I would have immediately said, "NO! Whatever deal you cut with Levitas, you will never get John Dingell to concur." But I didn't think that quickly.

"In that case," said the President, "since he's that close to an agreement, let's let Fred have a few more days." And with that the meeting was over.

The whole thing could have worked out so well. In fact, just a few days before this meeting the President had held a press conference, and in answer to a question about the Superfund documents that were being withheld, he had said, which was exactly the right thing to say, "I can no longer insist on executive privilege if there is a suspicion in the minds of the American people that it is being used to cover up wrong-doing."

I thought that was great. Of course, I should have known someone in the White House would manage to dilute it. I happened to be in the White House the day after the President made that comment, and David Gergen, Director of Communications, stopped me and said, "On that comment about releasing the papers, I thought you'd be pleased to know that I've just issued a correcting statement for the President." I was amazed by how little all those White House types understood of what was going on.

Another unsettling discovery was to learn that the media were now even more interested in me and what they insisted on referring to as "the growing scandal at EPA." Thinking (hoping?) they might be hot on the trail of another Watergate type of case, they intensified their coverage. Now, most mornings when I left for work there was at least one car parked on the street of the cul de sac where I lived, and if I'd had to go outside to get to my garage, I would have been stopped on the way and pressed for "a comment." The first morning I saw two cars outside my house I got the distinct feeling that, like a gathering of vultures, their number would soon increase.

In recent years so much as been written about the "pack mentality" of journalists that one hesitates to add to it, but as someone who was its prey, I know whereof I speak. What bothered me more than anything, as I indicated earlier, was the media's insistence on making me rather than the issues the center of the story, and their reluctance to do the work that would enable them to see that I was only one of several main characters. All the stories focused on me and my "defiance" of the committee; hardly anyone bothered to ask the folks over at the Justice Department anything more than perfunctory questions.

Clearly they thought I made the better story. A Reagan administration official is on the hot seat, and it's a *woman*. Can she take it? Will she be tough enough? You could plot the curve as it ascended.

Sometimes the press sent what appeared to be mixed signals. For example, in early November 1982 *U.S. News and World Report* said, "Gorsuch is faulted at the White House for being 'too aggressive.' " But in the year-end issue it reported, "the White House also said President Reagan was delighted with Gorsuch's tough stance [regarding the subpoenas] and the way she fought back."

I certainly hoped the President was "delighted," but I feared that some of his aides were not. I wasn't getting much positive feedback from my few contacts at the White House. For the moment the implicit instructions were, Steady as she goes, hold this course until we see how the negotiations proceed.

At about this time I had the meeting with my top program people, all the political appointees and their top staffs, the meeting that William Hedeman described earlier as being so emotionally charged. I do not have a clear recollection of telling them that I loved them, but I believe Hedeman's recollection. And I *did* love them. They had worked so hard, and come so far, and they had been so very loyal. All of them, that is, except Rita Lavelle.

13

L'Affaire Lavelle

From the beginning Rita had gone her own way. In an agency the size of EPA it takes some time before the Administrator learns if his or her wishes and orders are being carried out. When I began to get signals that Rita was either doing things that I had not authorized, or was not doing things I had told her to do, I did what anyone else in my position would do: I said, "Hey, what's going on here? Get in the game." And Rita always dutifully promised that she would straighten things out. But she didn't.

For example, I had told her that all public information and public relations functions were to be run through EPA's Office of Public Information. But I learned some months after the fact that Rita had hired several people who were actually functioning as her own p.r. department. Also, she had difficulty following the guidelines when it came to announcing and following through on enforcement actions, and she was not getting along at all well with the Regional Administrators, who had begun to come directly to me with their complaints. Their most serious complaint was the collective charge that she reduced their requests for funds to do emergency clean up work. At first I thought she was simply reflecting the kind of conservative frugality that the President (and I) espoused, and that he had charged all of us with implementing.

But as the months wore on I heard some of the complaints in detail, and it began to sound as if Rita were following a different drummer. Well before I could prove it, I had a nagging suspicion that Rita was inclined to take industry's side far too quickly. I knew the RAs often asked for more money than those of us in Washington thought they needed—after all, the more they spent on cleanup, the better they looked to the general public in their areas—but I was getting the impression that Rita's attitude went beyond the normal headquarters-versus-the-field kind of disagreement.

Another problem with Rita was finally brought to my attention by Cristy Bach, my personal assistant. Whenever I went off to speak somewhere, I required briefing papers from the various AA's so that I would have the latest information on the pluses and minuses in the program areas of the region I was going to visit. Invariably, Cristy informed me, the briefing materials from Rita Lavelle were either late or inadequate or both.

By late 1982 I was hearing enough complaints about Rita that I was becoming concerned. But every time I confronted her she had what sounded like a plausible explanation, and she promised to do better. Perhaps I gave her more chances than I would someone else because I knew she had inadequate management and policy background but hoped that she would grow; I don't know. I do know that because I was more than satisfied with the work of Bill Hedeman and John Skinner, I felt I could "afford" to let my problem with Rita slip down a few notches on my priority list.

Prior to the gala affair given to commemorate the second anniversary of the Reagan inaugural, we had an EPA dinner. It was a very successful affair, with a great deal of collegiality, and a feeling that though we were under a lot of heat, if the team stuck together we could make it through and even turn some of the bad publicity around.

That night was very special for me because it was also the night that Burford announced that he and I were going to be married in less than a month. We received many sincere expressions of congratulation, and probably drank too many toasts, but it was a grand feeling, and a grand night.

And then, in what was surely the worst possible timing, I found it necessary to fire Rita Lavelle, an action that lit the short fuse of a very large bomb. Actually, the bomb was a series of explosions, each one louder and more damaging than the last, which culminated in a devastating result.

On the Monday following the gala John Daniel came into my office, and said, "Did you notice that Rita and Bob Perry were off talking together half the evening? Maybe they are making up."

"No," I said, "I hadn't noticed, but that would certainly be welcome news. She really has caused more than her share of trouble."

Later that same day he was back in my office, and this time he had the picture in focus. "Sorry, Anne, but Rita and Bob are *not* getting on any better. In fact, they have a real problem, and it sounds serious as hell."

"For God's sake, what is it?"

"On Friday or Saturday Bob got a call from a *New York Times* reporter, and the guy really started to grill him about things Bob had supposedly done, or not done, regarding Superfund. It was all enforcement-sensitive stuff. After a while Bob got the impression that the guy was reading from a memo, a memo written about Bob *by* Rita. And everything in it was critical of Bob's performance."

"Good Lord! Get those characters in here right away, both of them!"

They'd barely sat down when I asked Rita point blank if she had had anything to do with such a memo. But I phrased it carefully, because by now I had learned that if you wanted a straight answer from Rita you really had to pin her down.

I told her what I had heard, and then asked, "Rita, to your knowledge, does any such memo exist? Either prepared by you, or by one of your employees?"

"Oh, my God, no. Never. I'm a team player."

"Okay," I said, "then this is very easily dealt with, though for the life of me I don't know why I'm having to tell you this. Get on the phone to that reporter who called Bob and tell him that no such memo exists, and that if he publishes anything of that nature he does so at his own peril."

"Okay," said Rita.

I knew Rita well enough not to leave it at that. The next day I asked John Daniel if Rita had made the phone call. He said he didn't know, but he would check on it. A short time later he had an answer for me: "No." I told him to get her back in my office.

"Rita," I said exasperatedly, "why the hell didn't you make that call?"

Her answer was that the reporter was either out of the office or his line was busy.

"Do I have to think of *everything* around here? Call his *editor*. And don't let the day end without taking care of it!" I was really mad.

On Wednesday I was out of the office, and when I called in one of the first things I asked John Daniel was if Rita had made the call.

"No," he said, and his gentlemanly Southern voice grew even quieter, which I knew meant we were talking about something very serious. "In fact, contrary to her usual demeanor, she came in this morning, and, very humbly, asked for our help."

"What?"

"Well, *my* help, I guess. She said that now that she's had a couple, three days to think about it, she *sort of* remembers that she *might* have written some notes that *could* be the memorandum in question."

My reaction was instantaneous. "John, that tears it. The woman is a liar. And what's more, she's a liar about something that was an attempt to discredit another member of our team!"

"I have only three rules of management," I stormed. John knew them by heart, but he wasn't about to interrupt. "One is that you never lie; another is that you don't undermine a fellow team member; and the third is that you do the best possible job every day. Now those are pretty easy to follow, but Rita has violated two out of three! I want her out of there before the sun goes down."

We began to learn more about the memo and the circumstances surrounding it. John learned that Bill Hedeman and another one of Rita's top people had heard of the memo's existence and also knew that a *New York Times* reporter had called about it, which meant the memo itself had been brought to Rita's attention before she was called into my office. That meant the lie was *very* premeditated, not something she could have forgotten, which made me even angrier.

We also learned that the memo contained one incendiary line, one statement that would cause the environmentalists, the Congress, and immediately thereafter the media—not to mention the

American people—to scream in outrage. The memo was basically a negative criticism of Perry's work in regard to Superfund enforcement actions. Rita wrote that by being so tough on companies that dumped hazardous wastes, Bob Perry was "alienating . . . the primary constituency of this administration, big business."

At the time it was hard to imagine a worse statement. From the very beginning that sort of "tilt" was exactly what our critics were accusing us of having. And it was that same accusation which I was working so hard to refute by cleaning up the internal paperwork backlog and getting new regulations on the books. But here was Rita saying the very thing that our opponents had been charging us with. It was patently untrue. Nonetheless, it would certainly look like a smoking gun.

When she wasn't faulting Perry for his actions, she was describing actions of her own that struck me as ethically and legally questionable. In one case after Perry had either concluded negotiations or reached an impasse with an offender, she had gone back to the company in question and suggested they continue to negotiate because they were close to an agreement. That one I had to refer to the Department of Justice.

From a strictly legal standpoint it's unethical for an attorney in an adverse position to go directly to someone who is represented by a lawyer. Of course, because she isn't an attorney, Rita Lavelle didn't have that exact problem, but it still looks very odd for an EPA official to do that.

Before I gave Rita the bad news personally, I thought it would be a good idea to tell the White House what my plans were. As it happened, John Daniel and I had a White House appointment the next morning so I arranged to see Ed Meese. What with all the rumors about Rita's "Meese connection," I was somewhat apprehensive; after all, he had held the Bible and sworn her in.

"Ed, I'm sorry, but it looks as if I have to fire Rita Lavelle. I've just learned that she did something very wrong and then she lied to me about it. I can't have people working for me who lie. I know it comes at a bad time, in fact it could hardly come at a worse time, because it makes things look even worse than they are."

Meese's response was immediate: "You've got to play your cards like they're dealt, Anne. You can't have someone working for you who lies."

To be honest about it, I was slightly disappointed that he didn't try to dissuade me. I wasn't at all looking forward to what would follow my firing her—Congress is screaming at the EPA Administrator, whom it already has under contempt, because she won't release certain Superfund documents, and then that same Administrator goes and fires the head of the Superfund program. In many ways it would have been a relief if he had talked me out of firing her.

Instead, all he added was that because she was presidentially-appointed, Senate-confirmed I had better go upstairs and tell Helene Van Damm, head of personnel, (and later our Ambassador to Austria) about it, so they could discuss it at the meeting of the senior staff scheduled for the next morning.

I wasn't too thrilled with that. "Look, she works for me. I know she's a presidential appointee, but I've never fired anybody in my life without looking him or her in the eye personally. But if that's the way you prefer to do it, then it's okay with me." And the next day the senior staff people—Baker, Meese, Deaver—met and approved Rita's firing.

I had an out-of-town trip that next day, but as soon as I got back to my office I called Rita in. It was a Friday afternoon.

John Daniel and John Hernandez were there, and we had a prepared press release for Rita as a "cover" for the fact that she was being fired. It announced that she was leaving to return to private industry in California. But first I told her point-blank why she was there.

"Rita, I want your resignation."

She gasped so loudly that it startled us. John Daniel told me later he was afraid she was going to have a coronary.

I handed her the press release. "Rita, as soon as this meeting is over, I want you to go to your office and draft a letter of resignation to the President. We have already talked to the people at the White House. But first, here is a press release we've prepared for you. You can make changes if you like."

Rita read it silently, and when she got to the part about her returning to private industry, she found her voice. "Am I bound by this?"

"What do you mean?" I said.

"What if I want to seek another job around here, or in state government?"

We let her reword it to say only that she was returning "to California to pursue other interests."

But I had to make things clear to her. "Rita, you must understand what this means, exactly. As long as I'm a reference, you're never going to work for any governmental entity. I'll make sure of it."

Of course there were tears. It was not an easy scene for any of us, especially for Rita.

Finally, when she'd regained some composure, she said, "Why are you doing this to me?"

"You know full well why I'm doing it. You lied to me, and you did so about a fellow team member."

"Oh," she said, "if you're still worried about that reporter from *The New York Times*, I've taken care of that. I convinced him the memo was written by somebody else, somebody on my staff, and without my knowledge."

"Rita," I said, stunned. "That's *another* lie."

Realizing her admission, Rita gasped, but said nothing.

"*Rita!*" I said. "You do not lie if you work for me. I don't know why you can't understand that."

I then gave her a piece of unsolicited advice. "If you're going to keep book on somebody . . ." she was giving me a blank look ". . . keep a list of negative criticisms, at least do it in your own handwriting, because that way nobody can add anything to it and claim you said it."

"Oh," she said, "but it *was* in my handwriting! I wrote it out before I put it on tape to be transcribed."

We never did find either the original memo or the tape, but what Rita's comment meant to me was that no one would ever know what really happened because all we had to rely on was Rita herself. And you simply couldn't believe her.

Rita was crying more openly now, and I asked her if she would like to go into the small conference room at the back of my office to compose herself. She nodded, and left the room. She did not return, but went downstairs to her office.

The last thing I said to her was, "I'm sorry it has come to this."

I learned later that Rita called all her key people together, and, still in tears, told them she had been fired.

William Hedeman, head of Superfund, was present at Rita's

highly emotional meeting. He recalls, "After several emotional breakdown periods, Rita told us that she had been called to Anne's office, been accused of lying, and told that she was to resign. She said she was given a copy of a press announcement indicating that she had decided to resign because her work had been completed, and that she would return to California. She said several times that 'This was all because of that stupid memo.' And she indicated that she had recalled the memo and that one of her staff had written it at her request. That was rather startling news to me, because a week earlier, when I had first heard a rumor about the memo, I went to Rita and asked her if it were true, and she said she knew nothing about it.

"I listened for some time, and then said to Rita that I felt she should leave immediately for the West Coast that evening, decline any interviews with the press, and simply put her experience at EPA behind her, and proceed with whatever she could do in California. Chip Wood, Rita's chief of staff, quickly responded by saying that the advice I was giving was wrong, that Anne could not fire her because she had been hired by and appointed by the President, and that the only person who could fire her was the President himself.

"Rita reacted positively to that statement by Chip and indicated that she was going to talk with Mr. Meese, and in our presence tried to get him on the telephone. Apparently she was only able to reach his secretary.

"The discussion began to ramble, and Rita continued to show a great deal of emotion. She finally excused herself, and asked that we return about fifteen minutes later to meet the new Acting Assistant Administrator whom Anne had designated, Mike Brown. When we got back, Rita had composed herself. She told Mike Brown that he would be able to work well with us, and she wished us all well. She then left, and it was the last time I saw Rita Lavelle until her trial."

Hedeman did, however, *hear* from Rita one more time that weekend: "She called me at home on Sunday night and told me to, quote, lay low, unquote, that she was going to 'come out fighting' Monday morning, and that 'all hell will break loose.' "

Rita was convinced that I did not have the authority to fire her, that only the President himself did, and that she should fight for her rights. And that—despite her several admissions of mendacity—was what she proceeded to do all weekend long. But it was a very curious time, because she refused to talk to anyone— not the press, not Joe Ryan from White House personnel—except certain powerful people in the White House. And they wouldn't take or return her calls.

All through Saturday and most of Sunday she kept trying to reach her "friends" at the White House—Meese, Baker, Deaver, plus others. I've been told that since these people had already approved her firing, they didn't call her back. Rita found plenty to do, though. She began to truck boxes and boxes of files out of her office.

I didn't think of it until Sunday afternoon. In fact, it was Burford who said to me, almost casually, "You did post a guard on her office, didn't you?" By the time I called, John Daniel, who'd received reports of the activity early Sunday afternoon, had already taken care of it.

What was removed? We'll never know for sure. Here is what John Dingell's committee would say about it, in their August 1984 report:

> In a late afternoon meeting on Friday, February 4, 1983, EPA Administrator Anne Burford [*sic*] handed Rita M. Lavelle, then EPA Assistant Administrator for Solid Waste and Emergency Response, a statement announcing Ms. Lavelle's resignation. Mrs. Burford informed Ms. Lavelle that if she did not resign, she would be fired. After her dismissal, Ms. Lavelle returned to her office to inform her staff.
>
> Beginning immediately thereafter and continuing throughout the weekend, members of Rita M. Lavelle's staff engaged in a concerted and comprehensive effort to remove official government documents, including Superfund case files, from Ms. Lavelle's desk and office. . . . Testimony before the subcommittee further disclosed that the unauthorized removal of government documents and files from EPA violated Federal law and obstructed several ongoing Congressional investigations. Testimony before the Subcommittee further disclosed that members of Ms. Lavelle's staff removed these important Agency records from EPA Headquarters with the full knowledge of Ms. Lavelle and, at least in one instance, at the active urging of Ms. Lavelle.

The Subcommittee also finds that Ms. Lavelle testified untruthfully before Congress about the removal of Agency
files and access to her files.
    . . . [Lavelle aides] Ms. Baldyga and Mrs. Janiszewski
gathered files from the top of Ms. Lavelle's desk, from the
lower right-hand desk drawer, and from Ms. Lavelle's cre-
denza. Mrs. Janiszewski gathered some files from the outer
offices of the Assistant Administrator and brought them
into Ms. Lavelle's inner office. Mr. Ingold directly super-
vised the gathering of the files. At one point, Mr. Wood
entered Ms. Lavelle's office and stated "the real bad stuff
is in my office. I gotta get that out."
    Susan Baldyga also recalls that Mr. Wood gave her three
packets of documents, including one pertaining to the Chem-
Dyne hazardous waste site, and one pertaining to the Seymour hazardous waste site, to give to Mr. Ingold on or
about February 4, 1983. The top page of each of these
packets had Ms. Lavelle's handwritten notes in the margin.
At the time Mr. Wood handed these three packets to Ms.
Baldyga, he stated, "Give these to Gene. I don't want them
in my office." He further emphasized that: "these could
really hurt Rita." Ms. Baldyga recalls giving these packets
to Mr. Ingold the night Ms. Lavelle was fired.
    All of the files collected by Ms. Baldyga and Mrs. Jan-
iszewski on Friday, February 4, 1983, were placed in three
briefcases. Among the files Mrs. Janiszewski collected were
files on Superfund sites, including Stringfellow (California),
Chem-Dyne (Ohio), Seymour (Indiana), LiPari (New Jersey), Burnt Fly Bog (New Jersey), Globe (Arizona), and Tar
Creek (Oklahoma). There were also files on the dioxin sites
in Missouri. In addition, there were files on Members of
Congress and high-ranking Agency officials.

    In regard to the files on agency officials, a footnote read: "Dur-
ing a Subcommittee staff interview on June 27, 1983, Ms. Baldyga
stated that Mr. Wood was into gathering what he called 'dirt.'
During Ms. Baldyga's executive session testimony, she explained
the meaning of 'dirt' as follows: 'Mr. Wood characterized it as
trying to solidify Rita's power base within the Agency. If anyone

knew any information on the different members of the staff, we were to report to him.'

The report continued:

> The documents gathered Saturday afternoon, esti-
> mated to be a stack two to three feet high, were placed in
> the trunk of Ms. Baldyga's automobile on top of the three
> briefcases gathered the previous evening. On Saturday eve-
> ning, Ms. Baldyga drove Ms. Lavelle to Carnegie's Restau-
> rant in Alexandria, Virginia, for dinner with members of
> Ms. Lavelle's staff. During the dinner, the staff members
> discussed, in the presence of Ms. Lavelle, the fact that Ms.
> Baldyga had documents in the trunk of her car. Following
> dinner, at approximately midnight, the three briefcases and
> other documents were transferred from the trunk of Ms.
> Baldyga's automobile to the trunk of Mr. Ingold's auto-
> mobile in the restaurant's parking lot. Ms. Lavelle was pres-
> ent and observed the transfer of the EPA documents. In
> fact, Ms. Baldyga and Ms. Lavelle had a conversation about
> the documents. Ms. Baldyga described this conversation in
> the following executive session testimony:

>> Mr. Frandsen. [Dingell Committee investigator]. Did
>> you ever ask Ms. Lavelle if she wanted to see the
>> materials that were in your trunk?
>> Ms. Baldyga. When I was transferring them from
>> the trunk of my car to the trunk of Mr. Ingold's car, I
>> said to her, "You should see the file here." And she
>> said, "I would rather not." We were just laughing and
>> she then walked to the passenger door of my car.

> On Sunday morning, February 6, 1983, Etta Janiszewski
> returned to Ms. Lavelle's office and for the first time re-
> moved Ms. Lavelle's strictly personal items, such as "stuffed
> animals." The Agency posted guards at Ms. Lavelle's office
> for the first time on Sunday afternoon, a classic case of
> closing the barn door after the horse was gone.

The question of whether or not I had the legal right to fire Rita Lavelle became moot on Monday, February 7, when President

Reagan fired her. But even that action did not take place without considerable backstage drama.

Once the decision had been made by the senior staff at the White House to back up my firing of Rita, Joe Ryan, a decent man who cared about all the people involved, tried to reach Rita to get her to come in and discuss the matter. He was hoping to reach an agreement whereby Rita would resign, rather than force the President to fire her.

Ryan had a problem. He couldn't get in touch with Rita. Her apartment was being manned by members of her staff, and they claimed she was not in and that they didn't know when she would be. But Ryan learned that Rita had a lawyer, one whom she had apparently hired sometime earlier, James Bierbower, Jr. I found it interesting that he had a great deal of experience in criminal law, which suggests Rita fully understood how serious her problems might one day become.

Ryan was able to reach Bierbower, who had represented several of the Nixon staffers implicated in the second wave of Watergate troubles, who said he would try to get her to call Ryan. But Ryan didn't hear from Rita over the weekend. There were many rumors floating around, the chief of which was that she would talk only to Ed Meese. But to this day I don't know if she did or not. And if she did, it certainly did not have the effect she'd intended.

By Monday the White House had a statement ready, which it wantd to release at the regular noon press briefing. Bierbower asked Ryan for "just two or three more hours." Ryan agreed, but when the lawyer either could not find his client or she refused to respond to his request, the deadline passed, and in late afternoon a release was posted outside the White House press office stating that Rita Lavelle had been fired by the President.

It was a sad affair for everyone concerned. And, saddest of all, it was not over. In some ways *l'affaire Lavelle* was just beginning.

14

SACRAMENT AND SACRIFICE

I did have one important respite in what was beginning to be an onslaught of problems: on Sunday, February 20, 1983, Anne McGill Gorsuch became Anne McGill Burford.

Somehow, Burford managed to find the only Irish-Catholic Republican Reagan-appointee judge in the District of Columbia. Well aware of the turmoil of our professional lives, Judge Thomas Hogan tried to make the ceremony that took place in his chambers as lovely as possible. And he succeeded.

The reception was equally lovely. Held in a huge ground-floor room at the elegant Four Seasons Hotel in Georgetown, it featured a string quartet and an open bar, not to mention pails of champagne and more food and wedding cake than anyone needed. In the credit-where-credit-is-due department, it should be noted that the reception was paid for by Robert, and arranged by Charlotte, my personal secretary, who *loves* to spend other people's money, and did so with style. She made a very special occasion even more so.

James Watt, who was Robert's best man, was funny and cheery the whole time. Strom Thurmond kept coming by and kidding Robert about how pleased he was that someone else had the good sense to marry a younger woman. When he began joking about whether or not we planned to have a family—Thurmond became a father again at the age of seventy-four—I just happened to see someone on the other side of the room I absolutely had to talk to.

Among the almost four hundred guests were, in addition to the political appointees I'd brought into EPA, several dozen of the top career staff members. Later I was surprised to learn that this was the first time that many of them had attended any event of a personal nature at the invitation of an EPA Administrator.

The wedding was an all-too-brief respite. I was scheduled to leave on Tuesday morning for Times Beach, Missouri, so obviously there was no time for a honeymoon. It was all but settled that in Times Beach I would sign off on the first "buy out" (the government's paying citizens for their homes and property) of an entire town in American—and perhaps even world—history.

Ironically, the trouble in Times Beach was caused by a substance that had been used for years to spray the roads in order to keep down the dust. As it turned out, that substance contained dangerous levels of dioxin. We had tested the soil, as had scientists from the Centers for Disease Control (CDC), and found very unhealthy levels of the dangerous substance, and then before we could decide exactly what to do, there was a flood, and the contaminated soil was washed inside peoples' homes, making a bad situation horrible. The people of the town were scared, and were looking to their government for help. At Christmastime President Reagan had promised that there would be some form of aid, and that the citizens would be the first to know the federal decision.

That decision was that we now had no alternative but to buy out the entire town. As EPA Administrator I was to make the official announcement, but the documentation and, in effect, the whole presentation was to be in conjunction with CDC and the Federal Emergency Management Administration (FEMA).

I expected an emotional trip, but I did not expect it to be as dramatic or as intensely emotional as it turned out to be. The whole experience was almost surrealistic, as if written by Kafka or, perhaps more accurately, painted by Munch, a man who specialized in depicting pain and fear.

One item of background information is particularly relevant, and, unfortunately, it involves Rita Lavelle; it is yet another example of the kind of trouble she was causing without my being aware of it. On February 3, the same day Rita was fired, she attended a very important three-hour meeting about the situation at Times Beach. The meeting was called by Lee Thomas, the head of FEMA, who was coordinating the various soil studies and monitoring their progress. Also representing EPA was Bill Hedeman.

Thomas gave them both a thorough briefing, being careful to point out that while the situation did not look good, the results were too preliminary and based on too little data for any definite conclusion to be drawn either way. However, as Hedeman later reported to me, it was clear things looked bad for the people of Times Beach.

On Saturday morning, February 5, Bill Hedeman was on the phone at his home in suburban Maryland when the operator cut in and told him he had an emergency call from a Congressman Young. Hedeman, who took the call immediately, was well aware of who Congressman Robert A. Young was—he represented Times Beach!

As Hedeman recalls it, "Congressman Young was quite concerned about what he had just heard on the radio, that Rita Lavelle had been fired. What so upset him was the fact that, as he related it, Rita had been in his office the previous afternoon and had advised him that the test results, the soil samplings, that had come in from Times Beach—the same ones that Lee Thomas had cautioned us not to talk about—were 'very good news,' in that they showed no problem."

Congressman Young would have been well within his rights if he had gone through the roof, especially considering the low opinion so many of his colleagues had of EPA and me at that very moment. But, in large part thanks to Bill Hedeman's careful handling of the matter, he cooperated fully when Bill told him that while we were still studying the test results, we were on the verge of taking action. And approximately three weeks later we did.

But first I had an important meeting at the White House with reference to Times Beach.

It was a day like all the days in February and March 1983— impossible. I'd had a fleet of meetings, and the only time I could find to talk to Hedeman and have him bring me up to the minute on Times Beach was in my car on the way to the White House. I believe the day was the Friday before my wedding.

Here is Hedeman's account of that ride. His memory, perhaps not surprisingly, is better than mine.

"In the weeks that followed Rita's firing, we had continued to get more soil samplings and more information regarding Times Beach. We had preliminary indications from the Centers for Disease Control that they would issue a health advisory based on this data if it survived a quality control review. That advisory would suggest the need to disassociate the entire town from the potential exposure to the dioxin contamination. As the data became more available, we had increasing evidence that the dioxin was very widespread throughout the town.

"Anne had an exceptionally busy schedule, and the meeting I had with her—I was personally handling the dioxin situation because Mike Brown, who'd been named as the deputy to replace Rita, had said to me that he had come in far too late to get directly involved—took place in her car on the way to the White House for a meeting. I went over with her the map that showed where the dioxin contamination had been discovered, and the concentrations of the samples we'd taken, and indicated the extent to which it had been dispersed throughout the town. I recommended to her that she select the buy-out option.

"After arriving at the White House we sat in her car for quite some time, reviewing the data. Finally she said to me, 'Okay, Bill, let's do it. First of all I want to advise several people in the White House that I have made this decision; secondly, I want to announce it personally, I mean I want to go to the town and meet some of the people who are involved; and, assuming CDC confirms their findings this weekend, I want to make the announcement in Times Beach.'

"She indicated that I should work toward the announcement that would occur on Tuesday, February twenty-second, so I spent the better part of that long weekend—it was the Washington's Birthday weekend—working with several of my staff people, personally writing the decision documents relating to the buy out of Times Beach. I spent all day Monday in the office with my staff putting the final touches on the decision memorandum, and conferring with Mr. Thomas at FEMA and also the Centers for Disease Control, both in Atlanta and in Washington.

"Everybody was working on their particular parts of this puzzle that had to come together by Tuesday. We had to have all the papers and documents in final form and ready for signatures by late Monday afternoon, because Anne and I and Lee Thomas were to fly to St. Louis together the next day.

"There was a great deal of media interest in what was going on, both as to Times Beach and also the whole situation at EPA. I did not tell any reporters of my travel plans, but that night one of them called my home and tried to learn, from my eight-year-old son where I was going and what airline I was using, and was persistent to the point of asking the *color* of the airline ticket jacket that the child had told him was on the kitchen counter."

When I got to the airport I had my hands full, because before I left I had to see that my two youngest children, Stephanie and J.J., got on the plane back to Denver all right. They told me how much fun they'd had at the wedding, and I told them how great it was to have them there, and that it wouldn't be long before we were all living together again. I could tell from their brave smiles that they were worried about me. As it turned out, they had reason to be.

As I walked down the concourse toward the TWA boarding area with Bill Hedeman, we were intercepted by Dale Russakoff of the Washington *Post*. At the gate, I met Lee Thomas for the first time, and encountered another reporter. The reporters began to press us about the plans for Times Beach, Russakoff being particularly persistent (although she denies this incident took place, I stand on my memory). I might not have minded Ms. Russakoff so much had she not chosen, from the very first time she interviewed me, to feign stupidity as to the facts and the issues involved. (I have to believe it was a ploy; no one employed by a major newspaper could be *that* uninformed about her own beat.) She wanted me to tell her what we had not even told the people of Times Beach! I was already very tired, and simply said, "Dale, you are so far out of it that's there no sense in trying to fill you in. Besides, the President has made a commitment that the people of Times Beach would be the first to hear our decision."

Hedeman and Thomas and I took seats toward the rear of the plane, and except for one quarter-hearted effort, the reporters left us alone. We had a considerable amount of work to do before we landed; it was the first time I had seen the finished version of the various decision documents that both Mr. Thomas and I had to sign. We worked hard for over an hour, and then I was ready to sign. I asked for a pen, and Bill Hedeman handed me his fountain pen.

I had written no more than the first few letters of my first name when the cartridge of his ink pen exploded, spraying me and the document!

I sat there for a full minute before I could speak. Then I said, "Okay, William, what do I do now?"

"Well," he said, shaking his head in dismay and amazement, "why don't you finish signing the document, and then we'll clean it, and you, up."

That's what I proceeded to do, with one last hitch. As I began to sign my last name, I heard Hedeman say, "Anne, wait."

"Huh?"

"You're signing the wrong name. . . ."

I looked down to see the familiar sweep of my capital *G*.

". . . your name is Burford now."

I shook my head, and for the first time signed "Anne M. Burford."

With the major paperwork out of the way, we began to talk of other things. I found Thomas a bright and likable man. He also seemed to be compassionate, which was essential to his main task of directing the evacuation of Times Beach. It was a good thing that I did like him, because a few days earlier I had been informed by Craig Fuller of Jim Baker's staff to see what I thought of Mr. Thomas as a "possible" replacement for Rita Lavelle. My reading of Fuller's tone, however, was: "We sure hope you like him, because you've got him."

Thomas and Hedeman and I talked of how we'd gotten into "government work," and discovered the unusual coincidence that one of the first public service jobs that each one of us had held was in the criminal justice system. So we spent the rest of the flight discussing various philosophical approaches to that knotty problem area in American life.

I have heard several of the people in our party describe the events of that afternoon, and the one word that keeps cropping up in each account is "bizarre." Congressman Young met our plane, and immediately led us to a meeting room in the airport terminal where we had a brief lunch with local and state officials and explained the decision to them, plus made sure such requirements as the state of Missouri's 10 percent portion of the buy-out would be met.

One rather strange feature of the meeting was that everyone knew there were vast numbers of media people hovering just outside the room, and all over the terminal, as well as at the motel where the next meeting was scheduled. But hardly anyone mentioned them, except when it came time to leave, and then we learned that the town officials had planned our escape.

For the first of what would be many times over the next several days and weeks, we were led through a series of doorways, exits, and entrances from one end of the airport to the other, and then into cars that took us to a large motel in Times Beach. We had eluded the press, but not for long.

What I could see of the city depressed me. Built on a flood plain, the houses were for the most part of second-rate construction, and seemed gloomy and dull. Of course, knowing that they were terribly contaminated and unfit for humans to live in did not add anything to my impression of them. One shudders to think of anyone having to live under those conditions, but somehow the meanness of the houses made it seem worse.

When we arrived at the motel we were again taken on a circuitous route in order to avoid the crush of reporters. Our first meeting, with the town council, was held in a large room in which all of the drapes had been tightly drawn so that the press could not see in. Their turn was next on the schedule, which had been set up by the Regional Administrator of FEMA.

The people of the town council took the news of the buy out quite well, almost philosophically, which must be very hard to do. They understood the rationale behind the decision, and they were appreciative of the fact that at the President's direction they were the first to learn the fate of their home town.

The press conference, in direct contrast, was a zoolike affair, an analogy suggested by the physical setup. The room was large, almost like a lobby, and had glass walls. The press and its prey (us) were on the inside, but lined up three, four, and five deep on the outside were the people of Times Beach, their anxious faces pressed up against the glass, peering in fearfully. The man from FEMA, who began the press conference by making several references to the goodness of the Reagan administration in saving the town, had placed speakers outside the room so the people could hear what was being said.

It was a terrible arrangement, just awful. I don't know why they didn't let the people come in, or why I didn't insist on it.

The members of the press were jumping up and down, shouting questions, many of which went far beyond the topic of Times Beach and the sad but historic event we were all a part of (typically, "How do you respond to the charge that . . . ?") And ringing the room were these faces peering in, able to hear but unable to ask their own questions about what was happening to them and their lives and loved ones. Through it all the FEMA official kept reassuring them, obsequiously telling them how the President really cared about them. The whole scene was definitely surrealistic.

Once again William Hedeman's memory of the scene will be more objective than my own.

> "The schedule called for us to meet first with the elected representatives of Times Beach for one hour, one to two P.M. as I recall, and then go from there to a press conference. All of this had been orchestrated by the Regional Administrator of FEMA. We met with the citizens as scheduled, and I felt that Anne was particularly compassionate toward them, and very personal in her remarks to them. She attempted to be not only sympathetic to their plight, and the delays they had experienced as we struggled with getting this data together, but also encouraging in terms of what this decision meant. I felt that she was extremely well received by those individuals, and she essentially handled virtually all of the discussion with them.
>
> "Then we embarked on what I consider to be one of the more bizarre events of my entire involvement with the Superfund program. We were guided down a series of what can only be described as secret passages, and into freight elevators in this motel until we ultimately wound up in a room that the press had assembled in."

The scene we entered was like something out of Kafka. The people of the town were not allowed inside the room where the mob of reporters awaited us, but instead had been herded into an outside courtyard. They pressed themselves up against the glass, their worried faces straining to connect the words, which were being broadcast to the loudspeakers on the inside. They seemed frozen in time.

"Anne began, and very quickly made the announcement of her decision to buy out Times Beach, and there was resounding applause and loud screaming noises coming from the large number of people in the courtyard. She then, because of the precedential nature of the announcement, began to describe why this decision had been made and the process behind it, and rather instinctively turned, and instead of addressing her remarks to the media, began to talk to the people in the courtyard through the windows. And I felt she would have felt far more comfortable having the press listening outside, and the people inside, instead of the reverse.

"And then, just as abruptly as it had begun, the FEMA official who had set up the conference terminated it. It couldn't have gone on for more that fifteen minutes. We were forcibly ushered out of the room, and through a second series of secret passageways into waiting cars and literally whisked away to the airport. It was unlike any press event I've been involved in or witnessed, and must stand as a classic example of how not to do such things."

I would see William Hedeman only one more time after that, and then almost two years would pass before we met again. But of course I did not know that then. I knew only that the days were beginning to fly by, and things were definitely not getting better. I had been afraid that firing Rita Lavelle would stir up the media, but I never dreamed it would ignite a firestorm of criticism and a rash of allegations against me and those who worked for me.

The rest of the "Times Beach week"—the first week of my life as Mrs. Robert Burford—would include trips to Arizona, California, back to Washington, D.C., and then on to Colorado, all of this between midafternoon Tuesday and Friday evening. There was to be a sort of second wedding reception for us in Denver on Saturday night. But in between I covered an awful lot of ground—not just physical, but also political, and even historic.

I was in Arizona for only two days, but it seemed longer. I had two speeches to make in Phoenix, one on Wednesday and one on Thursday, but that wasn't what exhausted me. What wore me down was a series of telephone calls that began on Wednesday. I was standing in the office of the Dean of the Arizona Law School when a call came from the White House. It was Jim Baker's number-one man, Craig Fuller calling to read me the names of several people whom he and his boss—but mainly his boss, I am sure—had decided should replace several of my high-level people at EPA.

Originally, Mr. Fuller seemed to be concentrating only on what he and Jim Baker perceived as the need to replace John Horton, my Assistant Administrator for Administration. There were allegations that Horton had used his government office, car, and employees for personal business, and other charges along that line, which ordinarily would have been handled fairly routinely by an internal investigation conducted by our Inspector General. But the current climate was different, and Fuller and Baker and others apparently had decided that changes had to be made, even if those changes involved only appearances.

I argued vehemently that we shouldn't replace people on the basis of allegations. Horton had been a good worker, a good supporter of the President, and he deserved better than that. What's more, I didn't even *know* the person Fuller was suggesting as his replacement. I recall I said that if this absolutely has to be done, then why not bring in Robert Broadbent, who was at Interior, and whom I thought to be a very able man. "No," said Fuller, "bringing in someone from Interior wouldn't look good." I managed to put Fuller off, explaining that it was time to make my speech.

That night, when I saw the hotel room—the hotel *suite*—I almost cried. Friends in Arizona thought perhaps Robert would be able to accompany me, and that maybe we could have a brief honeymoon in their beautiful state, so they reserved the Barry Goldwater Suite in the Biltmore Hotel. It all but knocked me out. The view was simply spectacular. Floor-to-ceiling glass walls in both the huge living room and bedroom provided a magnificent view of a wall of different mountains, Squaw Peak directly in front, then Camelback, and from the terrace I could make out South Mountains far off in the distance.

Unfortunately, Robert was not with me. My companion was Cristy Bach, who was nominally one of my two travel coordinators, but who was swiftly becoming, in the heat of battle, both personal aide and close confidant. Cristy was only twenty-three at the time, a fairly recent journalism graduate of Michigan State who had worked for the Governor of Michigan, but she was swiftly developing good, strong shoulders. And she was getting a very revealing look at what she had originally thought would be her chosen profession.

The next morning, before I was even dressed, I got another phone call from Craig Fuller. This time he had John Daniel on the line in a conference call from Washington, and he had added a few more names to the list of people he and Jim Baker wanted to get rid of—and they wanted me to go along with it, to make it look as if all of this was being done with my "blessing." At one point in the rather lengthy and acrimonious conversation I looked up and was startled to see all the natural beauty laid out before me. What a contrast, I thought. To see such splendor while hearing about such duplicity.

Now the White House insiders wanted to replace Mathew Novick, EPA's Inspector General, who'd been accused of being less than diligent, which I considered a very untrue and unfair charge, and they also had targeted Lee Modesitt, my Congressional Affairs man. Considering how Congress felt about EPA, which was in large part the fault of the White House and the Department of Justice and their damn executive privilege business, even Pope John XXIII would have made enemies in that job. To blame Modesitt was to miss the point.

Fuller kept pressing—there were more phone calls the next day—and finally I gave in. Even though I didn't know the new replacements, I agreed to their coming aboard after Baker's people promised to find a spot for Matt Novick at the Department of Energy. Modesitt was dropped down a notch within EPA, but at least he wasn't let go, which is what Baker's people wanted to do to him and to Novick. But John Horton was "asked to resign" and I let it happen. I will always consider that one of my biggest mistakes. He didn't deserve it, and I should have had more guts. Fortunately, he had several thriving businesses to return to, but that is not the point. I should have resigned then and there.

I gave my speech, and we left Phoenix immediately after.

The next morning, in San Francisco, while I was meeting in my hotel room with Sonia Crowe, my Administrator for Region IX, I got another call from the White House. This time we talked about more than just personnel matters. We discussed, heatedly, the ongoing battle over the documents. Even though the Justice Department lawyers had capitulated to (or cooperated with, depending on which side you are on) Mr. Levitas's committee, they were now in the midst of the very same battle with John Dingell's committee!

Incredibly, to my way of thinking, the DOJ lawyers and the White House were not about to give Dingell what they had so recently agreed to give Levitas. They seemed to think that Dingell would be satisfied with less. It made absolutely no sense on the face of it, and it was crazy in the context of the press furor that had erupted.

(Just how bizarre the press coverage had become was evident when we reached San Francisco. Also traveling on the same plane were the singer Tom Jones and his band. When he deplaned, he did so with a big smile for the crush of photographers and cameramen and reporters that he encountered. But his smile faded when he realized they were all for me. Or should I say "after" me?)

Papers across the country were running stories, many of them based on the leaks by EPA employees who were tired of hearing their agency accused of wrongdoing day after day but who figured with all that noise *something* must be wrong, stories that were little more than speculation as to what the "enforcement-sensitive documents" might contain. Suspicion had been great before I'd had to fire Rita, but now it seemed that everyone believed the worst. And here was the White House, on one hand replacing people with my apparent concurrence, and on the other saying it wanted to preserve the historic doctrine of executive privilege. It was enough to make a disbeliever out of anyone.

Sonia Crowe tried to get me to calm down, describing their actions as just more politics as usual. But I couldn't calm down. I was too damn angry.

I soon got another call from Fuller, and once again he had John Daniel with him. It quickly became apparent that Fuller and I were talking at cross purposes. I wanted him to get the message to the President that the idea of resisting the Dingell subpoena was all wrong, and that whoever was telling him to follow that course was misadvising him. Fuller, however, was more interested in lining up my *apparent* support for the high-level personnel changes at EPA.

In my half of the conversation, I told Fuller sharply, "This whole scandal will continue until the documents are turned over, and I don't think the President is being well served. And I don't think things will improve with the Levitas agreement. Why you people think so is beyond me. I think we ought to turn those goddamn documents over, or we're going to bring this President to his knees."

Fuller then began a strong push for my support of the personnel changes that Jim Baker was making at EPA. And as he did so, I kept thinking, "God, if John Dingell or some of the other Congressmen who've been beating on me had any idea that Baker was making PAS-level appointments at EPA without so much as checking with me, there would be some kind of hell to pay!"

Fuller said, "We can't let another day go by without appointing strong managers over there. We're up against the wall in needing to make this announcement today. We're holding off people who are saying more ought to be done."

I told him I thought the idea of having me announce the changes in the EPA staff was a big mistake. "I'm having a real problem with this. These are people I've never met. I've tried to put a good face on this whole mess against my better judgment. Frankly, I think it may be better to cancel my appearances and let you all make your announcements."

"Anne, we need your help in getting this story out."

"But you want me to say I approve of these changes, and I've never even talked with these people about working at EPA."

"Personally," said Fuller, "my heart goes out to you. And I don't like asking you to lie. I'll join with you on the documents question." And then he added, "The White House will do anything you want us to say or do."

"But you're *not* doing anything I want you to say or do!"

It was one of the most exasperating conversations I've ever had. Just before we hung up I reminded him, "I love this President, and he's being misadvised. You have given the Democrats an issue they can ride forever. Politically, this is disastrous."

With that I went off to make my speech to the Western Coatings Societies Symposium, where I encountered what was perhaps the worst media crunch of my entire time at EPA. In fact, it was at that speech that Cristy Bach was almost seriously injured when a camerman swung around and struck her with a "portable" TV camera.

Once again we found ourselves entering a hotel through garages and back hallways, working our way up to the room where I was to speak. Unfortunately, in order to get to that room it was necessary to cross a hallway and go through another room, and in that room was assembled a virtual mob of reporters and media people.

Earlier that day, back in Washington, Larry Speakes had made the announcement of the three "replacements" at EPA, and some of the press clearly smelled red meat. I told Cristy that I would have no comment for the press, and I told her to let them know that. I went on ahead.

As she recalls it, "There must have been fifty of them, at least that many. They were just pushing and shoving, and when they heard that she wouldn't talk to them, they began to move off to the balcony that surrounded the room where she was to speak. I told them there would be no comment, and they kept ignoring that and saying, 'Is she going to say something?' Finally, I said, 'What do you thing *silence* indicates?'

"When they began to move it was like a stampede. That's when I got hit with the camera as this guy moved past me. I almost got knocked down. And he didn't say a thing, couldn't have cared less! They were after a story and that was it."

The next morning we were back in Washington, and I met my "new team members" as soon as I got in. Lee Thomas, of course, I had met on the way to Times Beach, but the others were strangers. Out of curiosity I asked the others, "Now that you're here, who do you feel you are working for?"

"Oh," said one of them baldly, "we work for Jim Baker. We're just here at EPA to rescue you."

At the request of Fuller & Co. I held a press conference that day at which the new people were paraded before the media. I'd been asked to introduce them, and to say they were people "in whom I am well pleased." I handled the first part all right, but when I got to the endorsement, the words stuck in my throat. If I said them at all, which I doubt, it was in a mumble.

That was quite a day. Before it was over not only would I have met for the second time in several weeks with President Reagan, but I would also meet for the first time with Attorney General William French Smith in regard to the claim of executive privilege.

Of paramount importance in all of these meetings was the fact that the subpoena from John Dingell's subcommittee was returnable—it called for an answer, which meant my appearance with all requested documents—on March 10, only thirteen days away.

I had come back from my trip convinced that I had to make at least one more personal appeal to the President. On the night of February 24, while still in California, I told Craig Fuller I wanted to see the President the next day. He said he'd try to set it up. Also, Burford had suggested that I ask Senator Paul Laxalt for help, and the Senator kindly agreed to go with me to the White House to see his good friend the President. Some months later John Daniel would recall that meeting in testimony before Mr. Dingell's committee. It is a most accurate account.

[Congressman] SIKORSKI. Did the Administrator explain to you her hopes and what she expected to accomplish with the President?

Mr. DANIEL. Yes . . . her hope was to get the President to agree to a full release of all the documents.

Mr. SIKORSKI. Who was at the meeting with the President?

Mr. DANIEL. The meeting included the President, the Vice President, Senator Laxalt, the Administrator, and myself.

Mr. SIKORSKI. Where were Messrs. Fielding and Meese and Baker?

Mr. DANIEL. They were already out in California preparing for the arrival of the Queen of England who was coming in the next week.

Mr. SIKORSKI. What did the Administrator tell the President?

Mr. DANIEL. She made another very strong plea for release of the documents and she reminded him just as she had said the stories won't go away, with the agreement with Mr. Levitas, indeed they had not gone away and moreover there was nothing left of executive privilege after the agreement with Mr. Levitas.

There is no privilege left. That there is something there that someone still claims to be but there really isn't, and that he was not being well served by continuing to permit the withholding of these documents.

Mr. SIKORSKI. What was the President's response?

Mr. DANIEL. The President's response was I think very sympathetic with her position but he asked of her, what did Bill have to say about this.

Mr. SIKORSKI. Bill is who?

I still smile when I think of that question, because it was exactly the question I had asked the President. Up to that point Mr. Reagan had indeed been listening carefully and seemed to be quite sympathetic to what I was saying. I had the feeling that he was about to indicate agreement, that he would take my advice and order all the documents released to the Dingell subcommittee. But then he paused, and asked if I had talked to "Bill."

"Who's 'Bill'?" I said.

"The Attorney General, William French Smith," said the President, giving me a bit of an odd look.

"Oh," I said.

Mr. DANIEL. It turned out that Bill was Attorney General Smith and when she told him that she had never talked with the Attorney General about this, he turned to Mr. Fuller and instructed him to arrange for a meeting with the Administrator and the Attorney General to review the questions that she had raised.

Mr. SIKORSKI. During this whole period of time from September 1982 through February 1983 the EPA Administrator had never met with the Attorney General?

Mr. DANIEL. That is right, sir.

Mr. SIKORSKI. Did Mr. Laxalt raise any statement at this point?

Mr. DANIEL. Yes, sir, at the end of the meeting he approached the President and in a very quiet way told the President that the Administrator was correct and that the documents ought to be released.

Mr. SIKORSKI. Without any redaction?

Mr. DANIEL. Yes, just that the documents should be released to the Congress, all of them.

The meeting with "Bill" was cold, unproductive, and upsetting. The Attorney General was accompanied by Mr. Schmultz and Carol Dinkins, and by Craig Fuller and Dick Hauser from the White House. As the Attorney General was noticeably unsympathetic to my position, it was not a long meeting. I outlined why I thought the president was being ill served; Smith nodded and dismissed what I had said.

Flanked by his aides, who were dramatically placed in his huge office, the Attorney General made a brief statement, which sounded memorized, about the "historic significance of this privilege which has existed since the days of George Washington," and so on and on. I would have been tempted to laugh if the situation were different.

"But this is post-Watergate 1983," I said heatedly. "Not the days of George Washington. Your people have bargained away any remnants of the doctrine of executive privilege. I feel very strongly that these documents should all be released, and I feel equally strongly that the President is being misserved."

The meeting ended on a particularly bizarre note. With no warning or preamble, the Attorney General fixed me with a cold look and said, in an equally cold voice, "Your problems at EPA began long before you were required to assert executive privilege."

Stunned, I said, "How the hell would *you* know?"

That night Burford and I flew to Denver. We encountered mobs of reporters as we left, but we managed to shake them, and it was with a distinct feeling of relief that we saw Washington disappear beneath us.

The next night, at the Poundstones' home, Robert and I were congratulated by a hundred people, many of whom we had not seen for a year or two, which meant that the last time we'd seen them our lives had been a lot simpler. Still, I was not going to admit just how difficult things had become, at least not to the press.

The next day's Denver *Post* story of the "troubles" at EPA contained an insert by a feature writer. It said in part, "Mrs.

Burford, looking more relaxed as the evening wore on, reflected that when she told a reporter, 'Everybody tries to hit me with this "embattled" stuff. But the only people who are embattled are with the press. I was reading *The New York Times* on the way to Denver, and page after page, they seem to have almost everyone who's worked with me in my agency already convicted.' . . . Asked whether she planned to abide by her decision—announced earlier last week in San Francisco—not to resign as EPA head, she said, 'Hell, yes. I'm here and I'm feeling good.' . . . 'Gosh! You're looking great after all you've been through,' one woman on the receiving line said to Mrs. Burford, who wore the same brown dress as on her wedding day a week ago in Washington. And Mrs. Burford—who did look great—seemed genuinely glad to be among supporters for a change."

That comment was very true: I certainly was glad to be among supporters for a change. As to my boast that I was feeling good, I may have been at that moment, but the pace and the pressure were having their effect. Increasingly, I felt tired and, yes, put upon. But I'd be damned if I was going to admit that to a *reporter*.

15

WITH FRIENDS LIKE THESE...

To his credit the President resolutely denied all talk of "scandal" at EPA. But as February turned into March a lot of people must have thought he was whistling past the graveyard. Like mortar shells, one charge after another hit the airwaves and the front pages. And they all exploded.

There were charges, leaked of course and based on unnamed sources, that we were employing a paper shredder in the bowels of EPA to destroy incriminating evidence. Then another unnamed internal source said that I had held up the release of $6.1 million in cleanup funds due the state of California for its work on the Stringfellow Dump because it might have benefited Democratic Governor Jerry Brown, who was running for the United States Senate. What's more, it was also charged that as a way of justifying the Stringfellow deal, I also ordered that a Minnesota cleanup action be delayed for a year.

Eventually, after excruciating investigations by the EPA Inspector General, the FBI, and a federal grand jury, not a one of these charges made it into the pages of an indictment, or even a criminal or civil complaint. But at the time they *looked* horrible, and it was becoming more and more obvious that what we were dealing with here were *perceptions* and *appearances*, certainly not reality. But then bad press, when there's enough of it, takes on a hard reality of its own. And I had more than enough problems of the real variety to deal with.

Often, at the worst of times something so bizarre will happen that all you can do is laugh. I had been forewarned: in 1982, Congressman Boland, a Democrat from Massachusetts, called us before his subcommittee. He is an excellent chairman who knows what he wants, insists on getting it, and is not hesitant to give praise regardless of party lines when he gets the type of cooperation he seeks, especially with regard to budgetary matters, his special interest.

Following our three days of testimony, he said, "Mrs. Burford, I want to congratulate you on a very thoroughly prepared budget. This is the best budget presentation I have received from EPA. Now we would like you to submit to the committee in writing how you would spend an *additional* $50 million dollars."

I think that was the lowest day of my EPA life. It seemed to me that with that attitude on Capitol Hill we would never get out of the budgetary mess we were in. I called David Stockman and told him what had happened and asked him to issue a ruling prohibiting me and any other member of the Executive Branch from responding to that request. He did, but that did not deter the committee. EPA was given the extra $50 million anyway. Later, we spent days in an intense but ultimately successful lobbying effort to keep the full House from giving us another $70 to $80 million!

On the last day of February I was in Washington again, and facing the incredible (to me) fact that the Department of Justice was still determined to give Congressman Dingell *less* than it had given Mr. Levitas.

John Daniel and I had a discussion with Dick Hauser about what instructions we were to give any EPA employees who might be supoenaed by Dingell. According to Hauser, none of the "redacted" documents that had been given to Levitas were to be given to Dingell; that, he said, was the way he and Schmults and Dinkins wanted it. "Let him get them from Levitas," said Hauser.

"You must be nuts," I said, no longer caring about protocol. "I'm going to tell my people to do just the opposite. All members of Congress are entitled to anything given to one member of Congress."

Hauser said, "I feel uncomfortable about that." But later that day he called back to say that he had talked to Fred Fielding, and there had been a switch: Justice now took the position that any documents given to Levitas in redacted form could also be given to Dingell. But, he added, "We don't want anything going to Dingell that hasn't gone through the process."

As if I hadn't enough to worry about, February 28 was also the day that Craig Fuller told John Daniel that Jim Baker was "on the warpath" because of a speech I'd made in Colorado several days earlier, in which I'd suggested that Republican supporters urge the White House to turn over the documents. Any such remarks in the future, Fuller warned, would "hurt" me. What did he think I was already, *unscathed*?

March came in like a lion, with three events taking place on the first, each of which was decidedly serious.

John Daniel got a call from our Congressional liaison, Lee Modesitt informing him that Congressman Peter Rodino, Chairman of the House Judiciary Committee, had been quoted as instructing his staff to begin impeachment proceedings against Attorney General Smith "for obstructing a lawful Congressional investigation." The second event of more than passing interest was that John Dingell wrote to the President stating that Rita Lavelle had perjured herself in testimony before his subcommittee; he also said that Mr. Reagan should release the documents.

I was directly involved in the third event. That day I went up to the Hill. Based on the fact that the Justice Department-negotiated agreement with Congress had turned my agency into a "paper-producing factory," I wanted a supplemental appropriation. I told the legislators that my agency was crippled by the turmoil, that "we can't operate in this atmosphere." I also suggested that an independent commission be established to look into allegations of mismanagement in the Superfund program, because I was satisfied that with the exception of whatever Rita Lavelle might have done, we would all come out with a clean bill of health. (I knew as I spoke that Congress was not interested in sharing its oversight powers; there were already six different Congressional bodies investigating the agency.)

"As long as we have this circus atmosphere," I told them, "we will be inhibited from doing our job. So much of my staff's time is being spent in gathering documents for you that they have little time left for work." I told them "their time would be far better spent trying to clean up America," and I went on to defend the record of my twenty-two months as EPA Administrator. But I don't think I made many converts at that late date.

Here's an example of the way some of the Members felt: When I mentioned that the Justice Department would be checking out any allegations of wrongdoing at EPA, one Democrat responded by saying, "That's tantamount to letting the wolf count the chickens."

It was reported in the papers the next day, and on the morning and evening news, that at several points during my testimony my voice cracked, and that I "appeared on the verge of tears." I'd like to deny that. But it was true. Things *were* beginning to get to me.

It was at about this point that my friend Maiselle Shortly suggested I talk to her friend Linda Godsden, who had handled the press for Drew Lewis when he was head of FAA (Federal Aviation Administration). Linda was a real pro, and her suggestion was blunt and to the point: "Anne, you're getting killed in the press because they don't know you *want* to cooperate with the Congress. I think you ought to let all those White House types take a flying leap. So what you should do is to bag all the documents up, put them in a van, and truck them over to the Hill. But first you alert a TV crew!"

It was a great suggestion, and I almost followed it; I had John Daniel set it up. But then, at the last minute, I called Jim Baker, in a pang of conscience over breaking an Executive Order, even a terminally shredded one, and he had a fit. So I dropped the plan. But it would have had a *great* impact. And it would have made me feel wonderful, because the press coverage was definitely getting out of hand.

By this point I couldn't even get dressed without checking my dressing room window—one morning there'd been a reporter peering in! And the street in front of my house was now jammed with press people all day, every day. One morning at 6:30 I was awakened by a neighbor calling to see if I planned to call the police about the "traffic jam" on our little cul de sac. I said, "No, I don't need that kind of press either. But I sure wouldn't mind if you would call the head of the citizens' association and have him call the police." "But what are *you* going to do?" she persisted. "Me?" I groaned, "I'm going back to sleep."

But it was not a joking matter. Things were getting out of

hand. Cristy had been hit with a camera, I'd about had my eye put out with a boom mike that some enterprising sound person stuck into my garage. And a Washington *Post* reporter had even tried to reach my oldest son, Neil, at Georgetown Prep to "get his side of the story." (When I complained to her editor and he asked her about it, she lied and said Neil had called her first. She had "forgotten" that the headmaster had taken her call and her request. What's more, anybody who knew us was well aware that if Neil wanted to give his side of the matter to a reporter, it wouldn't be one from the Washington *Post*.) And every time we pulled away from the house, one or two tiny Le Cars were soon right behind us.

At my March 1 appearance on the Hill I had made one thing quite clear: What I termed the "miasma" surrounding EPA would not change until all the requested documents were given to Congress. Later that day John Daniel got a call from Craig Fuller who said he was going to discuss the White House response with Fred Fielding. The next day he called John again and said the White House would respond to the Dingell letter "along the lines of providing access," but he seemed to say that the White House viewed this as being less than complete access.

Here are the notes that John Daniel made to help him recall the events of March 2 when he was asked some months later to testify about them before Mr. Dingell's committee:

> Craig Fuller called again to say that Speakes in his press briefing that day was going to say: Congress can have complete access to documents in conjunction with oversight of EPA. Congress is not to be denied access to any document. This, of course, extends the Levitas agreement to all committees of Congress.

> Fuller noted that Speakes would down play the "process" [involved in the Levitas agreement, a "process" which was certainly less than full access].

> For AMG, I stated our non-concurrence. I said that we should respond that all documents would be turned over to Congress.

> Fuller said White House position is that they'll get the doc-

uments, have possession of redacted documents and can see them all. He said he couldn't see how Dingell could object.

JED [John E. Daniel] responded by asking why Dingell hadn't already accepted earlier offer? Fuller wanted Anne to "stick with this" through today; they can't go any further for now.

The next day was the worst I'd had so far. I was somewhat surprised to learn that Ed Schmults and Carol Dinkins had requested a meeting with me in my office at 6:30 that evening. Present at that meeting in addition to the two Justice Department lawyers were myself, John Daniel, Bob Perry, and one of his sharpest lawyers, Gerry Yamada. Also present for EPA was Lee Modesitt, my recently (and unfairly) demoted Congressional Affairs man.

Schmults, a large and rather ponderous man with a manner to match, set the serious tone of the meeting from the beginning. It took him very little time to get to the point. And it took me very little time to understand it: The Department of Justice was no longer going to provide me with legal representation in the fight with Congress over executive privilege! I could hardly believe my ears.

This is the conversation that took place, based on my memory and that of John Daniel, plus the notes he took at the time and later wrote out in somewhat more detail.

Schmults began by saying, "We have to make some adjustments in our representation of you as a result of your referrals for investigation and, ah, I feel what we, the Department of Justice, have to do is to give primacy to our investigative role, and wall off our criminal investigations from continuing and our civil representations . . . the rest of the department can't participate in White House counsel negotiations with Hill committees. Carol can't be privy to meetings regarding the investigations. That *may* present a problem of who from Justice goes up with the Administrator and Perry to hearings. . . . [Justice] can't fulfill that role anymore as it would muddy . . ."

"Wait a minute," I interrupted, having finally found my tongue, "are you telling me that I'm not entitled to DOJ representation

before Hill committees while fulfilling my role in answering subpoenas?"

"Yes."

"That's not what I was told when we got into this."

"We'll have to talk to Fielding and Hauser," he said.

Then I had a disturbing thought. "Am I under investigation?"

"Not at the present time."

"But then I am entitled to representation by the Justice Department. You can wall off another part of DOJ."

At that point Bob Perry made a suggestion: "You can withdraw
the President's order to withhold the documents."

"We can't do that."

I was getting madder by the second. "You got me into this
saying you could represent me against the contempt charge. Now
you say you can't."

"Our role has changed."

At that point my instincts may have taken over, for I said, "Put
it in writing by noon tomorrow."

Schmults's only answer was, "It's in the hands of White House
Counsel [meaning Fred Fielding] and Jim Baker, regarding executive privilege and the Congress.

At that point Bob Perry cut in with a question that I should
have asked myself, "Have you discussed this with the President?"

"No."

"I think," said Perry, "you have a moral obligation to recommend to the President to withdraw the order."

Schmults said nothing, and I sat there stunned. Finally I said,
"This is bizarre. You're saying that an administration official acting
under orders of the President is not entitled to Department of
Justice counsel!"

"I've told you," said Schmults laboriously, as if he were talking
to someone of below average intelligence who was having difficulty
following him, "we feel we have a conflict of interest."

Several people began to talk at once, with Gerry Yamada and
Bob Perry making no bones about how little they thought of Mr.
Schmults's message. When he repeated that "We can't represent
the agency and investigate it too," I said what so distressed me,
in light of all the bad publicity that EPA had been getting for
weeks: "This is going to look terrible."

At that point I got a call from Burford. Ordinarily Charlotte would not have put it through, but she knew he and I were scheduled to leave town that night, and we had already postponed our flight once. When I heard his familiar gravelly voice I realized instantly how much I wished he were there with me. I told him briefly what was taking place, and his reply was unprintable.

A few moments later I cut in the conversation to say to the Deputy Assistant Attorney General, "I've been told repeatedly that the existing order still applies, and that Justice was going to work it out with Dingell and everyone else."

He replied pompously, "The White House is assuming all responsibility for negotiating with Mr. Dingell."

There was another brief interchange between Schmults and my people, and then suddenly I heard a small cry from my secretary as the doors to my office burst open and in charged my husband. It was the first time he'd ever come into my office unannounced! "Damn it all," he roared, "you're the turkeys who got her into this!"

I thought Schmults's eyes would pop out. Puffing himself up, he said, "I came here for a scholarly discussion of the issues, not to be talked to rudely."

I realized things were not going to get better. "Wait a minute," I said, "let's close this discussion. I want your decision in writing."

There was some more talk, but basically the meeting had ended. I had the next-to-last word: "What they're trying to do . . ." I paused, and then two things hit me, with a force that was almost physical. "The only way I can avoid another contempt citation is to no longer be the Administrator." It was suddenly crystal clear to me that the only way the Justice Department could justify this new posture was to find that I had done something illegal.

Schmults said in a tone I found less than convincing, "That's not what we're up to. That's not why I'm over here."

Sure, turkey!

Things were getting increasingly strange. On the night of the Conservative Political Action Committee (CPAC) dinner, at which the President spoke, I was still in my office when I received a call from Burford telling me that I had to get over to the dinner immediately because President Reagan wanted to acknowledge me publicly from the podium before his speech. I tried mightily, arriving at the wrong hotel on the way, but by the time I got there it was too late.

The next morning the President called and said, "Anne, I just wanted to tell you how happy I am that Fred Fielding and the others have been able to work out this wonderful compromise with the House."

I lost my voice for a moment, and then said boldly, "Mr. President, I don't know who's advising you on this matter, but that was the *worst* agreement possible. It doesn't solve *anything*!"

His response was a stunned silence. Finally, he said something about how he just wanted to tell me how pleased he had been, and that was it. It struck me then—as it would again later on—that Mr. Reagan seems at a loss when the response to his first statement or question is unexpected. I don't mean to make too much of the prepared-script analogy, but it does seem he has great difficulty dealing with an "unscripted" response.

I was in a hell of a bind. The Dingell subpoena was returnable in one week, on March 10, and the White House and the Department of Justice were still talking about giving Dingell less than he had asked for. There wasn't a doubt in my mind that he would respond by citing me for criminal contempt, and, as Mr. Levitas had already proven, there would be no problem with getting the full House to go along. And now I didn't even have a lawyer! First, counselor Fielding convinced me to drop the private lawyer I'd hired to advise me, and now the Department of Justice had decided it could no longer represent me on the Hill.

What really infuriated me was the thought that not only had this same Justice Department talked me into spearheading the fight over the doctrine of executive privilege, but they had also tried their damnedest to get me to go on the lawsuit against the House of Representatives *personally* as a private citizen. At least I had the satisfaction of having won that battle; if I hadn't, my situation would have been even worse, though at the moment that was hard to imagine.

The immediate hours and days after that meeting were probably the scariest of my entire life. It had been apparent to me, and I think to John Daniel too, that the only way for me to avoid a second contempt citation was to resign as Administrator of EPA. That wasn't the scary part; what sent a chill down my spine was the thought that the only way the Justice Department could "win" was to make sure that I "lost." It was akin to the feeling one must get on learning the IRS is about to do an audit. I had to believe that the full force of the Justice Department plus the FBI looking into everything I'd ever done would eventually find *something*, and even if it wasn't bad, if it only *looked* bad, it could seriously disrupt my life, and cost me a small fortune in legal bills to defend the charges.

And what made those fears plausible was that every day there was a new "scandal" being uncovered by some enterprising reporter or leaked by someone. But now it appeared that the leaks weren't coming only from EPA. They were also coming from the *White House*! I had been warned that Jim Baker was "on the warpath" because two weeks earlier I had urged Western Republican leaders to let the White House and the President know they thought the documents should be turned over to Congress; but I didn't like the thought that he and his people would use such sneaky tactics to get back at—or get rid of—me. Ah, politics.

In addition to worrying about leaks, I had two other concerns. A major exception to the enforcement-sensitive restriction on Superfund documents that my people at EPA were pouring over daily was anything that might be construed as giving even the appearance of wrongdoing. And in late February and early March we found several of these. One of them, which I'll explain in some detail later, originated not in EPA but in the Justice Department itself. What's more, Rita Lavelle was still around, dropping what she hoped were new bombshells every few days, in an effort to build a smokescreen around her own troubles.

Was I getting paranoid? Hardly. Consider Deputy Attorney General Schmults's answer when I asked him if I were under investigation by the Department of Justice, his answer was "not at this time," which to me had sounded a lot like "No, but you will be." And certainly by this point I had no reason to trust the people at Justice.

The pressure was beginning to show. The weekend before, while out in California, I had been a guest on a talk show. To my great relief the majority of callers were very sympathetic to my point of view. Finally the support, to which I had grown unaccustomed, triggered a basic emotional response—I started to cry. Cristy Bach, who was with me in the studio, was astounded. It was the first time she had seen me cry. Later, she kidded me, "You're so tough, I didn't think you *could* cry."

On Friday morning, March 4, Cristy left early to do advance

work for a dinner speech I was to give that evening to the "1983 Biennial Louisiana Federation of Republican Women." As I feared, the tornado had already begun to touch down.

Cristy Bach has a vivid recollection of those last days and weeks:

"The intense press attention really started at Christmas, but since there wasn't much travel then, it picked up in January and February, and the more things got heated up, the worse the press coverage got. San Francisco was the worst as far as the press crush, and then on the Denver trip—not the last one, but the one prior to that—Anne got off the plane, and there was this huge crowd of people and press, and my heart stopped beating. Because she and I were walking up the runway, and there were all these cameras and reporters waiting.

"In New Orleans, on March 4, it was raining, and they were letting Anne out of the back of the plane because we had a limo waiting. I was standing under the wing of the plane, and we had to rush to get back to the hotel because we were almost late for her speech. We made it to the hotel, and my hair was all wet, so I looked and discoverd that when I was standing under the plane, oil had dripped into my hair. But there wasn't time to take a shower, so I quickly brushed my hair back and went to the reception and dinner with oil in my hair. It was awful. Under any other circumstances I would not have budged from that room until I'd showered and washed my hair!

"When Anne tried to walk into the dining room, the press was blocking her way, and they were walking backwards, as she was trying to walk in. It was just a zoo."

I remember that night rather well myself. The Republican women were very supportive, and that was a big help, but I was still wound up from my meeting the night before with Schmults and Dinkins. I had more than one drink following the speech. Trying to unwind, I kept Mike and Cristy up half the night talking. Cristy was supposed to get up for an early flight to Denver the next morning to arrange for the speech I was giving there, but finally I told her to forget about it and come with us on the later flight. It was just as well, because there was a huge thunderstorm that night, and she couldn't have made the early flight anyway.

As it had been mild in Washington and New Orleans, we had taken a chance and not packed our coats. When we got to Denver on Friday, with but one change of clothes, we encountered a major snowstorm that socked Denver in until Sunday afternoon. Frieda Poundstone met us at the airport, and again we went through a labyrinth to elude the press and get to her van for the trip to the hotel where I was to speak.

I gave the speech my best shot—these were Republican women and it was my home town—but I was showing signs of exhaustion by this point. All I wanted was to lie down for a while, but I had all sorts of people to see. And then, as it turned out, certain people wanted to see me.

16

WERE *THEY* TOUGH ENOUGH?

Up in the hotel room Steve Durham, my Regional Administrator for the area, asked me if he could speak to me "in private."

"Where, for God's sake?" I asked.

"Ah, how about the bathroom?"

We actually went into the bathroom and closed the door.

"What," I asked sharply, "is it that you couldn't say it in front of Frieda?"

He said, "Joe wants to talk to you."

Other than my father, I knew only one "Joe" in Denver important enough to be identified by his first name. Joe Coors.

"Fine, but why the secrecy?"

"Because I don't think he wants it known."

I assumed that Coors wanted to hear first hand what was going on, so I put a quick call in to John Daniel (it was by then 3 A.M. Washington time) telling him to get the latest and most complete chronology of the whole battle, and get on the next plane for Denver. I knew Joe Coors well enough to know that all this was pretty unusual. Joe had supported me in both my political races, and I had met him any number of times socially over the years, but he and I had never had a conversation about any political issue, ever.

The second thing that was unusual was that he wanted me to

come to his home. I had been there before, but again only on social occasions, and I'd never known him to do any work at home.

Of course I agreed to go. I waited until John Daniel arrived, and then Frieda's husband Mel, a very sweet guy, insisted on driving us up there himself and waiting, even though it was still snowing like mad.

Joe asked me to join him in his study. It was the first and only time I'd ever been in that room. I settled in, thinking I'd be there quite a while, as it was a long story to tell to someone who hadn't been in on it.

With no preamble Joe Coors said, sort of blurting it out, "They want you to resign."

" 'They'? Who are 'they'?" It was all I could think of to say.

"People very close to the President."

"But why are you doing their dirty work for them?"

With a half-smile he said, "I never could refuse Ronnie anything."

My response was, and to this day I am amazed that I had the presence of mind to think of it, "What's in it for me, Joe? What do I get out of it?"

"You get out."

"That's not good enough. Six months ago I tried to get an appointment with the President to offer to step down after the first two years of his term, but I was never able to get in to see him for that purpose. That 'get out' deal would have been fine six months ago, but not now. It's not enough."

"What do you want?"

For some reason I had the answer ready. "I want three things. I want my people, the people I hired, taken care of—no wholesale firings; I want my legal bills paid; and I want a reappointment to a decent post in this term of this administration."

He said, "I'll make sure you get all three of those things."

Moments later the meeting was over, and I was back in the car. I looked at my watch and was startled to see that the whole thing had lasted less than half an hour.

That night on the evening news President Reagan was quoted as reaffirming his "strong support" for me. I did not hear it, as Cristy and Mike Sawyer, my other traveling companion, and John and I were having dinner. Suddenly, there was a waiter with a phone saying he had a call for Mrs. Burford. It was Holly Coors,

Joe's wife, and she said, "Oh, Anne, I just heard the President on television, and he said he supports you. Isn't that good news?" Obviously Holly had not been eavesdropping at the study door that afternoon.

Getting out of Denver was worse than arriving there, because the storm had canceled a lot of flights. On Sunday, when the weather cleared, the airport was mobbed. I finally managed to get seats for me and Cristy, but I left John Daniel and Mike Sawyer to fend for themselves. As soon as the "No Smoking" sign went off I reached for a cigarette, and was about to perform my other ritualistic habit—asking Cristy Bach to hand me some EPA documents to work on—when I realized that my life had just changed. It may not have been official yet, but I had no doubt that it would take no more than a few days for the verbal deal I had struck with the White House, through Joe Coors, to take effect.

I realized with a start that I would have to learn a new, or at least a different, routine. For the past two years, minus two months, I had followed the same pattern. Never one to rise too early or to come into focus very quickly when I did rise (I kidded Burford when we got married that "I do floors and windows, but I don't do mornings") I usually arrived at EPA at 9:30 or 10:00. Generally I made about two speeches a week, so I was often out of the office or out of town at midday. When I was there, meetings with staff, or testifying at budget hearings, or returning phone calls (I never let a day go by without returning all my phone calls) usually consumed all the time until about 6:00 P.M. Then, when the phones shut down and things got quiet, we got down to the real business. All my Assistant Administrators knew they could get to see me, and have my full attention, between six and eight at night. I had an open-door policy. Of course, one had to get by Denise Mitstifer, my personal secretary who kept my schedule. Denise, whose job it now takes three full-time people to do, became known as the Dragon Lady of the Twelfth Floor.

And at the beginning, before we had the full complement of AAs in place, John Hernandez and I seemed to be the only ones there. We ran everything but the elevators. I was running the Air program, Superfund, and Toxics, and he was running Water, Drinking Water, and Research and Development. I personally reviewed every State Implementation Plan that came up, and they were usually several inches thick.

Most of my careful reading and study was done on airplanes. In order to do that, however, I'd had to change my usual pattern. Prior to coming to EPA, when I flew I was like so many other people—order a drink, have dinner, and read a novel. But as Administrator I'd put Cristy between me and anybody else, and take out about four inches of paper. Poor Cristy, she hardly had any room in her luggage for clothes because I made her carry so much paper. But I could get through an enormous amount of reading that way—regulatory drafts, regulatory packages, scientific literature, plus anything relative to the decision-making process. And when you sit atop a pyramid of ten thousand people with every major decision having to be made by you, an enormous amount of paper makes its way to your desk. (I had a policy of getting anything out of my office in one week, two weeks maximum. I was determined to avoid the bureaucratic clutter that had plagued earlier EPA administrations.) I would pray for long flights, because they meant I could get that much more work done.

So it was a very strange feeling, on that flight from Washington to Denver, to realize that for the first time in almost two years I really didn't have to spend my airtime busily and carefully reading some document. I didn't like the feeling.

I was anxious to see Robert again. He had spent most of that day getting recommendations for me for a new lawyer. As strange as it may sound, I would have been willing to go before John Dingell's subcommittee, four days away, without a lawyer. I still believed *that* strongly in my promise to Ronald Reagan. I had agreed to assert the doctrine of executive privilege, which now lay in tatters, thanks to the ineptitude of the Justice Department lawyers, and even though I had clearly been arguing for full release of the documents, I would nonetheless be ready to go before the committee and explain the President's position.

I was still that much of a loyal team player.

But that would have been a very unwise thing to do. There was too strong a scent of blood in the air, and too many wild allegations being made, for me to take that chance. So Burford had spent the day frantically searching for a good lawyer.

But first we had to get home from the airport, no small task as it turned out.

I called Robert and said, "Don't come and get us or send a driver, we'll just hop in a cab."

"Hold on," he said, "the street's crawling with press. It's been that way all weekend long, even though it hasn't stopped raining in two days. There are all sorts of cameras and reporters."

I told Cristy, who said, "Let's go to my house. It's only five minutes from yours, and then I can drive you home. They don't know my car."

That sounded like a good idea, so we hopped in a cab. We hadn't gone but a few hundred yards when the cabbie said, "You're Anne Burford, aren't you?"

"Yes."

"I thought so," he said, smiling, "I recognized the ring." Evidently, the large diamond Robert had given me televised well.

We got to Cristy's apartment house, and climbed into her snappy little Firebird. But first we called Robert and warned him, "Wait four and a half minutes and then press the button for the garage door!"

He did just that, and moments later Cristy came flying around the corner, tires squealing, and reporters looking up as we flashed past and—*zap!*—into the garage. Down went the door, and we were safe at home. They'd spent the entire weekend in the rain, and didn't have a single picture to show for it. I didn't feel a bit sorry.

(As recently as the week before I had been a real softie with what may have been some of the very same media people. Somehow I'd arrived at EPA when they weren't looking, and I'd gotten up to my office untouched by a single lens. But they sent a representative who moaned that they would get in trouble with their editors and bosses, so I actually went back down, had my driver take me around the block, and then got out, slowly, so they could get their footage of me arriving at work.)

Robert had some good news. He thought he had found a good lawyer. His name was Douglas Bennett, and he had been recommended by former Congressman Mike McKevitt who had been a DA in Denver. Bennett, a partner in the Atlanta firm of Powell, Goldstein, Frazier and Murphy, was in the Washington office, along with Stuart Eizenstat (and others) who had been Domestic Affairs advisor to President Jimmy Carter. What we liked about

Bennett's firm was that it had a good mix of Republicans and Democrats. Bennett himself knew Washington ways, having been in the personnel office in the Ford White House. I had an appointment to see him Monday afternoon.

But first I was determined to go to the beauty parlor. I was not going to let a pack of reporters keep me from my appointment. I told Cristy to be prepared for another stock car run on Monday morning.

She proved more than equal to the task. I fought through the crowd to her car, ignoring all comments, and we took off. We'd gotten only a few blocks away when Cristy looked in the rearview mirror, and said, "Nuts. We're being followed." This time it was both of the little Renaults.

As Cristy recalls it, "Being followed gives you the creepiest feeling. I'd never been followed before. I really hated it. But I drove as if I were on TV, because I decided to lose them in the middle of Memorial Bridge, but it was too hard to do with two of them. I did manage to lose one, though.

"I was supposed to just drop Anne off, but when we got there I said, 'I can't leave you with those guys following you.' So I parked, and when Anne went into the building, I just blocked the door so they couldn't come running in. These two reporters came plowing into me, but I just stood there and blocked the way. They couldn't get by. People were forming a small crowd, wondering what was going on. One reporter said, 'Hey, we're just trying to do our job,' and I said, 'Hey, so am I.' Several days later I'd hear from his boss.

"Anne did manage to get her nails done, but before we could get out of there, the phone had started ringing, with calls from reporters who had learned she was there and wanted to get her to make a comment.

"When we pulled out of the garage there was a car waiting to follow us. There was probably one at every exit. So off we went to EPA, and when we got there the reporters were all over the place, and I pulled right up to the door. If they hadn't moved I would have run right into them. Later my mother called me from Detroit and said, 'What are you doing? We saw you on television almost running over reporters!' So I let Anne out at the door. I was really mad, because we had a guard who was supposed to stop cars, but he just let the camera crews keep driving on by.

"Anne asked me to come up, and stay with her, just sit in her office while she had her meetings, and then we left EPA and went over to Doug Bennett's office. And Anne never came back."

From Monday through Wednesday, the day I resigned, the press crunch ws incredible. James Watt finally gave us some of his security people—an unmarked car and a driver, and another guy or two, Interior employees, who were tough guys, but very nice. (Cristy, who now works at Interior, sees them from time to time around the building, and they reminisce.)

The Monday session with Doug Bennett threatened to turn into an all-nighter. I was determined to get him to understand the full story in one sitting, and he made a valiant try.

Several times Doug protested that he had to get home because it was his son's birthday (he has six children), but even at that I kept talking, kept trying to get him to see the full picture and as many of the ramifications as possible. He faced the task not only of defending me in the event that the Justice Department went after me on some misconceived—or trumped-up!—charge, but he also was going to be dealing with the White House in negotiating my resignation. I wanted a clear understanding of the terms of our agreement, and he would be the one to talk with them. I was finished talking to those people, with one exception.

The night wore on, and I kept talking and talking, and finally Cristy got mad. "Look," she said, "you're so tired you can hardly talk straight. Go home and get some sleep." Doug Bennett was relieved to hear that, though Burford, who had been there almost from the beginning of the meeting, was kind of annoyed. Like me, he felt that it was very important that Bennett know as much as he could, because of the seriousness of what might happen. Finally I took Cristy's advice. I was too tired to go on.

Bright and early the next morning we were back in Doug's office, and we stayed at it all day. I did not let my office know where I was, and when it turned out I needed some papers, I had Cristy call John Daniel and have them driven past a corner in downtown Washington where she would be standing. He kept asking her where I was, but she wouldn't tell him, because then he could honestly tell the press he didn't know. And the press was out in force looking for me; my "friends" over at the White House were tripping over one another leaking the news that I was about to resign—or even, according to one version, be fired.

Cristy recalls, "John was really worried about Anne, and kept asking me over the phone where she was. And I just kept saying, 'I can't tell you. Anne's going to have to tell you. You're a lawyer, you should understand.'"

Finally by Wednesday morning Doug had reached everyone he had to reach, and had received all the assurances. Joe Coors reported that Meese had agreed to the payment of my legal bills, and there was approval of my two other conditions. So that was it. Resignation was real. All that remained was for me to tell the President, and I insisted on doing that in person.

So about five o'clock on a gray March afternoon four of us went over to the White House—Cristy Bach, Doug Bennett, Robert Burford, and me—where Jim Watt met us in Ed Meese's office. Ed didn't have much to say, but his manner was gentle, and I will always remember that gratefully.

Shortly before we went upstairs, Craig Fuller came into Meese's office. Several days earlier Fuller's face had been front and center on page one of the Washington *Post*. If he wasn't the King of Leakers, we didn't know who was. He started to say something about how sorry he was, and then he looked at Cristy and me, and quickly read the looks of pure hostility on our faces. He stopped in midsentence, and backed out of the room.

When the call came that the President was ready to see us, we learned that the meeting would take place in the family quarters. That meant we had to use a hallway that ran right past the open doorway to the press pool, which was packed with reporters who had been gorging on rumors for days. Ed Meese cleverly used his girth to block the view of our passing by on our way to the elevator.

As we went upstairs I was aware of being in control of myself, and I promised myself that I would definitely take the high road. I would say only that I realized that my resignation was being requested and that was fine with me, but that the President should know he was being terribly misserved by the people who had been advising him on this matter, that the people who worked for him had not been working in his best interest.

The President received us upstairs, and said little, so I began right away. I said, "You truly are being badly misserved by the people who have been advising you on this. Also, I have to say that I think having my friends," by which I meant Joe Coors, "do the dirty work of your staff at the same time you are on television saying you support me is, really, a less than honorable way to do business. I resent it, and I thought you should know that. But I am willing to resign, under the terms that have been agreed upon."

The President listened quietly to what I had to say, which did not take long. Although he was dressed informally, and was "at home" rather than in the office, he was noticeably ill at ease; the situation was unpleasant. He wanted to accept my resignation, not to hear criticism of his staff or *any* discussion of EPA. He made a comment that I can no longer recall, and that was it. We all got up and left. We could not have been there more than ten minutes.

When we returned to Meese's office, who should be standing out in the hallway but Fred Fielding and Dick Hauser. "Anne," said one of them, "look what we have. It's our agreement with Congressman Dingell, signed, sealed, and delivered. Here's your copy." I just stared at them, and without saying a word I went in to Meese's office to call my children and tell them that I had resigned as Administrator of the Environmental Protection Agency.

First I called my people at EPA—John Daniel and my AAs, Kathleen, Eric, and Tod—to let them know that the White House had agreed to protect their positions. And then I made the more difficult calls—to my chldren—to tell them I had resigned as Administrator of the Environmental Protection Agency.

Stephanie and J.J., who were out in Denver finishing the school year, took it fairly well. At least they sounded as if they did. It was probably better that they weren't any older and that they were not in Washington. Neil, on the other hand, got very upset. Halfway through Georgetown Prep, and smart as a whip, Neil knew from the beginning the seriousness of my problems. He also had an unerring sense of fairness, as do so many people his age.

"You should never have resigned," he said firmly. "You didn't do anything wrong. You only did what the President ordered. Why are you quitting? You raised me not to be a quitter. Why are you a quitter?" He was really upset.

"Honey, relax. It isn't everything it appears to be. I can't explain it all to you now, but don't be upset. There are other things going on that I will tell you about when I see you. I'm just fine."

We managed to get out of the White House without the press stopping us, and returned to Doug Bennett's office. It was abundantly clear that we could not go home, as there would be reporters and cameras everywhere. And by this time the press knew where Cristy lived, so we couldn't go there either. Lee Stillwell, Senator Armstrong's very able press man, the one I'd wanted to hire twenty-two months earlier, who had been an unofficial media adviser to us for the past week, was in Doug's office. Lee suggested that we spend the night at his townhouse in nearby Arlington (which he occupied with his brand-new bride, Roxanne, who could not have been more gracious in a situation few people would have been able to handle). So that's where we spent Wednesday night, talking and drinking, and eventually sending out for Chinese food, which I hardly touched. I may have shed a tear or two, but I did not break down. At least not then.

And when the news came on we all got a kick out of seeing my secretary Charlotte reading the announcement of the press conference I had scheduled for the next day at noon. It would be my last official contact with the press.

I knew the crowd would be immense. There were dozens of mikes on the podium in front of me when I walked in to give my statement. The noise level was almost scary, with the sound of cameras clicking and bulbs flashing being the least of it. There was that audible undercurrent of noise that one hears only from a large and excited crowd.

Because I had no desire to go back to EPA—and the anticipated size of the media mob—we had rented a ballroom in the nearby L'Enfant Plaza Hotel. But even that room seemed small with everyone jammed into it.

Shortly before I "went on" I had a kind of reunion with John Daniel and a few other of my top people in a room off the ballroom. I had been out of touch with them, purposely, since Monday. It was great to see them.

I did shed a few tears, which were then conspicuously displayed on all the news shows and on front pages across the country, but I believe I held up pretty damn well.

I said, "Shoot, I can't even work anymore. All I can do is read news clips and figure out how to get dressed in the morning without TV camera crews in there. That's not right. That's not good government. It's killing me."

I described my meeting with the President the night before, and I related how I had told him I believed we *had* made real environmental progress during my twenty-two months at EPA, and how he had responded that "it didn't seem to be getting out in the news media." And I said that I had told him I agreed with that observation, an understatement if ever there was one.

"You guys haven't printed it," I told them, "but this President has a strong commitment to the environment, and so do I."

I added, "I became the issue, and I never intended for that to happen."

Because I had already resigned as Administrator when I called the final press conference, EPA would not pay the room rental. I ended up paying the L'Enfant Plaza Hotel $1,000 of my own money.

Most of the questions were, once again, subjective: Did I feel victimized? Was I a scapegoat? The last question was, "Do you have any regrets?" Burford grabbed the microphone and said, "Only that we didn't take our honeymoon."

At the end of the twenty-minute press conference, the press burst into applause.

To me, that was the ultimate irony.

Part IV

AFTER THE DELUGE

17

JUST THE FACTS

In late September 1983, six and a half months after my resignation, I testified for the last time before Congressman Dingell's Subcommittee on Oversight and Investigations. For a variety of reasons the mood was very different now. Although there was the usual press crunch, neither the attitude of the reporters nor the questions of the Members were blatantly confrontational. But then there was very little to be confrontational about. Congress, and in a sense the press too, had gotten everything it wanted.

Consider what had happened in that half year:

> Rita Lavelle had been indicted on four counts of perjury.
> EPA had a new Administrator and a whole new team.
> Congress had been able to see everything it wanted to see.
> The environmentalists were quiet.

From my standpoint the more important story was what has *not* happened. Looking at the fuller record, from the day I resigned until the day this is being written (spring 1985) the so-called "Scandal at EPA" has produced a rather meager harvest of wrongdoers. But you would not have found many people back in 1983 who anticipated such an outcome. Nor have you read any headlines to that effect since then.

Consider this picture: in the March 21, 1983 issue *U.S. News & World Report* listed the "chief allegations":

Mismanagement. The agency is accused of moving too slowly to act on information that the highly toxic substance dioxin had been mixed with waste oil and spread through hundreds of sites in Missouri in the early 1970s. . . .

Conflict of interest. Rita Lavelle, former head of EPA's Superfund for cleaning hazardous-waste sites, is alleged to have influenced negotiations with her former employer, a major contributor to the dump. . . .

Missing funds. An audit of the 1.6 billion-dollar Superfund found that 53 million dollars could not be accounted for. . . .

Stringfellow acid pits. Former EPA chief Anne Burford is accused of playing politics in delaying until after the 1982 election a 6.1 million-dollar grant to clean up a hazardous-waste dump site in Riverside, California. Agency officials deny their actions were aimed at keeping Democratic Governor Jerry Brown from claiming credit for the cleanup in his campaign for the Senate.

Improprieties. Both Lavelle and John Todhunter, EPA Assistant Administrator, were frequently wined and dined by officials of companies the agency regulates. . . .

Political influence. Reagan appointees, critics say, methodically got rid of dozens of agency science advisers they regarded as environmental radicals. . . .

Personal financial gain. A long-time friend and part-time adviser to Burford is accused of improperly helping draft waste-dump rules benefiting his client. . . .

Unethical conduct. An EPA employee tipped off a chemical company on what the agency would settle for in negotiations to end a toxic-dump lawsuit. . . .

Shredded documents. EPA officials allegedly brought in

two paper shredders to destroy incriminating documents
sought by congressional investigators. . . .

Quite an indictment, eh? Not quite, for no indictments followed. With the exception of the case against Rita Lavelle, not a
single one of those charges, which a reputable national magazine
felt comfortable enough to repeat in print, resulted in a criminal,
or even a civil, charge.

As part of his research for this book my collaborator John
Greenya filed a Freedom of Information Act request with EPA
in order to find out what actions had been taken following my
departure. He asked for "all investigative reports produced by
EPA's Inspector General's Office regarding all appointees of former Administrator Anne Burford, both during and after her tenure as head of EPA."

When contacted by EPA and asked for specific names, Mr.
Greenya responded with a list of thirty-four, including those of
consultants (such as Jim Sanderson) as well as actual appointees.
Of those thirty-four people, there were no investigations, and
therefore no reports, on eighteen of them. Of the remaining sixteen not a single one of the investigations resulted in a recommendation for prosecution. Not Jim Sanderson. Not John Todhunter. Not John Hernandez. No one.

And what about Anne Burford? Mr. Greenya filed a separate
FOIA request for any investigations involving Anne McGill Gorsuch or Anne McGill Burford or Anne Gorsuch Burford—whatever. That request produced a single file, the results of the 1982
investigation into my actions involving Thriftway. Again there was
no charge or indictment. The FBI, which conducted its own investigation of me and five of my top aides, didn't charge or indict
anyone, either.

Skeptics might say that no one other than Rita Lavelle was
indicted because the critics were mollified by my resignation. Anyone who believes that is either very naïve or very uninformed.
When five Congressional committees, and the Department of Justice itself through the FBI and a grand jury, are investigating you
and a number of other people, you can be sure that not all of those
inquisitors are going to be satisfied with a single resignation. Nor
would they accept a whitewash. That brings me to one of the main
reasons I hired Doug Bennett, not simply to help me retire with

grace, though he did that too. At the time of my resignation on March 9 I faced the immediate prospect of answering the subpoena from John Dingell's committee the next day, but the resignation relieved me of that duty. (Also, as I mentioned, on my way down from seeing the President for the last time, Fred Fielding and Dick Hauser greeted me with the news that they had just worked out a compromise with John Dingell regarding the documents; additionally ironic was the fact that it turned out to be essentially the same compromise that EPA lawyer Gerry Yamada had worked out, but which Fielding and Hauser had rejected.)

In a sense, though, the Dingell committee subpoena was the least of my worries. Doug Bennett's main concern as my lawyer involved what he termed a "dual track." As he put it in a 1985 interview, "We had this contempt of Congress citation, which attached to her as 'Anne Gorsuch Burford,' not as Administrator of EPA, so it stayed with her as an individual person. Getting that thing lifted was number one on our agenda, because that's a criminal offense, a no-fooling-around kind of deal which entails presentment to a grand jury and the possibility that an indictment could be returned. That was the first aspect. The second was that we knew there was an ongoing investigation and that she was going to be called as a witness by several committees. John Dingell, Elliott Levitas, and the Judiciary Committee had all indicated to me that they planned to call her, though as it turned out only the Dingell Committee did.

"They wanted her testimony in regard to the various allegations that had been made, many of which she had referred as Administrator over to the Justice Department, some of which had been referred from Capitol Hill, and even some, I think, from the White House. And the Justice Department was charged with the responsibility of looking at all these charges, which they did, and eventually they came out with a report that found no grounds for indictments in any of these areas. But the work we did entailed going back and restructuring Anne's whole tenure at EPA, in order to determine just what had happened in regard to such places as Stringfellow, and Riley Tar, and Globe Mining in Arizona, and to such people as Jim Sanderson and a host of other people of 'lesser visibility.'

"Then, after she testified before John Dingell's Committee, the other committees decided not to call her, or to go forward, because of her testimony before Dingell's Committee, and because they hadn't found anything independently. But my representation of her took up, virtually, the rest of 1983, about nine or ten months."

Getting the contempt citation lifted put Doug Bennett in the record books: he had to, and did, engineer the production of an act of the House of Representatives. Not the least of his problems was having to deal with Congressman Howard—my old friend— and his refusal to lift the contempt citation. In Washington, grudges, valid or otherwise, die hard.

Back to the results of the FOIA request. The single report in the file did not involve the Stringfellow site. It had to do with Thriftway, the small New Mexico refinery that had sought a relaxation of the rules governing lead content. And it was an investigation that took place, and was resolved in my favor, while I was still in office. Acting on a request by former Congressman Toby Moffett, a Connecticut Democrat who was about to leave his House seat to make an unsuccessful run for the U.S. Senate seat held by Republican Lowell Weicker, EPA's Inspector General, Matt Novick, made the initial inquiries, and then, wisely in my opinion, went outside the government for a legal opinion as to whether I had done anything wrong. The lawyer who wrote the report was David Webster, once a partner of Edward Bennett Williams (a high-profile Democrat), and he concluded that my actions were clearly within the discretionary scope of my powers as EPA Administrator, and that no law had been broken. That was the end of that.

There is, however, an interesting footnote to the Thriftway matter. In July 1982 I was called to testify before a rather unusual ad hoc collection of House members who had an interest in EPA. Not all of them were there; John Dingell refused to join the club. But James Scheuer of New York was there, along with New Jersey's James Florio, Toby Moffett, and others. Florio chaired what was actually a joint committee hearing of five subcommittees.

I had not been testifying for very long when I noticed something unusual. Ostensibly the subject matter was to be a broad range of EPA oversight matters; however, all the questions were about Thriftway. And then I noticed something even more unusual. As one Congressman finished his questioning, there would be a pause, and some conferring with the member next to him, and then a Congressional staffer would transmit a piece of paper from member to member, who would pick up the line of questioning where his predecessor had left off. Suddenly I realized what they were doing: They were trying to set me up for a perjury charge! I had already given a sworn statement on Thriftway to the Inspector General. The committee also swore me in when I began my testimony. Obviously they were trying to *elicit* contradictory testimony which, if I gave it, would be perjury. The ploy was so obvious that I almost laughed. But as I had nothing to hide, I had nothing to fear, and I simply answered their questions, and left.

Unfortunately, there is a footnote to the footnote. This turned out to be the hearing that resulted in the resignation of Lester Brown, one of former Congressman Moffett's top environmental aides. After the record of the hearing had been printed several Republican Congressmen complained that their testimony had been altered. After an investigation it was learned that the aide had altered their testimony, and, confronted with the evidence, he resigned.

Lester Brown had worked for Moffett for eight years. As the Waterbury *American* reported, "The changes, restricted to testimony of Republican lawmakers, were found in final transcripts released in June of subcommittee hearings reviewing enforcement policies set by then-EPA administrator Anne Burford. The number and nature of the unauthorized changes is not public information, as the issue is under investigation by the House Ethics Committee and the U.S. Justice Department. The altered quotes apparently had no effect on the subsequent shakeup of top-level EPA officials [I wonder how the paper determined *that?*]. But the inaccurate and misleading statements in the transcripts could have caused future problems, as the testimony is now part of the official history of those hearings. Brown, a noted expert on hazardous waste issues and the co-author of the recently-published study, 'Hazardous Waste in America,' resigned after writing a letter to his superiors saying he had made some unauthorized changes."

I continue to worry what might be the effect of that altered testimony, seeing as it resides within the House Ethics Committee and the same Justice Department that so willingly sold me down the river. I have never, nor has Doug Bennett, been able to obtain copies of that testimony!

Back to those "chief allegations," that list of crimes that never were. Stringfellow involved something that supposedly happened in August 1982, although the allegation cropped up during my last weeks in office. The case gained little credit for those who pointed the finger.

It took a while before I would learn the genesis of the Stringfellow accusation. In essence this is what happened. In the last two weeks before I resigned certain White House advisers who had concluded that I had become a liability to the President put out the word that they would welcome any revelations of serious misconduct on my part, any "smoking guns." Ever eager to please the White House, Ernie Minor—the same Ernie Minor who wanted to run EPA for me when I first came to Washington—went to Dick Hauser of Fred Fielding's office and told him that his friend and Council on Environmental Quality coworker Al Hill had told him an interesting story about a remark I was supposed to have made the previous *July*. But it was Minor, not Hill, who went to the White House with the story. Talk about hearsay.

Hearsay or no hearsay, Mr. Hauser could hardly wait to get in touch with the Justice Department. The next day he sent the following memo to John Keeney, a Deputy Assistant Attorney General in the criminal division. Headed, *"EPA Investigation,"* it read:

March 4, 1983

The following information came to our attention late yesterday afternoon. It is forwarded for whatever action you deem appropriate in connection with Justice's consideration of allegations relating to the Stringfellow Acid Pits.

Ernie Minor, a Member of the Council on Environmental Quality, has advised that on August 4, 1982, he participated in a luncheon on board the *Sequoia*, in which EPA Administrator Burford, Secretary Watt, (then) Under Secretary of the Interior Hodel, EPA Staff Director John Daniel, CEQ Chairman Allan Hill were attendees. (Minor states that former Secretary Edwards and Deputy Secretary Ken Davis also were present for part of this luncheon.)

Minor advises that to his best recollection Burford stated, during that luncheon, that no money would be released for a Stringfellow (California) clean-up until after the elections. Minor advises that CEQ Chairman Hill recollects Burford stating, "I'll be damned if I am going to let Brown take credit for that (Stringfellow clean-up)."

For your information, I orally advised Ted Olson of this information last night.

The only problem with the Minor-Hauser smoking gun theory is that their implied conclusion is all wrong. I *did* delay making the grant to clean up the California site, but it was for perfectly valid reasons that had nothing to do with Jerry Brown's Senate campaign. As I told the investigators, I may have made a flip remark about not wanting "to give Brown a gift," but—and this is a point no one mentions—had I made that grant under those circumstances, it would undoubtedly have been a gift had it been given to anyone—and an illegal one at that.

There were four reasons why I declined to make the grant to Stringfellow at that time: (1) the majority of the $1.6 million was a reimbursement, not a grant for future work and therefore no one's health was jeopardized for lack of additional work; (2) several items for which they were claiming reimbursement were the subject of an unresolved audit; (3) it was one of the largest Superfund grants and thus would be subject to intense public interest and press coverage, but the briefing papers were so inadequate and in such disarray that I couldn't have begun to answer the most elementary questions; and (4) there was no evidence in the briefing papers that there had been any effort to identify the responsible parties and pursue enforcement against them, a necessary precondition.

Without dragging the explanation out any longer, let me simply quote from a portion of the Justice Department's report on their investigation of this horrible crime:

Investigative Results

The investigation established that a luncheon was held aboard the Sequoia on August 4, 1982. In addition to Mrs. Burford, persons aboard the Sequoia that day included the Secretary of the Interior, the Secretary of Energy, the former Secretary of Energy, the Deputy Secretary of Energy, the Chief of Staff for EPA, the Executive Assistant to the Secretary of the Interior, and the Chairman and a Member of the Council on Environmental Quality. The FBI interviewed these individuals, and only two witnesses recalled Mrs. Burford's making comments of a political nature about Governor Brown; the other individuals on the Sequoia denied any recollections of Mrs. Burford's making such comments. One witness recalled merely that Mrs. Burford had said something to the effect that she was not going to do any political favors for Governor Brown. Likewise, another witness recalled that in the course of a discussion about Governor Brown's Senate campaign, Mrs. Burford referred to six million dollars which EPA was to pay to the State of California, and she said that she believed that Governor Brown would claim credit for California's receiving this money should it be paid. This witness expressed his opinion that Mrs. Burford clearly implied that she was going to hold back the six million dollars to avoid assisting Governor's Brown's election efforts; however, he was unable to provide any evidence to support that opinion or that Mrs. Burford actually held back any EPA money from the State of California to avoid helping Governor Brown.

In addition to interviewing individuals on the Sequoia, the FBI interviewed those EPA officials assigned to EPA's Region IX headquarters in California and EPA's headquarters in Washington, D.C. who were in a position to know about the decision-making process involved in the Stringfellow matter. None of these interviews disclosed evidence establishing Mrs. Burford held back EPA money to avoid helping Governor Brown with his campaign for the Senate.

Analysis

The allegation against Mrs. Burford raised the possibility that she had committed a criminal misdemeanor violation of a federal election statute. As pertinent to this allegation, 18 U.S.C. section 595 prohibited Mrs. Burford from using her official authority for the purpose of interfering with, or affecting, the nomination or election of Governor Brown for the office of United States Senator. Since no competent evidence was discovered that Mrs. Burford engaged in the prohibited conduct, the investigation of this matter was closed.

Doug Bennett likes to point out that there were more than fifty pages in that FBI report "on the investigation of alleged violations of law by present and former officials of EPA," of which only two and a half pages pertain to my conduct. And I like to point out two more facts: it involved only five people who worked for me at EPA—John Todhunter, Louis Cordia, Robert Perry, John Horton, and Jim Sanderson; and each of them was cleared of any wrongdoing. But you never read a headline or a story to that effect. Allegations always make better reading, and, of course, they sell more papers.

Speaking of interesting reading, I recommend all three volumes of the report of the final hearings of the Dingell committee's investigation of EPA, but especially the third volume. Entitled "Investigation of Superfund and Agency Abuses," it covers "the withholding of EPA Superfund files, the claim of executive privilege, and the management of the Superfund program." As Phil Shabecoff of *The New York Times* commented wryly in an interview for this book, "That volume has been the source of any number of 'news' stories."

One of my particular favorites involves a story that has never been given the wide circulation it merits. What makes it initially intriguing is that it also involves lawyers for the United States Department of Justice, as well as several EPA attorneys. And what makes it *very* intriguing is that the matter somehow, and very conveniently, got lost within that same Department of Justice. As best I can reconstruct it, this is what happened. In mid-February 1983, a time of great heat and very little light, EPA's first line of checkers, while searching through Superfund documents to determine what could or could not go up to the Hill, ran into several handwritten memos that appeared to contain evidence of wrongdoing.

The file made its way up the chain of command until it reached me, and I agreed immediately that it looked suspicious. The notes had been taken the previous September 7 at a meeting of EPA and Justice Department lawyers in the office of Carol Dinkins (who, from the evidence in the notes, apparently was not present). The notes reflected, in three separate cases, an understanding that someone at the meeting had clearly said that the decision to fund certain Superfund sites should be made *before* the upcoming elections, in order to gain political advantage and good faith.

One note contains the words "election tracking"; another says, "Oct. 8 is our political deadline"; and the third contains the sentence, "C.A. [probably consent agreement] not signed, won't be signed in the near future (could be signed again in Nov—when not so hot)."

A decision to fund (or not to fund) a Superfund site at a certain time for purely political considerations, which is obviously wrong, had been discussed. And, which to me is far worse, such a discussion took place in the presence of Justice Department attorneys—at a time of intense public and media interest in the possibility of wrongdoing at EPA—and not one of them raised an objection!

That was the first problem. The second involved what happened to the "case" after we discovered it.

When the document in question was brought to the attention of Bob Perry he called John Daniel immediately (I was out of the office), and said, "John, we've got a document here that you need to look at right away."

As John recalls it, "When I got down there and saw it, I said, 'Bob, ship it to the Hill. Prepare a transmittal letter for Anne's signature, and get it over there right away,' because clearly it was outside of the President's executive order. And I also told Perry to advise Justice that we were sending it to the Hill.

"So he called Carol Dinkins, and when she heard what it was, she said, 'Well, seeing as all this is a criminal matter now, and we are in the investigative stage, *we*'—meaning the Department of Justice—'should be the one to send it to the Hill.' That sounded appropriate to Bob Perry, so when she said, 'Why don't you bring it over?' he did so. But when he got to her office he found not only Carol Dinkins but also Ed Schmults, the Deputy Attorney General, which indicated to him that this was a pretty high-level matter.

"Perry gave the document to Dinkins who then gave it immediately to Schmults, and the clear understanding was that they would see that this important information got to Congress, and they would let the people in their criminal division know about it so it would not in any way interfere with their criminal investigation.

"Well, that document did not make it to Congress until long after Anne had resigned. Something like September or October, six or seven months later. And, in fact, it might never have made it over had it not been discovered by some of John Dingell's own people who had been given carte blanche permission by Bill Ruckelshaus, the new EPA Administrator, to look through any files they wanted to.

"And when they found it, and read the notes that indicated that the people at this meeting were talking about scheduling the announcement of Superfund grants to coincide with the 1982 elections, their eyes popped out. They wanted to know why this information, which was clearly not enforcement-sensitive and clearly not covered by the executive order, had not been given to the Congress.

"By this time I was a private citizen again, but I got a call from the Dingell committee, and I had to go over and testify as to what I knew about the matter. And then it hit me—we had discussed this very same matter in front of William French Smith, the Attorney General himself, on the evening we met with him at the suggestion of the President! It was at the Department of Justice, and Anne was arguing that we had to turn over the documents to Congress, and she said, 'Why we just found a document, for example, that is clearly outside the order and needs to be sent to Congress, and we're going to have lots of instances like that, and you people have given me no guidance on how to deal with that . . .'

"And at just that point Carol Dinkins interrupted her, and said, 'There's no need to worry about that, we'll see it gets there, we're taking care of that.'

" 'I'm not questioning that,' Anne said, 'I'm just concerned that we have no process . . .'

"And again Dinkins interrupted her, and in front of the Attorney General and Schmults, and while at least both she and Schmults knew what was in the document and how explosive it could be, repeated that they were taking care of it. Anne could see that this line of reasoning was not getting her anywhere, so she went on to another.

"But the point is that this was hardly a matter that slipped through the cracks because people didn't know about it. From the standpoint of the Justice Department's awareness, first there was the original promise on the phone to Bob Perry, then after Perry took it over there Dinkins and Schmults told him they would take care of it, and then right in front of Attorney General Smith Dinkins again promised to take care of it—and nothing ever got done. The only reason it was even found is that Dingell's bleary-eyed people just stumbled onto it as part of a page-by-page search."

To me, there is no question that the Department of Justice purposely held back that document from the Congress. I cannot say if Attorney General Smith had any knowledge of what was in the document, but both Carol Dinkins and Ed Schmults—lawyers who at one time were both second only to "the General" in the Department of Justice—did.

What is ironic is that this happened at the very moment I was being held to the strictest of standards with regard to my conduct and that of my people at EPA, so as not to give the slightest hint or appearance of wrongdoing. And my "judge," in addition to the Congress, was the same Department of Justice that conveniently mislaid an important piece of evidence that would have brought embarrassment, or worse, to some of its own people.

Consider how it looked: As John Daniel says, "Clearly, there's something wrong with it from the standpoint that these are *lawyers* involved who are supposed to be litigating a case, or preparing to, and where was their judgment on this? Why didn't one of them say, when they heard reference to 'election tracking,' 'Hey, wait a minute, I'm not going to have anything to do with this, and I'm going to report it to Miss Dinkins and we're getting the hell out of this'? or 'I'm turning this over to the U.S. Attorney, or to Congress'? But no, instead they all just sat there and wrote down their little notes, and they did their little duty to meet their election delivery dates. It's just so easy to see why something like that is dead wrong, law or no law."

John is exactly right.

I also agree with the way Congressman Sikorski characterized the matter in the final hearing of the Dingell subcommittee. His last question to John Daniel was, "So that incident fell into some black hole, never to be referred to in the report that was produced in August of this year [1983] by the Department of Justice?" And John answered, "I have not seen any reference to it, sir."

I would be remiss if I did not address myself to the role of the media in my "downfall." One central fact should be understood:

In the almost nine years that had elapsed since the unraveling of the Watergate case, no Washington story received as much coverage as the "Scandal" at EPA. I'm told that from 1973–74 until the last half year of my tenure at the Agency, late 1982 to early 1983, more reporters and crews were assigned to my story than any other. Except for Patty Hearst's, I can't recall any story anywhere in the United States that received as much attention.

In part that's understandable. Once the issue of executive privilege was raised, and reporters began to hear and then write about "withheld documents," the parallels were in place. But that explains only the *extent* of the coverage. It does not explain its quality, or lack thereof. One of the main reasons why so many people are surprised to learn that there weren't more fires under all that smoke is that the massive coverage alone suggested the presence of substantial wrongdoing. Another reason is that much of the coverage was sensationalistic, offering allegations as facts, and implying that charges would certainly lead to convictions.

It is important to keep in mind that the memory of Watergate loomed very large in the minds of many of the journalists who covered EPA and me. Some of them had covered Watergate, while others, younger people, were in school at the time and made their decisions to become reporters because of that event and all the excitement it generated. So perhaps I should take a philosophical attitude when recalling their excessive zeal. But I find that hard to do.

One expects me to complain about the press. But certain members of the press have also expressed reservations. Two articles in respected publications—the *Columbia Journalism Review* and the *Washington Monthly*—contain criticisms of the nature of the press coverage in this case that should disturb any fair-minded person.

Of course I disagree with the author of the *CJR* article's thesis that there was wrongdoing at EPA that the press failed to uncover but I do not disagree with his statement that: "In the competition for leads, hearsay became a valuable commodity. Wide publicity was given to unsubstantiated accusations of lawbreaking that emanated from secret Congressional hearings. Stories that had rattled around Washington for months without a home suddenly became big news. Intense attention was sometimes focused on minor pecadilloes, while particularly damning information was slighted. Reporters and camera crews maintained a vigil at the homes of prominent EPA officials, waiting in vain for candid breakfast interviews. It was, in short, a classic episode of pack journalism, with great shortcomings as well as distinctive successes."

And I most certainly agree that, ". . . the twenty or so reporters assigned to cover the EPA on a regular beat were primarily interested in the views and behavior of only one person: Burford." He was dead right that in the heat of the last weeks of battle, "Hearsay crept into print almost immediately, abetted by the irresistible spectacle of numerous congressmen waving startling accusations of federal wrongdoing."

Another reporter who makes this point is Joe Davis of the *Congressional Quarterly*. He covered the whole affair, and feels that while "There were some good reporters and some good reporting, it was hardly journalism's finest hour." Davis recalls an instance in which Congressman Scheuer of New York stepped out of his office with a release for the scores of reporters jamming the hallway, and said that, "while we would have to trust him on the accuracy of the charges, which had to do with the existence of a 'hit-list' of career employees at EPA, he would be holding hearings very soon which would substantiate them. On that basis, I would not use the story, but almost all of the other papers ran front page stories the next day featuring the charges. The hearings he'd promised were never held, and, to the best of my knowledge, those particular charges were never substantiated."

What Mr. Davis reported about Congressman Scheuer did not surprise me. I had learned something important about the man through one of my Congressional Affairs people who'd had a conversation with one of Scheuer's top aides not long after Rita Lavelle testified before the congressman's subcommittee. According to the Hill staffer, Scheuer was offering me a deal: if I would fire Rita, he would not bring charges of perjury against her. I was startled by his offer, which amounted to a federal crime (it is known technically as misprison of a felony, meaning one fails to report knowledge of a felonious act). I sent back word that I would make no such deal, and that was the last we heard of it. But it gave me a very negative impression of Congressman Scheuer and the people in his office.

"Too often," concluded the author of the *Columbia Journalism Review*, "reporters merely wandered from one press conference to another, preparing news accounts that conveyed a sense of struggle without steering the audience to the truth through the presentation of relevant facts. In succumbing to this comfortable routine they functioned essentially as mouthpieces for different viewpoints, and it was their sources, not their own or their editors' judgment, who determined what appeared on the front page or the evening news broadcast. It takes time and energy—not to mention a willingness to walk down blind alleys—to reach deep into the federal bureaucracy and extract stories that make news rather than merely reflect it. Journalists need not wait until the pack descends and the smell of blood is in the air."

During an interview for this book, Phillip Shabecoff told a significant anecdote about that same pack approach and mentality.

"It was about a week or two before Mrs. Burford resigned, and George Tames, a *New York Times* photographer with something like thirty years of experience, and I were standing in a hallway of one of the House buildings, along with maybe fifty other reporters, waiting for her to come out of a hearing. Instead of coming out the door we expected her to use, suddenly she appeared at the far end of the hallway. So the group of reporters started to walk after her, and when she turned the corner of the corridor, walking quickly, there was a moment's hesitation, and then they all started to run. I turned to George and said, 'I'm not running after anybody.' He did, though, because we needed a picture. When he came back he looked at me and said something that turned out to be prophetic. He said, 'She's gone. In this town, when the pack starts running after you, you're *gone*.'"

Joe Davis recalls that at one of the Senate hearings involving me and EPA he counted at least fifty print reporters and fifteen television cameras. As he points out, once a camera crew has been sent out, it is highly unlikely it will return and say, "There really wasn't a story today."

Another point can be made. I can remember any number of hearings in which important testimony, especially regarding the budget, was slated to follow mine. But as soon as I had testified, the cameras were turned off and packed up. That's hardly good journalism.

"It was not," says Davis, "the most illustrious chapter in the history of journalism. People were entirely too ready to convey charges and allegations without finding out the other side. Some of the charges that got printed toward the end had been made years before and ignored by the press, and it was only the added insinuation of criminal wrongdoing that propelled them to the front page, even though some of the charges were relatively minor, such as using government property for personal use. A number of individual reporters did very good jobs, people like Howie Kurtz of the *Washington Post*, and Phil Shabecoff, Al Gordon of the *Rocky Mountain News*, and Bill Kronholm of the Associated Press. There were a lot of good journalists working on this story, and they did some of their best work, but eventually they were just outnumbered. And some of the reporters got overwhelmed. For the last few weeks, typically, there were several developments a day.

"At one point, the *Washington Post* had eight different people, in either single or joint bylines, on this story, and that was before it snowballed. When you have that kind of situation, you know there *will be* a story. And, EPA's posture was to be not very forthcoming, which also didn't help matters. There was not a lot of candor in many of its statements.

"The whole sound and fury was over before anything was looked at carefully, and before it went through the legal process. In that sense it is accurate to say that Anne Burford was abused. Part of the problem with the coverage was that journalists have a tendency to be generalists, not specialists, and it *was* a very big job. Often you had to be in two places at once. The press was not able to deal with that whole record, and in fact it was even hard for any committee of Congress to do that. My point is that Mrs. Burford deserved to be questioned, but it should have been for the *right* reasons."

Phil Shabecoff agrees. "No question, there was pack journalism. But there was a lot of very good work done, too. Almost as soon as the executive privilege battle began, we started to hear stories about how the White House was going to screw her. I think that the conduct of the White House in this affair was without question reprehensible."

18

RITA REVISITED

What to say, at this point, about Rita Lavelle? As this is being written she has just begun to serve her six-month term (at a minimum-security prison in her home state of California), and it will probably sound unkind of me to add to the record of charges against her. But that is exactly what I am going to do.

When I fired her I felt sorry for her. In fact, I continued to feel sorry for her for well over a year after that. However, I have learned some things in just the last few weeks and days that make me so angry at Rita Lavelle that I have lost all remnants of sympathy. It is now undeniably clear to me that Rita Lavelle was an EPA team member in name only. Her real allegiance lay elsewhere. The problem is in determining exactly where, for evidence exists to indicate at least two "bosses" other than my agency—private industry and the White House.

First let's review *exactly* why Rita Lavelle is in jail, for I have found that with the passage of time many people are no longer clear on just what it is she did.

In very abbreviated form, this is what happened. Before coming to EPA Rita had worked for Aerojet General, which turned out to be one of the companies that had dumped hazardous wastes at the Stringfellow site. She testified under oath before both the House and the Senate that she had recused herself from any dealings with Stringfellow as soon as she learned that her former employer was one of those firms.

But it was proven that she had continued to deal with the Stringfellow matter for weeks after the date she said she had recused herself. And because of this, on August 4, 1983, she was indicted on the following counts: 1. knowingly making a false statement to the Administrator of EPA (her statement to me regarding the date that she knew of Aerojet's involvement); 2. obstruction of a proceeding before a Congressional committee (her affidavit to Congress "memorializing" the above date); 3. perjury before the Senate Committee on Environment and Public Works; 4. perjury before the Subcommittee on Public Works and Transportation of the United States House of Representatives; and 5. perjury before the Senate Committee on Environment and Public Works (regarding election tracking on Superfund grants). She was acquitted on the last count. All the counts stemmed from the fact that she continued to be involved with the Stringfellow case after the date she knew of her former employer's involvement.

On December 1 of that same year a federal jury in Washington, D.C., convicted her of four felony charges after a two-week trial concluded with seven hours of deliberations. She was convicted of two counts of perjury, one count of filing a false statement with the EPA, and one count of obstructing the investigation of a Congressional committee.

As the report of the Dingell committee summarized it, "A review of the entire record demonstrates that Ms. Lavelle continued to participate actively in the Stringfellow case after being pointedly told that her former employer was listed as a waste discharger and possible responsible party at the site. The record further shows that Ms. Lavelle attempted to cover up her unethical conduct by making a false statement to this Subcommittee and testifying untruthfully before Congress."

She was sentenced to six months in jail, and a fine of $10,000. She was also sentenced to five years' probation, and to perform community service while on probation. She appealed the conviction, but it was affirmed, and in April 1985 she began to serve her sentence. On the day she went to jail she was quoted as saying she had been framed. If she said who framed her, it was not reported.

When she sentenced Rita Lavelle, Federal Judge Norma Holloway Johnson explained why she was insisting on at least some time served in jail: "After full consideration of all these factors, Ms. Lavelle, and the fact that you indeed violated the public trust, that your perjury actually offends and strikes at the very core of the trust that had been conferred upon you, the fact that you still cannot apparently admit to yourself the injury you caused the Federal government—it is not just a matter of the injury you caused yourself, but the injury that you caused to all of us as citizens of this country—it is my view that probation is inappropriate."

It's possible that Rita Lavelle got off easy. The Dingell subcommittee was interested in several other areas that might well have led to her being indicted on other counts, but was stymied by missing documents. Among the actions that interested them were Rita's "election tracking" efforts, her keeping of what she called a "Stars and Chits" list (which they called "a record-keeping system to record her political successes," but the way I heard it was actually closer to a "who-owes-me-what" list), and the amount and extent of her contacts with the White House. It is the last of these items that most interests me, especially because of something neither John Daniel nor I knew until the research for this book was almost completed.

Both Chairman John Dingell and former Congressman Elliott Levitas (he lost his bid for reelection in 1984 and now practices law in Washington and Atlanta with the Atlanta firm of Kilpatrick and Cody) were kind enough to agree to be interviewed by John Greenya. Each had something interesting to say about Rita Lavelle's extramural activities, especially Mr. Levitas.

Rita was questioned by Dingell's people about the extent of her contacts with the White House while she worked for me. The report says:

> The Subcommittee's investigation has determined that Rita M. Lavelle's contacts with White House officials were far more extensive than either they or Ms. Lavelle have acknowledged to date. However, the Subcommittee presently is unable to draw conclusions about the substance of the conversations between Ms. Lavelle and various White House officials. The Subcommittee's efforts to explore the full nature and extent of these communications have been

hampered significantly by a lack of cooperation from Ms.
Lavelle and the White House. Currently, the White House
is preventing the Department of Justice from providing the
Subcommittee with White House memoranda and other
documents relating to contacts of White House officials with
Ms. Lavelle and other EPA officials. The Subcommittee has
not had the opportunity to question Ms. Lavelle, and our
investigaion has revealed that on the one occasion where
she did testify under oath about her contacts with White
House officials, she testified untruthfully.

The report also pointed out that several newspaper stories in
early and mid-1983 said White House Counselor Fred Fielding
was conducting an investigation of contacts between senior presidential aides and EPA to see if there had been any political manipulation of EPA programs. In fact, Chairman Dingell wrote Mr.
Fielding on September 9, 1983 for a copy of any report he might
have written on that topic, and Fielding responded orally admit-
ting that "he had not prepared a written report summarizing the
results of his inquiry into White House contacts with EPA officials." That hardly surprised me.

What *did* surprise me was what Mr. Levitas said. Testimony
before several committees indicates that Rita had had "numerous"
conversations with Craig Fuller, another Reagan aide who went
back to the California days, and who served in the very important
position of Secretary to the Cabinet, which meant not just that he
saw the President daily, but that he was one of the favored few
who sat with the President at the end of the day. But the number
given by Rita's secretary, an estimate of maybe ten or a dozen,
and those over her fifteen-month stay, did not seem excessive,
though had I known it I would have wondered why she needed
to talk to Craig Fuller even that many times.

However, Elliott Levitas told us that his recollection, based on
the logs of Rita's telephone calls made from her EPA office, was
that she called the White House about *150 times*—and most of the
calls were to Craig Fuller!

John Daniel was stunned when he heard this. He said, "I would
have had much more reason to call the White House than she,
and I worked for EPA much longer, but I bet I didn't make *half*
that many calls to the White House." As for me, I probably made

no more than fifty such calls, and only a handful were to Mr. Fuller.

When asked if his recollection of the number of her calls to the White House was similar to that of Elliott Levitas's, Chairman Dingell said, "I cannot give you an answer on that. But I can tell you that as Rita Lavelle was leaving the Agency, she walked out with boxes of records and papers, and we do have testimony that she did hold a number of meetings, not only with Craig Fuller and others at the White House, but she did also hold meetings with top personnel at the Department of Justice."

Later Dingell added, "She was apparently a very busy lady, and used the telephone extensively, and traveled extensively around Washington to discuss with people what was going to be done, not only on the production of papers and documents, but also on a number of matters and policy decisions relative to timing, and where the grants would be made. She walked out, according to testimony, with a goodly number of boxes of documents, and we'd love to get them. I'm afraid they have now gone to a more permanent and unavailable depository."

Clearly, I should have put a guard on Rita's door the minute I fired her. Based on recent court decisions some of the things that Rita may have taken, such as phone logs and probably also her "Stars and Chits" lits, are considered personal papers, and therefore hers to keep. But what intrigues me is the sheer volume of stuff that according to the testimony of her aides she took with her. Some of that *must* have been EPA papers.

Another fair assumption regards her phone contacts with the White House. With 150 phone calls going *one* way, there has to be some kind of response from the other side. You don't make the second phone call if the first one isn't productive if it does not involve some kind of interchange. It defies logic to think that she called Craig Fuller 150 times and Craig Fuller said *nothing* of substance.

Another point needs to be made here: Those communications were definitely outside established channels. Period. What are "established channels"? Anything that was developed for legislative policy was developed in Cabinet Council, which I attended for EPA, and it's all there. There's a channel for it. Second, in communicating what's going on at EPA we had a regular channel of communication. Weekly reports went out over my signature to the Secretary of the Cabinet, Craig Fuller, which included anything of substance. But 150 phone calls to Craig Fuller does not fit in to any established channel of communication between EPA and the White House.

I knew Rita was talking to people at the White House extracurricularly, but I had no idea of the volume. And I certainly didn't assume that there was flow *back* from the White House, which there has to have been with this many phone calls. Also, none of my other Assistant Administrators went directly to the White House about anything.

As far as her meeting with Justice Department officials goes, I'm appalled (unless she met with Bob Perry about enforcement cases—I never heard of any such meeting.) Even though it was a Superfund document that was being withheld, it was not a Superfund issue at any time. It was an issue that was dealt with through the Administrator's office at all times. The only other party that would be involved would be the Office of General Counsel. God only knows what those contacts were about.

Congressman Dingell, former Congressman Levitas, and I— plus their people and my people and a host of others—went a lot of rounds together, but like good fighters we held no animosity. Basic policy disagreements over the approach that I brought to my management of the Environmental Protection Agency still exist, and probably always will (we do come from different parties), but there are no personal hard feelings as a result of our tough encounters. How they feel about the other major players in this drama is another matter entirely.

Here are a few of the things John Dingell said when he was interviewed for this book on May 1, 1985:

"We have to keep educating White Houses this way. It's a continuing battle between the Congress and the White House over the availability of information to which the Congress is fully entitled, a problem that has gone on since the earliest days of the Republic. And, regrettably, what happens is that people get confused about the issue, and usually send up [to the Congress] some other unfortunate soul to suffer the grief that is associated with carrying out the administration's policy with regard to the availability of information.

"Interestingly enough, this thing got blown out of any proper size in what was really a very unfortunate way. Superfund, an amazingly complex piece of legislation, was coming up, and I had Michael Barrett, the chief counsel of my investigative subcommittee, call down there to EPA and ask for five files, in different parts of the country, and request the information—just send the files up—because this matter was going to be in Mr. Florio's subcommittee where he was going to commence writing a piece of legislation. The genesis of this was entirely normal; there was no tip, no speculation of wrongdoing, no nothing.

"So Michael called down to EPA's general counsel, Mr. Perry, and asked him, in my name, to deliver the files. Mr. Perry said he would have to call back, and when he did he said he had been instructed by the Justice Department to send all the files over to [Justice] and to keep no copies. This was exactly what happened to us on the ITT-Geneen investigation, which was actually the precursor of Watergate.

"There was no way in which I could stand still and tolerate that kind of behavior on a matter of this sort at that particular time.

"So we proceeded immediately to go through the orderly process of issuing subpoenas to compel the production of that information. Our efforts were totally unrelated to actions being taken by Mr. Levitas and his subcommittee of the Public Works Committee, which was engaged in a similar but different inquiry relative to their responsibilities under the law. And that is the genesis of this whole unfortunate event.

"At no point during the course of this proceeding did we ever ask for more than a limited number of files. Now, Mr. Levitas asked for a lot more files, but he was proceeding in his own investigation, and I'm not sufficiently familiar with what he was doing or whether it was good policy or bad policy that I'm prepared to describe exactly why he proceeded in the fashion he chose or we chose. We allowed the matter to rest, and did not even proceed toward a contempt citation carrying the matter to the House floor because of the termination of the Congress, and simply commenced to proceed to address the question in the new Congress. Whereas, in fact, as I remember it, Mr. Levitas got a vote [of contempt] on the House floor on this issue, and of course

then the untoward and unfortunate events commenced with regard to that particular matter insofar as they affected Mrs. Burford. . . .

"The Justice Department's lawsuit against the House of Representatives was entirely worthy of these incompetent bunglers
that we have to deal with down at the Justice Department. The
idiots not only relied on the Nixon case, a losing case, but they
misquoted it! They cited the case for points that were 180 degrees
from the rationale of the case.

"Their behavior was shameful in other principles, too. Remember, they told Mrs. Burford and other people there at EPA
that they would refuse to represent them. That's inexcusable.
They got them miles out on a limb that folks up here were sawing
off busily, and they were diligently looking the other way, and
saying, 'Well, you'll have to get yourself a private lawyer.'

"Interestingly enough, the same people that were advising them
they had to get a private lawyer are now rushing out to get the
government to pay the rather luxurious charges of private lawyers
who represented them in cases of relatively minor merit, such as
Mr. Meese's case. And not only did they do it to her, they did it
to rank-and-file government servants. . . .

"The Justice Department, having asserted these extraordinary
postures in their briefs, then absented themselves and left these
people, who were doing what they were instructed to do, to suffer
the consequences, including potential criminal liability and other
liabilities without the advantage of counsel to which they were
fully entitled. Shameful behavior.

"Why did the Justice Department bring that lawsuit? I have to
say that it was probably amateurism carried to an extraordinary
degree. Lawyers like to argue lawsuits, and when they're paid by
the taxpayers to argue lawsuits without any personal consequences
for them. And without having to maintain a reputation for success
or failure in lawsuits, they are quite free to argue absolutely asinine
positions with no merit in the full assurance that they will not lose
clients, and that if anybody goes to jail or suffers misfortune, it's
not a matter of particular concern to them. It's sort of a Pontius
Pilate syndrome."

When asked if he had drawn any conclusions as to the extent
of President Reagan's awareness of the problems at EPA, Dingell's
answer had both a historical and a current reference. "It's difficult

to tell what any President, rather especially this President, is aware of."

Then he continued, on the question of who knew what, behind the scenes. "It must be observed that there were continuing discussions which went on during this matter, rather, during the events that led up to this matter, which involved people at EPA with people in the White House and people in the Justice Department. I don't believe that has ever appeared in public testimony."

Chairman Dingell pointed out that the whole affair was not neatly and cleanly resolved by my leaving office, or even by the appointment of Bill Ruckelshaus as my successor:

"The sequel to this, of course, is the appointment of her successor and the rather different policies he was able to lay in place with the concurrence of the administration. This got him great credit, and left her in a rather unfortunate posture. But the sequel is also the fact that the Congress tried to write a new Superfund law, with different funding provisions relative to cleanup. We are, by the way, still struggling with the damned issues relative to Superfund—hazardous waste—and we are finding a continuing flow of fresh and horrifying problems. The number of waste dumps has grown astronomically since she left office. Many of these dumps were there but just were unappreciated at the time. We have found that ground water contamination is a very serious problem, and it is one which may exist into geological time. And this is a precious resource that we have no right to defile for the future.

"The particular vignette we're dealing with is but part of a much larger panorama, though now there is a new cast of characters and new portrayal of old issues and new issues, and new battles with new participants over old issues and new issues both. Hopefully, when we get done we'll write ourselves a decent piece of Superfund legislation that will move us toward a rational cleanup of this mess we've got here."

John Dingell also had some last thoughts about me, and the drama in which I played a central part.

"In a very real sense she was the victim of almost a Greek tragedy. Now, I'm not going to describe whether I agreed with her on all matters with regard to the administration of the agency. That's an entirely separate discussion. And it's not my business to tell you justice was done or not done. That is a court function, and not a power that I think ought to be trusted to Congress. As for 'getting away with something,' that's done every day by persons from mendicants to White House personnel and executives. It's done from the captains of industry to the poorest welfare mother.

"But Anne Burford I don't think got away with anything."

Elliott Levitas was also kind enough to give us a good deal of his time. Interviewed in his Washington law office in late April and early May 1985 he was candid, complimentary, and very "educational."

"When I became chairman of this subcommittee the Superfund program had just recently been put in place, and one of the things I felt needed to be done was to take a look at the new programs *before* they got out of whack, in order to make them workable, rather than just doing a retrospective autopsy on them. And to use oversight as a means of making corrections and improvements in the program before the thing went down the tube. Too often oversight goes back and picks the bones of the deceased.

"So I decided in 1981 to start really just an oversight review of the hazardous waste program and some other programs that were being administered by EPA at that time. And as far as I was concerned it was just a routine exercise in oversight. . . . And I was not aware at that time that Dingell's people were also interested.

"So I put some top people on what was just a routine investigation. Then, right in the middle of it, there was a decison made by EPA, by Anne Gorsuch, permitting sanitary landfills to be used to receive liquid waste ["liquids in landfills"], and I was very upset about that, and immediately called a hearing, right in the middle of this routine investigation, and that was when some red flags began to be thrown up.

"This is the spring of 1982, and we're still conducting the investigation on a plodding basis. And then, boom, the door got closed. And after several conversations with people at EPA, with Mrs. Gorsuch and with some people at the Justice Department, I realized we were going to have a fight, not only about the program itself, but we were headed for a major fight over the executive-Congressional prerogatives. And I had no inkling that was coming, absolutely none.

"It seemed to me that on this issue, to raise questions of executive privilege about documents that no President of the United States will ever see in his life was a little bit specious. When something like that begins to surface I get pretty suspicious, so I realized pretty early on that we were headed for a showdown.

"At that point I began to think they were hiding something, not necessarily Gorsuch, but more likely the White House. Or the Justice Department. The White House *and* the Justice Department. That was the sense I got from how this thing was being played out. We weren't talking about contras operating in Nicaragua, and we weren't talking about atomic bomb secrets, we were talking about the Superfund program. We were talking about documents which most people wouldn't understand if they saw them, they were so technical in nature. So I knew there was some problem there, at least on one level, and maybe on two or three levels.

"But I made it very clear that we were going to get those documents, and we were going to let the chips fall where they may. So I went to my committee and laid it all out for them, and let them know quite early on that there was going to be a showdown on this thing. I did not believe then that the administration would bring it to the point that it eventually did, because it just made no sense.

"We sort of negotiated from afar with Mrs. Gorsuch, and I never got the feeling that it was her decision not to provide us with the documents. I did get the impression that she was too good a Reagan soldier. And she knew, in my opinion, that what she was asked to do was neither right nor made good sense. And yet she went along with it.

"One conversation sticks in my mind. It was after the subpoena, and I had no animosity toward Anne Gorsuch, none whatsoever. She was a very bright woman, but I felt she was giving greater respect to a man than she was to the law, and I felt she, as a lawyer, should have known that. And that's one of the places where she and I parted company. But I remember when we got to the point where this thing was going to have a showdown, I made one last effort to head this thing off. And by this time I had figured this thing out.

"A, the White House *did* have something to hide; and B, the Justice Department was looking for a fight, and wanted to win in an executive privilege struggle with the House, and they just picked this one. But they picked the wrong one, and the wrong guy.

"What did the White House have to hide? There *were* political considerations taken into account in the Superfund program. There *was* a certain mismanagement of that program. There *was* White House involvement—you don't have 150 conversations that are logged (forget how many are not logged) between an Administrator for hazardous waste programs and a deputy to the Chief of Staff of the White House [without it]. That's Rita Lavelle and Craig Fuller, among others. I don't know if that's on the public record, but the documents are there.

"So I think there *were* things to hide. But I think, more significantly, the Justice Department, and if I had to say who, probably Ted Olson, or maybe a civil bureaucrat, decided that there had to be a fight over executive privilege. They had backed down on two or three instances. They had backed down on this issue in the Carter administration with the Department of Energy, they had backed down on this issue with Jim Watt, and by golly here it was again, and they were going to take a stand on it.

"Back to my story of the conversation. It was shortly before Mrs. Gorsuch was supposed to appear before my subcommittee and bring the documents, and I was doing everything I could to head that off. All I wanted was the documents. I know that she has said publicly that I was on a partisan, political exercise, and all I can say, though it's very self-serving, is that's not the case. It never dawned on me that we would end up in the situation we did; all I wanted to have was an investigation of the Superfund program.

"Anyway, I realized that she was headed for some real serious problems, so I called her one afternoon, and I don't recall if she called me back or if I reached her in her official car, but she was on her way to the airport. And I said to her, not unaware of the fact that telephone calls over the radio around here are routinely monitored, 'Anne, has it occurred to you that you are being set up in this matter?'

"There was a very long silence on the other end of the phone, and then she said, 'Well, we ought to talk about this when I get back in town.' She obviously didn't want to talk about it then, and under those circumstances. But we never had that conversation.

"On the day she came before my subcommittee and was cited for contempt, she was accompanied by Ted Olson. And I said to him before we got started, more for *her* benefit than his, 'Mr. Olson, how can you represent Mrs. Gorsuch here today and advise

her what to do and what not to do? Isn't there a conflict of interest
there? Because in the event Mrs. Gorsuch, acting on your advice,
places herself in contempt of this committee and ultimately in
contempt of Congress, the Justice Department is going to have to
prosecute this woman.'

"I was trying to make the point that the Justice Department
had a different agenda, had a different role to play, than Anne
Gorsuch."

Mr. Levitas also had some observations to make on the lawsuit
filed by that same Department of Justice.

"I've got to believe that that lawsuit represents the *nadir* of the
legal reputation of the Justice Department of the United States.
It was an absolute absurdity. You never knew whether to just hold
it in contempt or utter disdain, from a legal point of view, or to
view it as a very pernicious action on the part of any administration. And, of course, that story still hasn't been fully told.

"Eventually it was obvious to me that this woman was being
set up, that the Justice Department was looking for a fight, and
they decided to do this one, and then they proceeded to do a
terrible job, and she was just caught in the middle. I would quarrel
with Gorsuch on her policies in running EPA, but she was doing
exactly what Ronald Reagan wanted her to do, from beginning
to end. The policies of EPA were not the policies of Anne Gorsuch,
they were the policies of Ronald Reagan, or whoever it is that
makes policy in that administration. And she was doing them.

"And I have said repeatedly that I don't buy off on the Nu-
remburg defense. Just because someone tells you to do something
is no defense if you know it's not right. (And they didn't really
give her a stellar group to work with.) So Anne and I would part
company on those issues, but as far as the big issue is concerned,
there's no question in my mind that she was a victim of that, that
she was set up, and that it was the White House and the Justice
Department."

Just as Congressman Dingell had done, Mr. Levitas could not
resist pointing out several ironies in the way things turned out,
especially in view of what the Justice Department's intentions must
have been.

"What the Justice Department did as a result of its efforts is,
instead of enhance the position of executive privilege, they probably did as much to eliminate and certainly erode that doctrine

than had been done in recent years, in modern memory. They may have, in effect, done the opposite of what they set out to do.

"This matter was one of the major Constitutional confrontations, certainly since Watergate, and one of the key Constitutional confrontations of this century. We were going eyeball to eyeball, and there was going to be a showdown. And really I was very sorry for Anne, that she got into this thing. She wasn't the person who should have been in the dock. It should have been somebody else. But she let herself stay there, and she's got to bear the consequences of it.

"And this was not a casually taken action on our part. I gave more deliberation and thought to what to do and how to to it; we had different ways to proceed. We could have held her in contempt of Congress through the inherent power of Congress, and not even go through the procedure of having the matter referred to the U.S. Attorney.

"I remember before we made that decision of what to do, not only checking out the precedents on the inherent power of Congress to hold a person in contempt, but what would be done if that occurred. Who would go out and arrest Mrs. Burford? And where would she be incarcerated? I checked out the location of the old jail in the Capitol Building. I actually went and met with the Architect of the Capitol, and he took me around and showed me where they used to hold prisoners. There was nothing casual about this matter at all.

"What has the Justice Department done on this Constitutional issue? For the first time in history a Cabinet-level official was held in contempt of Congress. Now *that* is a precedent that this administration has gained for itself. We went through almost two hundred years as a Republic without ever having a Cabinet-level official be held in contempt of Congress. And they managed to push us to the point, this time, to do it.

"And it was all handled so callously. At the end it was like the Russian sleigh ride—the administration would keep tossing another person off of the sleigh to keep the wolves at bay."

Another person with very strong opinions on this matter about the actions of the Justice Department and, indirectly, the White House, is Stanley Brand. Now a lawyer in private practice in Washington, Mr. Brand was the attorney for the House of Representatives (his official title was Counsel to the Clerk of the House) from

1977 until 1984. He was at the heart of the battle over the papers, and he recalls the entire fight with undisguised passion.

Asked for his opinion of the Justice Department's lawsuit, he said immediately, "It was a joke. It was frivolous. It was like something I'd have expected from someone who hangs around Fifth Street or St. Elizabeth's [a mental hospital] and files a nuisance suit. It was poorly done, it had to be amended three times, it charged causes of action that were blatantly outside the realm of good lawyering. If anybody had looked at those cases and statutes they would have known better. They had the wrong officers named, such as the Sergeant at Arms when it was the Clerk of the House. It was all screwed up. Shoddy work."

A similar opinion was given by Rex Lee, former Solicitor General of the U.S. When asked, after a speech, if there was truth to the rumor that the Justice Department hadn't appealed its case because it was so weak and so poorly done, Mr. Lee said, "That's what I've heard."

Brand has a vivid recollection of the moment he learned the Department of Justice was going to sue the House of Representatives. "I was on the floor of the House—moment of drama—we were going forward. We were almost voting; in fact, the vote may have already been running. The vote to hold Anne Gorsuch in contempt. Then somebody runs up and there's this big confab with Elliott Levitas and Jim Howard and me and maybe even John Dingell and the Speaker's Counsel and a host of others, and he said, 'They are preparing to go into federal court and sue us, and try to enjoin us,' and this and that. And I said, 'Boy, that's terrific.' They all looked at me as if I were crazy. And I said, 'That is the worst thing they can do, and my strategy is going to be to embarrass them, to get it dismissed as quickly as possible, and show that they built this thing on a house of cards.'

"Before the citation for contempt it was clear to me that she was not making the calls. In fact, in her off-the-record discussions with the members she was willing to cooperate but was being restrained from cooperating. I always sensed that she would have been a reasonable person had she been allowed to be. Not that she didn't agree with the overall philosophy, but I think what happened was the legal ideologues in the Justice Department took over and said, 'This is a great test case, and she's the guinea pig, and she's a loyalist.' And they took advantage of her, knowing she was a loyalist, and did not disclose to her the risks of what was going on. And for her part, and with all due respect, and I don't mean this in any derogatory fashion—she might even admit this in a candid moment—I think she was a little naïve about Washington and what was likely to happen to her, and felt that with these great guys from the Department of Justice behind her she was going to be able to weather the storm. But she didn't really understand the rough-and-tumble of Washington life. That may be the only legitimate lesson that people can take away from her personal experience—that you come into Washington, and though you may believe very strongly in your principles, and believe very strongly that you're doing the right thing, you have to be very careful, because they will denude you in one minute. In fact, somebody once asked me what I thought about what happened to Anne Burford, and I said, and it may sound flip but I mean it in a serious way, it was like that Italian movie, 'Seduced and Abandoned.' I think that's exactly what happened to her. And she's hardly alone in that hall of fame of people who have been chewed up and spit out by the milieu here in Washington."

Brand has a very unfavorable opinion of the way William French Smith's Department of Justice titled its lawsuit. "The caption is ludicrous. It says, 'The United States of America, care of the Department of Justice, 9th and Constitution.' That's like writing to Santa Claus at the North Pole. Who the hell do they think the United States is? It's not some GS-18 appointed down in the Department of Justice. It's the sovereign elected representatives, that's who the United States is. If in an interbranch dispute they want to say, 'Congress versus the President,' I'll buy that, but what I won't accept is that they're the United States and we're some bunch of rump politicians who have no status under the Constitution. That's exactly the arrogance we were fighting in that suit, and it goes back a long way to the separation of powers suits, but I think it was part of their undoing."

He feels that the men behind the whole idea were "Teddy Olson and Larry Sims. They were the brain trust down there who wanted to teach the Congress a lesson. I don't know if they dealt the doctrine of executive privilege a death blow, but they set it back, and they set it back in several documented ways. Never again will anybody in the executive branch be able to file a civil suit with a straight face."

When asked about William French Smith's role in all of this, Brand almost laughed. "He was a part-time Attorney General. I don't think he had much to do with it, I don't think he understood it. I think his boys came in, Olson and Sims, sold him a bill of goods, he sold the President a bill of goods through the legal counsel [Fred Fielding], and they were off to the races. If you wanted to hide something from Mr. Smith, put it in a law book. I really believe that. His testimony on this was singularly uninformed—no concept of government or how it functions, or of the case law, for that matter. I just don't think he understood what it was all about.

"As for the President, I don't think he did either. He made some critical judgments which showed that he was a smart politician, that he wasn't going to make the mistakes that Nixon made. When he saw that he was getting into a position that was a loser, he cut his losses. Unfortunately, that meant jettisoning his people, whom he had steadfastly said he was going to stand behind. And that's unfortunate. But he knew enough to do that. I think cutting his losses saved him, saved him a lot more grief, because it was building to a head. I was getting questions from members saying, 'Well, gee, what's going to happen if the President is . . .' and 'What's *his* role in this?' and 'We now think there is White House involvement in EPA matters,' but they cut us off at the pass. Again, at Anne's expense. But that's where it was going."

19

THE THREE PROMISES

I have *almost* come to the point where I must address the question of ultimate responsibility in this matter, and I confess I do so with a degree of reluctance. But first let's look at what happened to the three promises made to me by Joe Coors on the day he communicated the President's request that I resign. To recapitulate, I was promised that my people would be protected, that I would be given a new position before the end of the first Reagan administration, and that my legal bills would be paid.

This is how things stand in the spring of 1985. My people were all fired, most immediately accompanied by the full flush of press and Congressional allegations of wrongdoing, plus one or more Inspector Generals' investigations to contend with. Others were fired a bit later, and few were allowed to die lingering deaths in do-nothing jobs. Despite the promises of the White House, Mr. Ruckelshaus saw to it that highly competent people—such as Kathleen Bennett, my head of the Air office, who'd been promised another, and equal, position—were dismissed. And though he has never complained publicly, Dr. Eric Eidsness, my AA for Water, who got the same treatment from Ruckelshaus, received a pariah's welcome from industry when he looked for a job in the private sector. And these were people about whom absolutely no suggestion of wrongdoing was ever raised. So much for promise number one.

Thanks to the media the public already knows what happened in regard to promise number two. But as usual that account lacks a certain, ah, fullness. This is what actually happened. In the spring of 1984, a year after my resignation, Joe Selgato, a very decent guy who works in the White House personnel office, was conscious of the fact that the promise had been made, and he came to me and said he wanted to fulfill their promise. After explaining I wasn't after a full-time position, I asked for a list of vacancies on committees and commissions and boards, and they didn't have one. A while later he got back to me with a makeshift list of *membership* vacancies, among which were included the National Advisory Committee on Oceans and Atmosphere and the board of the Kennedy Center.

The crux of this appointment was personal professional rehabilitation, pure and simple, a public showing that I still had friends in this administration. With that in mind I said I'd take the Kennedy board.

"Sorry," they said, "those appointments are Mrs. Reagan's personal property."

"Well, then I don't see anything on the list that interests me."

Soon Joe called back and asked me if I would be interested in the chairmanship of the Oceans and Atmosphere Committee. I had to think about that for a while. It was a powerless body; and, as an advisory board, it had no executive, legislative, or regulatory power. The administration had indicated its opinion of the committee by requesting zero funding for it three years in a row. What's more, it was filled with Carter Democrats. But their terms were expiring, and the White House planned to replace everyone. There were no plans to fund it, but Congress continued to do that for them. Joe suggested that with new members and me as the chair, perhaps we could turn out a quality product.

I agreed, but then I added a warning. "When my appointment is announced there will be reaction to it and probably a whole lot of negative criticism."

The response to that was, "Oh, Anne, you think you're so g.d. important, such a high-profile political figure. You're yesterday's news."

"Okay," I said, "maybe that does sound vain, and if so I beg your pardon, but it is still my political judgment that when you announce my appointment as chairman of that committee, the fit will hit the shan."

Not only did they disregard my advice, but once again the White House staff showed its colors. There was a two-pronged reelection strategy designed to counter the bad press regarding EPA, that had the President do two things: visit the Chesapeake Bay to say how he was going to clean it up (an effort that had been deleted from every one of the President's prior budgets) and invite a select group of environmentalists to the White House for lunch. The crack White House staff announced my appointment a day or two before the environmentalists were to have their special lunch with the President!

The uproar, especially from the environmentalists, was even worse than I had predicted. One of them announced he was going to boycott the presidential lunch. Cooler heads got him to reconsider, but he (and the others) spent the entire time berating the President for having the insensitivity to name me to anything connected with the environment. And then Congress got into the act; resolutions were introduced in both chambers calling for the President to rescind the appointment.

In reaction to all of this, in a speech in Denver I made some off-the-cuff remarks about the committee itself (the most widely repeated quote was my characterization of it as a "nothingburger") that only fueled the blaze. The President had underlined its lack of importance by refusing to ask Congress to fund it. Also, in preparation for the appointment I'd gone back and read the committee's annual reports, and it appeared that the biggest thing it had ever done was to recommend improving the National Weather Service by buying all the stations touch-tone phones because they are computer-compatible, something anyone who'd taken an elementary course in computers could have suggested.

However, if there is one thing that the Washington establishment cannot stand, it is to have one of its institutions characterized as powerless or silly. And this one was both. All I was doing was calling it like it was.

What did these stalwart folks in the White House do when faced with yet another chance to stand tough? They caved in. But for a *second* time they hadn't the guts to come to me themselves and ask me to bow out. Once again they went to my friends.

This time it was three female friends—Maisell Shortly; Anne Graham, an Undersecretary in the Department of Education; and Sally Buikema, who worked at the Republican National Committee and is currently at the Department of Energy. All of them urged me, in my own best interest, to get out.

"It may well be," I said, "but I'm sick and tired of those people using my friends. It's the same old Joe Coors bit on the part of the gutless wonders in the White House, the same ones who demanded to know if I were tough enough."

So I told my friends the answer was no. This appointment was not for the President, it was for me. It didn't matter what the liberal press said; the reappointment said something to the people that I needed to have something said to. So I no longer stood to lose anything, and, by this time, I was used to all the frenzied press attention. I stood my ground.

On August 1, I went to the airport to pick up J.J., who had spent some time with his father in Denver. While there, I heard a page for "Anne McGill," my maiden name. It was Burford, from his office, saying, "One of the neighbors just called, and there are fully fifty reporters in front of the house."

We ducked the press by changing our plans—instead of having friends over to our house, we went to theirs, and then to dinner at the 1789 near the Georgetown campus, despite the fact J.J. had emerged from the plane wearing his most beat-up soccer shorts and a shirt to match.

The next day John Herrington, then head of White House personnel and today Secretary of Energy, called and asked if he could come over to my house. I said yes, and bit my tongue, because this was the same John Herrington who prided himself on not returning phone calls. I called Burford and told him he might want to come home—maybe someone would need to be called a turkey again!

Herrington came out, and told me that he thought it might be in the best interests of the President, and in my best interests, blah, blah, blah, if I stepped down. I said, "Forget it. And besides that, I deeply resent your going to my personal friends to effect your public business."

Then he said, "I am going to be in the White House personnel system for a long time, and if you see fit to withdraw, I promise you there will be bigger and better things down the road."

By now I had had enough. I said, in agreeing, "John, I want you to remember that I never asked for it. I want you to remember what you voluntarily promised."

He nodded, and that was that. I withdrew my name. After the election I got one phone call from Joe Selgado, asking me what John Herrington, his boss, had promised me. I told him to ask Herrington. He called back, and asked me if I would like to come in to the White House personnel office "just for a chat." I went, we "chatted," and that's the last I've heard about promise number two.

Promise number three. As of this writing I owe Doug Bennett and his former law firm $211,295.01. That doesn't count the $20,601.24 that Burford and I have paid in monthly interest, for a total of $231,896.25. There has been a lot of talk about who should pay the fees—should it be EPA, or the Department of Justice, which has a well-stocked fund for this very purpose—but to date no one has taken action.

The man who could change all this with a stroke of his pen is Presidential Counsel Fred Fielding, but he has done nothing, which is no surprise, since he was the architect of the whole disaster. The President was recently quoted as saying, in a news conference, that he favors the payment of my fees. And now that the government has paid the massive fees that Attorney General Meese incurred while the subject of an investigation by a special prosecutor fees more than twice as large as mine, simple political reality, if not fairness, would suggest my lawyers be paid. But nothing has happened. I feel certain that by the time this book appears I will have had to file suit to compel payment of those fees.

20

LOOKING BACK AT
WONDERLAND

I received an expensive mid-life education. But was it an education I needed to acquire? In some ways I would have preferred my illusions. Look at some of the truths I came to see: Congress's lack of concern with and its lack of accountability for the terribly serious budgetary problems of this country; the virtual disappearance of the Constitutional doctrine of executive privilege; the prevalence of personal, as opposed to political or philosophical, agendas; loyalty, and the lack of thereof, as practiced in Washington politics; and the depths to which certain environmental lobbyists will sink to play on the very real concerns of the American people for their environment.

In reference to Congress's dereliction of its budgetary duty, I think it's important to point out that while I was in office, in every Cabinet area except defense, Congress gave the President *more* money than he asked for in his budget request. I wonder how many Americans realize that it is unlawful for the head of an agency of the government like EPA to willfully spend *less* than Congress has appropriated.

As for executive privilege, I agree with Stanley Brand's comment that as a result of the futile and pathetic efforts of the Justice Department lawyers, "in the future, no one will be able to bring

273

a civil suit based on executive privilege with a straight face." A once proud traditional protection has been effectively lost because of the inept legal work within the department that is charged with being the government's lawyer. Were I still in government, I'd be plenty worried. Even though I'm not in government, I'm *still* plenty worried.

As for the press, I am told that there *are* good, honest journalists who do their homework, get their facts straight, and keep their biases to themselves. Unfortunately, I have met only a very few of them. The vast majority, in my opinion, do not work hard and let opinion into their news copy on a regular basis. As for fairness, let me cite just one example. When I remarried while in office, I was in the heat of a fierce, historic confrontation with Congress over the direction the President wanted me to take EPA. The *Washington Post* chose to run a cute editorial that had to do with my name change:

"In the midst of a grand Washington ruckus, with the cymbals crashing, the trumpets sounding and the hounds baying, the person at the center of it has quietly gone and done a very unfair thing; she has changed her name. It's a real possibility that about 75% of the people . . . are going to see that somebody named Burford is now the head of EPA and conclude that either (one) Anne Gorsuch has been fired or (two) this has all gotten too complicated and the hell with it.

"No feminist would admit it, but Mrs. Burford has availed herself of a refuge no male officeholder could ever hope to use."

So much for respect for privacy or fair play. The title of that clever editorial? "Remember Mrs. Whatshername?"

It both scares and sickens me to realize that *policy* of the United States government can be determined by the front page of the *Washington Post*. If they did it at EPA, they can do it again. Perhaps this time at the Department of Defense? One of the things that my case so clearly illuminates is that the press prefers to cover personalities rather than issues, and as a result public trust, which is essential to good government, does not rest on fact and reality. It can so easily be manipulated by allegation and distortion. I really feel that the time has come for the press to clean its own house.

What is one to say about the environmental extremists? I am convinced that we made an honest and responsible effort to seek a reduced budget while at the same time producing more environmental protection. But we were never given credit for that effort or for any of our accomplishments.

Why not? At the risk of sounding paranoid, let me state that our good work was not properly reported because the press bought the charges and the rhetoric of the environmentalists without checking for substance. When I entered EPA, zealotry poisoned every aspect of environmental protection and made intelligent judgment of the issues nearly impossible. We brought science and scientists into EPA to a greater degree than ever before, but we did not get credit for it.

If you think I am exaggerating, let me quote one of the best-known and allegedly most respected of my environmental critics, Jonathan Lash, who was the senior staff attorney for the Natural Resources Defense Council in Washington, and who wrote a book lambasting the environmental protection policies of the Reagan administration.

Since the end of 1984, Lash has been the environmental commissioner for the state of Vermont. In a recent interview that ran in the *Boston Sunday Globe*, he admitted that some of the decisions he has made in his new job "would have enraged him in his previous job. Lash said he 'would find it very difficult to go back and do the work I did before because an important part of being an effective advocate is to undermine the credibility of the government and, if necessary, the personal credibility of the people involved. . . . I think it was absolutely necessary to undermine the credibility of Anne Burford of the Environmental Protection Agency.' "

Absolutely necessary to undermine my *personal* credibility? And people wonder why I ascribe a large part of the blame for my having to resign to the tactics of the environmentalists. Given Mr. Lash's admissions, what other conclusion could I draw?

What is the current status of the Environmental Protection Agency? I would bet that the average intelligent newspaper reader or television news show viewer believes that the turmoil at EPA has resulted in a much-improved agency. Indeed, any fair-minded person, no matter what his or her politics may be, would hope that we didn't go through that incredible maelstrom only to end up where we began.

Unfortunately, that is just what happened. As a matter of fact, in many ways, the situation at EPA is now worse than when I was in office.

William Ruckelshaus is long gone. The new administrator is Lee Thomas, the former head of the Federal Emergency Management Agency (FEMA), with whom I flew to Times Beach in 1983 to announce the buy-out of the town. Lee Thomas is a good and decent man, but he is doubly handicapped in this administration by being a bureaucrat and a registered Independent, which means he has very little, if any, political clout.

Another way of assessing the situation at EPA is that of the eight top offices in the agency, excluding Thomas's own, *five* are vacant. All eight top spots require PAS appointments, which means the president appoints them and the U.S. Senate has to approve them. Of these eight, only three are held by people whom the President has sent to the Senate for confirmation.

How is Mr. Thomas able to run the agency with any sort of control or autonomy?

Some observers feel that Congress has usurped the prerogative of the Executive Branch, and is in effect running EPA by virtue of legislative deadlines on a myriad of regulatory programs. If that is the case, it is a curious oversight on the part of a supposedly conservative president.

Frankly, it appears obvious to me that the President and his close advisors are simply ignoring the Environmental Protection Agency and its many mandates. I just have to wonder why the environmentalists are so quiet. Having "driven" me from office, are they now resting on their laurels? Or have they satisfied their private agendas?

This is a funny town, Washington. Or had you already figured that out? What happened to me, and to the people who worked so hard for me, was scandalous, but what is happening to the Environmental Protection Agency is worse. And now, with the Ice Queen gone, no one seems to be paying any attention. No one seems to be standing up and asking the right questions. Maybe no one is tough enough.

21

REFLECTIONS OF A PRIVATE CITIZEN

I am often asked if I am bitter about what happened. I am *not* bitter. Despite the outcome, I had quite a ride. The President gave me an opportunity to serve the country that only a select few have, and we did not squander that opportunity. We made every minute of that twenty-two months count, even when we were besieged. To be able to say that gives me a true sense of accomplishment. I can tuck that under my pillow at night; it makes me feel good.

We brought about regulatory reforms, advanced the cause of New Federalism, and, most significantly, produced more environmental results with fewer people and dollars.

Reagan let me be Reagan.

It was a challenging and exciting time, and we had a hell of a lot of fun. Let me cite two incidents that always makes me laugh. As it happens, they both involve Jim Watt.

One day not long after I resigned, Jim insisted on taking me and Burford and my two younger children out to dinner. Jim chose the restaurant, a pizza house on Wisconsin Avenue. It was a pleasant enough place, though they seated us right in front of a huge bank of loudspeakers, through which came rock song after rock song. We were about halfway through the meal, when I noticed that J.J. and Stephanie were having a hard time keeping their faces straight. Later, when we were alone, I asked them what was so funny. J.J. said, "Didn't you notice? All they were playing were Beach Boys albums!" Jim Watt, who knows only hymns and anthems, never noticed.

The other Jim Watt story, which is both humorous and kind of poignant, is probably better told by Jim himself:

"It was during the crisis time, the time of the worst Congressional pressure against her, and I said, 'Anne, you're not using all the tools at your command to whip those members of Congress. They're demagoging you. They don't care about the truth. But you're not using all the tools at your command. You must wear that purple dress, and go up there and be a feminine personality.' And she was very beautiful then, as she is now, and she has these gorgeous eyes, and I said, 'The first Congressman who goes after you, I don't care what he says, you *flash* those eyes, and you come out with all the hostility you can muster, and you point right at him and say, "You wouldn't *dare* ask that question if I were a man! You're a *sexist!*' "

"She refused to do it. And I said, 'Anne, if you do, that's the only thing that will dominate the evening news. What's more, he won't be able to defend himself. There is no defense for a man charged with that. Whether it's true or not is irrelevant. You will have taken the initiative, and any member of Congress you charge with being a sexist will be guilty in the public's mind, regardless of the facts. You women have that advantage over us, and you must use it. Those members of Congress are being cruel and unfair to you. You've got to fight them.'

"But she said, 'Jim, I can't do that. It's not fair. I didn't get my job because I'm a woman.'

"We had this session over and over again. I even wrote out the exact wording on a slip of paper and handed it to her and told her to carry it in her purse and practice it at lunchtime and coffee breaks and to and from work, so when the question comes you don't have to think about it, you can just nail the Congressman. But she did not have the courage to defend herself as she should have defended herself.

"Is there discrimination in America against women? Absolutely. And those members took advantage of it, and tried to demean her as a woman whom they thought would not be tough enough to take it.

"She is tough, though. She was much stronger than I thought she was. I didn't think she would be as strong as she is. She was tough, she was able, and she was loyal. But she refused to defend herself with the tools at her command. She would have whipped those little wimps had she done it. But she didn't do it, and I still fault her for it.

"The only criticism I have is that she did not play the woman's role. She tried to think that she was in a man's world, and they played unfair with her, and she didn't take the proper steps to defend herself, or she'd have backed them off. It would have meant getting down in the gutter with them, which she was unwilling to do. But meanwhile they got her."

At the close of the final hearing before John Dingell's subcommittee in September, 1983, at which I testified, Mr. Dingell told me:

> The Chair would like to observe that your testimony today and the testimony that was received yesterday with regard to the performance of the Justice Department, your behavior with regard to presentation of the documents to this committee, and your advice to the administration on those matters are clearly corroborative of each other. And the Chair is of the view that had the matter been left in your hands—the production of the papers, books and records that were requested by this committee—very probably none of us would have found ourselves in the train of events that has brought us to this point.
>
> The ironic thing is that your advice was not heeded and vast problems arose. Had your advice been heeded, the problems would not have arisen. It becomes plain that many who failed to heed your advice and who bear major responsibilities for the unfortunate situation we found in the confrontation between the Congress and the White House remain in the administration to continue advising the President on the conduct of his policies. The Chair observes that this is a curious and at best an ironic set of circum-

stances, one which I believe ill serves the country and I think quite clearly ill serves the President himself.

John Dingell raised an extremely important point. Who *are* these powerful people who remain in the administration to continue advising the President on the conduct of his policies? Well, certainly, one of the most powerful is Fred Fielding, who is still the Counsel to the President. In many ways, the President's perception of the people who run his administration is dependent on the information and advice given him by Fred Fielding, a fact that will always worry me. Fielding's chief aide is still Richard Hauser. Hauser is a decent man, but he will never contradict his boss.

David Stockman resigned as the all-powerful head of OMB in the summer of 1985, and joined a Wall Street banking and brokerage house. But his influence and the network of aides still in government will continue to play a major role in the behind-the-scenes running of the country as long as Ronald Reagan is president.

Jim Baker, in a major role change, is now the Secretary of the Treasury. He will continue to wield great power, silently, for the next two years at least. Craig Fuller is now the chief aide to George Bush, Ronald Reagan's heir apparent; I used to like Craig a great deal, but after learning about his frequent phone conversations with Rita Lavelle, I have to lump him along with all the others I've met in Washington who follow a private agenda. One of Craig Fuller's chief aides is Fred Khedouri, the man who asked John Hernandez if he were willing "to bring EPA to its knees." So the major players are still very much in place, very much in power.

Ed Schmults and Ted Olson have left the Department of Justice and returned to the private practice of law, as has William French Smith. Also now practicing law are Stanley Brand and Elliott Levitas. John Dingell remains a powerful figure in the U.S. House of Representatives.

Rita Lavelle is in jail. But her presence is noted. Her framed photograph is on the wall of Joe and Mo's, a popular Washington restaurant, with the inscription: "I enjoyed every bite, even when I paid."

My staff is scattered. John Daniel practices environmental law in the Washington office of an Ohio law firm. Kathleen Bennett,

John Todhunter, and Eric Eidsness are back in private industry. Bill Hedeman is still the head of Superfund. Cristy Bach is an aide to Don Hodell, Jim Watt's successor as Secretary of the Interior. As for Watt himself, he has an office in Washington, and advises new, and often minority, businesses on the intricacies of working with the federal government. Burford remains as head of the Bureau of Land Management.

That brings me to the President. At my final press conference the day after I resigned I said that the President and I shared a commitment to environmental protection. I had made that statement many times before, and I had always meant it sincerely. I am afraid that if I were called on to make that same pledge today, though, after what I have been through and after what we have learned researching and writing this book, I would have to qualify it.

Certain facts just cannot be ignored. For one thing, the President has never made a major environmental address, one in which he devoted the full text of a major speech, or remarks at an important event, to the environment. Frankly, after five years of silence, even I have to question his commitment.

We did try to get the President to make an environmental speech. My people drafted and polished several speeches for him to give on environmental protection, but none was ever made. I later learned why. James Watt, to whom we submitted the speeches as head of the Cabinet Council on Natural Resources and the Environment, admitted that he had never sent them on to the President. Why not? "Because I couldn't get Mike Deaver to involve the President in environmental matters," Jim confessed.

Clearly my agency did not get the support I expected. Indeed, in my twenty-two months in office I probably spent less than a total of two hours with the President, most of which was spent discussing executive privilege rather than matters of direct concern to EPA.

Ronald Reagan is touted as being the greatest team player, the greatest loyalist of his own administration. If that is the case, we are all in deep trouble. As Stanley Brand so aptly pointed out, when Congressional criticism began to touch the Presidency, Mr. Reagan solved *his* problem by jettisoning me and my people, people whose only "crime" was loyal service, following his orders. I was not the first to receive his special brand of benevolent neglect, a form of conveniently looking the other way, while his staff continues to do some very dirty work. The current management vacuum at EPA is a direct result of Presidential neglect. Those slots would not be vacant if there were a real concern for the environment.

When President Reagan asked me to head the Environmental Protection Agency, I understood that he wanted me to carry out his policies of New Federalism and regulatory reform, and to get better environmental results with fewer people and less money. I took the job because I wanted to bring a politically conservative approach to solving the management problems of environmental protection. And I took the job because I thought Ronald Reagan shared that philosophy.

Having to face the fact that he does not is probably the hardest thing I have had to do, and I am still uncomfortable with it. Ronald Reagan has always been a personal and political hero of mine, and concluding that he doesn't care about the environment hurts.

As for me, after a bout with the blues (and a *lot* of support from my family and good friends) I got back up and dusted myself off, and am now in business for myself, representing clients on a variety of matters, only one of which is environmental law. It would take a miracle to get me back into public life, and, for the moment, that's just fine with me. As the saying goes, I already gave at the office.

APPENDIX

HIGHLIGHTS OF THE ACCOMPLISHMENTS IN THE OF-
FICE OF PESTICIDES AND TOXIC SUBSTANCES, 1981–1983:

—The inherited backlog in safety review and registration actions was reduced by 100%. In 1982, the pesticides office experienced a 30–50% increase in requests for actions yet did not fall
behind. This was primarily due to the development of improved
management services for the office.

—The first Registration Standards were issued as part of a
program (initially authorized by Congress in 1972) under which
all pesticides registered before 1972 would eventually be reexamined, and each pesticide would be reexamined every five years.
The program, as established, would have accomplished this goal
by 1989.

—The Special Reviews (formerly known as Rebuttable Pre-
sumptions) which were initiated in the 1976–1978 period and left
unfinished were completed.

—The first guidelines for the development of pesticide safety
data were issued. (They, too, had originally been mandated by
Congress in 1972.)

—The first standard pesticide safety data requirements were
issued (also mandated in 1972 by Congress).

—The first Guidance for Use of Peer Review of technical issues were issued (in response to a Congressional mandate of 1980).

—During the 1982 and 1983 fiscal years, statutory deadlines for actions under pesticide laws were met on a routine basis for the first time.

—The backlogs in decision-making on the testing of existing commercial chemicals were eliminated.

—Guidelines for chemical safety data development were issued.

—Chemical reporting rules requiring manufacturers to provide production-and-use information on chemicals being considered for additional safety testing by EPA were promulgated.

—Rules covering transport and disposal of dioxin were promulgated.

—Rules requiring inspection of schools for friable (easily reduced to powder) asbestos, plus the notification of parents and employees, were promulgated.

HIGHLIGHTS OF THE ACCOMPLISHMENTS IN THE SUPERFUND PROGRAM, 1981–1983:

—The National Contingency Plan, the national blueprint for management of the Superfund program, was promulgated. The plan also established a national response network at the regional, state, and local level for governmental response to episodic releases of hazardous substances into the environment (July 16, 1982).

—A National Inventory of U.S. hazardous waste sites, which initially included over 12,000 sites and which has grown to include over 21,000, was established.

—A ranking system (the Hazard Ranking System) which is used to prioritize hazardous waste sites for Superfund attention, was established.

—Using that system, we established the first National Priority List of 115 Superfund sites on October 23, 1981. The list was expanded to 160 sites on July 23, 1982, and further expanded to include 418 sites (December 30, 1982).

—We undertook emergency removal actions at 104 sites, at a total cost of $25.5 million.

—We developed a systematic approach for reviewing all sites in the national inventory.

—At sites on the National Priority List, we initiated 64 remedial investigations and feasibility studies, eleven designs, and eleven constructions.

—Six sites on the National Priority List were cleaned up. (This number has not increased as of July 1, 1985.)

—We entered into an agreement with the Army Corps of Engineers to oversee the design and construction of all federal lead Superfund clean-ups.

—We established management systems to track expenditures of all Superfund money for cost recovery purposes.

—We actively promoted industry's awareness and use of design specifications for prototype technology both to destroy and to manage hazardous waste developed by EPA's research and development program, including the mobile incinerator, the mobile soils washer, and a mobile water treatment unit.

—Major settlements were reached with responsible parties at Superfund sites, including Chemdyne, Ohio, involving a total surface clean-up and commitment to do the RI/FS for groundwater contamination; Seymour, Indiana, involving total surface clean-up of 60,000 abandoned drums of waste; and total remediation of four sites in Michigan at which the Velsicol Corporation was the responsible party.

HIGHLIGHTS OF THE ACCOMPLISHMENTS IN THE OFFICE OF AIR, 1981–1983:

—Through management streamlining, the backlog in State Implementation Plan revision was reduced by 98 percent.

—New Source Performance Standards (NSPS) now move faster through the procedural pipeline, and production time has decreased by 14 percent.

—We streamlined the certification program, which greatly reduced manufacturer and EPA workloads, allowing concentration on product improvement and issues that directly affect air quality.

—During 1982, we published seven final NSPS, as opposed to the ten which had been published in 1976–1980.

—Final regulations on lead phasedown were published, which will mean a 34 percent reduction in lead emissions over the old proposed regulations and a reduction of more than 127,000 tons of lead.

—A major radiation standard concerning Uranium Mill Tailings was published, and a Notice of Proposed Rulemaking was published for establishing a High Level Waste Standard.

—During fiscal year 1982, 23 additional states accepted full delegation for the NSPS program, bringing the total to 31.

—Fully 90 percent of all applicable NSPS have been delegated to the states.

—NESHAP delegation has increased 32 percent and 44 state and local agencies have accepted delegation of the PSD program, in increase of 13 during the 1982 fiscal year.

—As of March, 1983, only 7 percent of the statutory sources were out of compliance in the enforcement area, and 2 percent more are on compliance schedules.

—The targeting of enforcement resources toward the most significant violators has made significant progress since start-up in 1981. Of 531 sources identified as significant violators, better than 50 percent have been brought into compliance or placed on compliance schedules.

HIGHLIGHTS OF THE ACCOMPLISHMENTS IN THE OFFICE OF WATER, 1981–1983:

Under the Effluent Guidelines for Best Available Technology (BAT) to control toxic substances, there were three separate guidelines: 1. new source performance standards for a new facility as yet unbuilt; 2. BAT for existing facilities; and, 3. industrial pretreatment standards, for industries that discharged into a municipal sewage system. Therefore there are three regulations for each one of the twenty-one industry categories.

—Of the total universe of industries for which effluent guidelines were to be issued, when we took office only one had been proposed. So the effluent guidelines for all twenty-one of these industries were produced and promulgated during our time in office.

—This effort represented, from 1981 to 1983, an estimated 882,000 consultant man-hours. Total dollars spent on effluent guidelines, going back to 1976, were $123.5 million, of which an estimated $80 million went for industrial studies necessary for producing the toxics effluent guidelines. Yet only one BAT guideline had been promulgated (for the timber industry).

HIGHLIGHTS OF THE ACCOMPLISHMENTS IN THE OF-
FICE OF SOLID WASTE, 1981–1983:

—First national set of regulations controlling land disposal
- covering land fills, lagoons, injection wells, and waste
  piles.

—First national survey of hazardous waste management practices
- survey of amount of waste generated and number of
  people subject to regulation.

—Proposed first national uniform manifest system.

—Regulatory reform
- correction and simplification of regulations pursuant to
  Paperwork Reduction Act

—Delegation of administrative responsibility to 35 states.

To put it simply, while other administrations had been trying
for years to get those guidelines out, we were the people who
did it.

—The following regulations or guidelines were made final or
proposed during my time in office:

- trihelomethane settlement for safe drinking water;
- advanced notice of proposed rulemaking for volatile
  organic chemicals for drinking water;
- advanced notice of proposed rulemaking for interim
  primary drinking water standards;
- reform of the water quality management regulations;
- reform of the water quality standards regulations;
- reform of the state grant regulations;
- the settlement of the National Pollution Discharge Elim-
  ination Permit System regulations, and the deconsoli-
  dation of the same regulations;
- reform of the construction grants regulations of the
  National Ground Water Policy;
- the audit and close-out of a backlog of 500 construction
  grant projects between the time I took office and February of 1982;

- the publication of eight health advisories for unfamiliar contaminants in water supplies;
- the addition of eight construction grant delegations to state agencies, which brought the total up to 45; and,
- the adoption of a four-phase regulatory strategy for controlling contaminants in drinking water, a strategy that is playing itself out just as we wrote it.

As I mentioned in the book, this list is not a complete catalog of all that we accomplished. But it is a listing of real accomplishments, hard achievements. We are all proud of it. Unfortunately, none of these significant environmental achievements was reported.

INDEX